T0301747

Open Innovation and Knowledge Management
in Small and Medium Enterprises

Open Innovation: Bridging Theory and Practice

ISSN 2424-8231

Series Editors: Anne-Laure Mention *(Global Business Innovation, RMIT, Australia)*
Marko Torkkeli *(Lappeenranta University of Technology, Finland &*
INESC TEC, Portugal)

The series aims to contribute to knowledge creation and more importantly, to knowledge accumulation, through the combination of multiple streams, perspectives, disciplinary approaches and diverse backgrounds. In doing so, it departs from the current body of literature adopting a purely academic perspective on Open Innovation, and thus restates the importance of anchoring Open Innovation research into the reality, practices, challenges facing firms and policymakers. This book series covers multiple perspectives, such as measuring and assessing the impact of Open Innovation, dealing with organizational matters and culture, designing strategies, policies, incentives and measures to support and implement Open Innovation, and discussing the advantages and limitations of adopting Open Innovation strategies.

Published

Vol. 3   *Open Innovation and Knowledge Management in Small and*
Medium Enterprises
edited by Susanne Durst, Serdal Temel and Helio Aisenberg Ferenhof

Vol. 2   *Open Innovation: Unveiling the Power of the Human Element*
edited by Anne-Laure Mention and Dimitrios G Salampasis

Vol. 1   *Open Innovation: A Multifaceted Perspective (In 2 Parts)*
edited by Anne-Laure Mention and Marko Torkkeli

Forthcoming

Digital Innovation: Harnessing the Value of Open Data
edited by Anne-Laure Mention and Vera J Lipton

Open Innovation and Knowledge Management
in Small and Medium Enterprises

Editors

Susanne Durst
University of Skövde, Sweden

Serdal Temel
Ege University, Turkey

Helio Aisenberg Ferenhof
Federal University of Santa Catarina, Brazil

World Scientific

NEW JERSEY · LONDON · SINGAPORE · BEIJING · SHANGHAI · HONG KONG · TAIPEI · CHENNAI · TOKYO

Published by

World Scientific Publishing Co. Pte. Ltd.

5 Toh Tuck Link, Singapore 596224

USA office: 27 Warren Street, Suite 401-402, Hackensack, NJ 07601

UK office: 57 Shelton Street, Covent Garden, London WC2H 9HE

Library of Congress Cataloging-in-Publication Data
Names: Durst, Susanne, editor. | Temel, Serdal, editor. | Ferenhof, Helio Aisenberg, editor.
Title: Open innovation and knowledge management in small and medium enterprises / edited by
    Susanne Durst (University of Skövde, Sweden), Serdal Temel (Ege University, Turkey),
    Helio Aisenberg Ferenhof (Federal University of Santa Catarina, Brazil).
Description: New Jersey : World Scientific, [2018] |
    Series: Open innovation: bridging theory and practice ; volume 3
Identifiers: LCCN 2017054849 | ISBN 9789813233584 (hc : alk. paper)
Subjects: LCSH: Small business--Management. | Knowledge management. |
    Diffusion of innovations--Management.
Classification: LCC HD62.7 .O64 2018 | DDC 658.4/038--dc23
LC record available at https://lccn.loc.gov/2017054849

British Library Cataloguing-in-Publication Data
A catalogue record for this book is available from the British Library.

For any available supplementary material, please visit
http://www.worldscientific.com/worldscibooks/10.1142/10806#t=suppl

Desk Editors: Herbert Moses/Alisha Nguyen

Typeset by Stallion Press
Email: enquiries@stallionpress.com

Printed in Singapore

To Guido

Susanne Durst

To Hulya, Efe and the coming baby Cem due in
December 2017

Serdal Temel

To my deceased grandparents, my parents Isaac
and Ester Aisenberg Ferenhof, and my sister Elaine

Helio Aisenberg Ferenhof

Preface

Almost four years ago, Serdal found a paper written by Susanne on university–industry collaboration, and just three minutes after reading the paper Serdal sent an email to Susanne saying that *"the way you are looking at university industry collaboration is different than mine and I am very impressed. I think there are lots of things we can learn from each other and we can publish very interesting papers in collaboration"*. This email was responded to by Susanne in less than three hours and has since then created an academic collaboration that is based on trust and reciprocal "empowering".

Having met only once, communication between Susanne and Serdal takes place primarily via email and skype chats. In the meantime, this has led to the publication of three books chapters, three papers, and now this book. A rather similar collaboration is found between Helio and Susanne, who run weekly video calls in which ongoing projects are discussed or new ones developed.

We, the editors, believe that a collaboration that is based on trust, expertise, long-term commitment, as well as mutual benefits is essential for developing successful outcomes. And despite all seriousness, we make sure we have fun too!

The present book is the outcome of our decision to take on a new challenge, to expand our academic collaboration with other colleagues from different countries and different backgrounds, and to find a way to develop our joint research interests which are open innovation, knowledge management, and small businesses. We hope that this book will be considered as relevant by readers interested in the topic not only in the involved countries, i.e. Germany, The Netherlands, Sweden, Brazil, Spain, Iceland, Hong Kong, and Turkey, but also in other countries.

We like to thank our Universities, University of Skövde, Ege University, and Federal University of Santa Catarina that made possible this project.

Susanne Durst
Serdal Temel
Helio Aisenberg Ferenhof
August 2017

About the Editors

Helio Aisenberg Ferenhof is a Doctor in Production Engineering from Universidade Federal de Santa Catarina, UFSC. He has a Master's Degree in Knowledge Management from UFSC, an MBA in E-Business from FGV/RJ, is a Specialist in Didactics for Higher Education from SENAC/SC, and has a Bachelor's degree in Computer Science from UNESA. Currently, he holds a Visiting Professor position at After Graduation Program of Communication and Information Technology (PPGTIC) at the Federal University of Santa Catarina (UFSC) Campus Araranguá and is also an associate member also an associate member of the research group of Knowledge and Innovation Management (KIM) at the School of Business at University of Skövde. His research areas include Knowledge Management, innovation, intellectual capital, project management, service management, product development, and computer science. Before joining academia, he worked as a system developer, system analyst, project manager, and consultant in different industries. In 2010, he received a prize of innovation from Nancy-Université -INPL, "Prix d`innovation — à l'évenément international — 48H pour faire émerger des idées".

Susanne Durst is an Associate Professor (Reader) at the School of Business at the University of Skövde (Sweden) and Professor of Business Administration at Universidad del Pacífico (Peru). She is also the leader of the research group Knowledge and Innovation

Management (KIM) at the School of Business, University of Skövde. Her research interests include small business management, SME business transfers, knowledge management, knowledge risk management, and corporate governance. She has been conducting several national and international research projects on company succession, corporate governance, and knowledge management in SMEs and public organizations. Her work has been recognized through different awards, including the Transeo Academic Award in 2012, and she has published in international peer-reviewed journals. Before joining academia, she held different designations in private enterprises of different industries and of varying size.

Serdal Temel earned his PhD from Dokuz Eylul University, Department of Economics. He has been working as a researcher at Ege University Science and Technology Center since 2000 and is responsible for university–industry cooperation, technology transfer, R&D, and innovation projects. Dr. Temel worked as a manager of the Aegean Innovation Relay Centre (IRC-Ege), which was one of the centers within the EU. Dr. Temel has taken an active role in over 30 national and EU projects and has more than 35 articles and book chapters on innovation, R&D, university–industry collaboration, and entrepreneurship published in international peer-reviewed journals. Currently, he is Vice Director of Ege University Technology Transfer Office and Head of Ege University Department of Innovation and Entrepreneurship and Visiting Associate Professor at Southampton University Business School. Dr. Temel is also a recipient of the prestigious Newton Advanced Fellowship.

About the Contributors

Joaquín Alegre is a Professor of Innovation Management at the Department of Business Management "Juan José Renau Piqueras" at University of Valencia. His teaching and research interests focus on the innovation process within organizations. Innovation, knowledge, organizational learning, and entrepreneurship are frequent topics in his research. He has published his findings in journals such as *Research Policy, Technovation,* and *International Journal of Management Reviews*. He has served as an Associate Editor at *European Management Journal* for three years (2013–2016). Since 2015, he coordinates the University of Valencia Doctoral Programme in Business Management. He currently leads a research project on Open Innovation and entrepreneurship in SMEs financed by the Spanish Ministry of Economics and Competitiveness.

İlker Murat Ar is an Associate Professor in Business Administration, Karadeniz Technical University, Turkey. He received his BS and PhD in Business Administration from the same university. He teaches courses in operations management and operations research. His research interests are focused on innovation, technology, R&D management, and logistics.

Niels Dijkman graduated in Financial Economics in 1997 from the Vrije Universiteit (Amsterdam). He started his career in (investment) banking. In 2007, he was appointed as Sector Banker Food at ABN AMRO Bank. He cooperated in various publications on business strategy and sustainability. Currently, he works for a specialized Food & Agri consultancy firm in the field of total/true cost Accounting.

Ingi Runar Edvardsson is a Professor in Management at the School of Business, University of Iceland. He received his PhD in Sociology from the University of Lund, Sweden. His research and publications focus on knowledge and human resource management, outsourcing, regional universities, SMEs, and Nordic labor markets. He has presented his research at several international conferences, including Decowe: Development of Competencies in the world of work and education, International Forum on Knowledge Assets Dynamics; International Labour Process conference, and European Regional Science Association. His articles have appeared in *Employee Relations, International Journal of Knowledge-Based Development, Journal of Knowledge Management, Knowledge Management Research & Practice, International Journal of Entrepreneurship and Small Business, International Journal of Knowledge Based Organizations, International Journal of Research in Open and Distance Learning,* and *Scandinavian Journal of Education Research.* He has also published several book chapters.

Anabel Fernández-Mesa is an Assistant Professor at the Department of Business Management 'Juan José Renau Piqueras' at University of Valencia in Spain where she teaches subjects related to strategy and innovation management. She has also been a researcher at the Institute of Innovation and Knowledge Management (INGENIO, CSIC-UPV). She holds a PhD in Business Management from the University of Valencia. In 2012, 2014 and 2015, she was a Visiting Researcher at Erasmus University (Rotterdam). Her research interests focus on organizational learning, innovation, entrepreneurship, and dynamic capabilities from a strategic perspective. She has published articles in journals such as *Technovation, Industrial Marketing Management,* and *International Business Review* among others. Recently, she has been leading a research project on innovation at the individual level financed by the Valencian Community.

Frances Fortuin graduated in biology from the University of Groningen in 1978 and defended her PhD thesis on the alignment of innovation to business strategy in 2006 at Wageningen University. Frances Fortuin is a non-executive member of the Board of Bartiméus, one of the largest institutes for the blind and visually impaired in The Netherlands, and guest researcher at Wageningen University in the Netherlands. Until 2016, she was senior project manager responsible for the Innovation Expertise Centre of Food Valley NL. Her research interests encompass innovation in chains and networks.

Ana García-Granero has a Degree in Economics and a Master's in Business Strategy. In June 2013, she obtained a PhD in Business Management from the University of Valencia. She has been a researcher at INGENIO (CSIC-UPV) and Grenoble Ecole de Management (GEM). Currently, she is an Assistant Professor at the University of Valencia, where she teaches courses related to business strategy. Her main research interests include open innovation, ambidexterity, organizational design, and top management teams. She has published in journals including *Innovation: Management, Policy & Practice, European Planning Studies, Thinking Skills and Creativity,* and *Journal of Business Research.*

Elsa Grímsdóttir is a Doctoral Student at the School of Business, University of Iceland. Her research interests focus on how SMEs identify and create new knowledge and how these activities result in innovation. Elsa has a Master's Degree in Management and Strategic Management as well as in Human Resource Management from the School of Business at the University of Iceland. Elsa has researched and written articles on the importance of corporate culture in the merging of companies and of the storage and dissemination of knowledge in companies.

Ilka Heinze holds degrees in Business Administration and Psychological Research Methods (MSc., UK). After gaining about 20 years of professional experience in HR Management, she now works as a freelance HR consultant and lecturer in management. Her research projects focus on entrepreneurship and management.

Thomas Henschel is a Professor in Management Accounting at Hochschule für Technik und Wirtschaft in Berlin, Germany. He has served as a faculty in Edinburgh Napier University, UK, City University Hong Kong, China, and Hochschule Merseburg, Germany and was a Visiting Professor at the School of Business, University of Skövde, Sweden. His research focuses on corporate governance and risk management in small firms. He has published extensively in a variety of journals and led a number of consultancy projects. Thomas Henschel is also engaged in technology transfer to small and medium-sized enterprises. He was working as an Auditor for Ernst and Young before moving to the academia.

Rongbin W. B. Lee is the Chair Professor of the Department of Industrial and Systems Engineering and the Director of the Knowledge Management and Innovation Research Centre of The Hong Kong Polytechnic University. He has pioneered the research and practice of Knowledge Management in various industrial sectors in Hong Kong, including manufacturing, trading, public utilities, and health care, and has conducted research projects in knowledge elicitation and mapping, unstructured information management, and organizational learning and innovation. Professor Lee and his team have launched Asia's first on-line MSc. Program in knowledge management, as well as the Global MAKE (most admired knowledge enterprise) Award in Hong Kong and Mainland China and chair the annual Asian Knowledge Forum. He is currently the Chief Editor of the *Journal of Information and Knowledge Management Systems* (Emerald) and the *International Journal of Knowledge and Systems Science* (IGI Publishing).

Onno Omta graduated in Biology in 1978 and defended his PhD thesis on the management of innovation in the pharmaceutical industry in 1995 (both at the University of Groningen). In 2000, he was appointed as Chaired Professor in Business Administration at Wageningen University. He is also a (co-)author of many scientific articles on innovation management. His current research interest encompasses entrepreneurship and innovation in chains and networks in life sciences.

Francisco Romera is an International PhD Student from University of Valencia (Spain) and University of Portsmouth (England). His research interests include knowledge transfer, open strategies to innovate, sustainable development, and innovation and management of entrepreneurial ventures. He is currently focusing on the relationship between open innovation and technology transfer in entrepreneurial ventures and their processes of commercialization through new product development.

Victor Scholten is an Assistant Professor in Business Administration at Delft University of Technology, the Netherlands. Before joining Delft University of Technology in 2007, he held the position of Assistant Professor at Erasmus University in Rotterdam. He received a PhD in entrepreneurship in 2006 from Wageningen University, The Netherlands. His current research interests are in strategic business venturing and corporate entrepreneurship. He is particularly interested in the interplay between entrepreneurship and strategic management: the balance between opportunity and advantage seeking behavior.

Ardalan Haghighi Talab is a Research Fellow in the department of Values, Technology and Innovation at the faculty of Technology, Policy, and Management at Delft University of Technology, The Netherlands. His current research interests are in support innovation systems via knowledge management. He is particularly interested in knowledge typologies and their link to transfer mechanisms: A tailor-made mechanism based on the knowledge type. Ardalan has extensive experience in data science, including econometrics and network analysis.

Haley Wing Chi Tsang graduated with a double degree — BEng (Hons) in Industrial and Systems Engineering and BBA (Hons) with a major in Marketing from the Hong Kong Polytechnic University. She is currently an MPhil student in the Knowledge Management and Innovation Research Centre at the same university. She previously worked in a global financial services company providing risk management and portfolio optimization solutions for major investment houses. Her work was awarded the 'Best Paper and Presentation' in the master and doctoral colloquium in the 8th European

Conference on Intellectual Capital held in Venice, Italy, 2016. Her research interests include intellectual capital, risk management, and knowledge management, and she is conducting a global study of knowledge risk in various industrial sectors.

Cees van Beers is a Professor of Innovation Management and Head of the section Economics of Technology and Innovations. He holds a doctorate in economics from the Free University Amsterdam. He worked at the University of Leiden as an assistant professor, the Institute for Research on Public Expenditure in The Hague as a senior researcher, and as associate professor on innovation economics at Delft University of Technology. He also worked as consultant and expert for several international organizations such as the OECD, FAO, and the World Bank.

Contents

Introduction

Susanne Durst, Serdal Temel[†], and
Helio Aisenberg Ferenhof[‡]*

**University of Skövde, Högskolevägen 1, 541 28, Skövde, Sweden
and Universidad del Pacífico, Lima, Peru
[†]Ege University, Erzene Mahallesi, Gençlik Caddesi,
35040 Boronova, İzmir, Turkey
[‡]Universidade Federal de Santa Catarina, Campus Reitor,
João David Ferreira Lima, Florianópolio, SC 88040-900, Brazil*

1. Outline

This book aims to shed light on the interplay between open innovation (OI) and knowledge management (KM) issues in small and medium-sized enterprises (SMEs). With the proliferation of the OI paradigm and against the backdrop of the increasing number of external knowledge-transfer activities, the management of knowledge is more important than ever for innovation and firm performance, a situation that holds for any type of organization. In fact, KM is no longer a pure intra-organizational activity but constitutes a vital interface function between the organization and its external partners/stakeholders.

You may say this sounds nice, but what makes the present book one that should definitely be read? Well, because even though the fields of OI and KM have been extensively studied both on general levels and with regard to large companies, when SMEs are considered, this is not the case: Our understanding is still underdeveloped. This is reinforced when the interplay between OI and KM is addressed: Our understanding is even more limited. Therefore, we, the editors, believe that our book is timely and will hopefully contribute to raising awareness regarding this promising and relevant topic.

2. Structure of the Book

Throughout the book, readers will obtain both a broad overview of the two main concepts, namely, OI and KM and its interplay. In addition, research will be presented by leading international researchers in the field, which will help the readers develop and/or expand their understanding of this phenomenon. This broad approach can also support in broadening the mindset regarding the topic under investigation and its application. Thereby, this book will primarily focus on SMEs and their approach with respect to the interplay in question.

In order to achieve our aim, the book consists of 10 chapters that are divided into three parts. The idea behind Part 1 is to introduce the main concepts, namely, SMEs, OI, KM and the interplay between OI and KM in SMEs. This is followed by Part 2, which provides empirical research insights into the phenomenon of interest. The book concludes with Part 3, which addresses promising future avenues regarding the study of OI and KM in SMEs.

In the following, we will briefly highlight the content of the individual chapters.

In Chapter 1, "Small and Medium-sized Enterprises", Thomas Henschel and Ilka Heinze introduce the readers to smaller firms, their specific characteristics, and their management. Ilker Murat Ar continues with Chapter 2, "The Concept of Open Innovation", in which the author presents OI as a way for organizations to become more collaborative and competitive. The chapter also highlights the need for paying attention to the risks of OI. Helio Aisenberg Ferenhof gives in Chapter 3, "Knowledge Management", an introduction to the term. Thus, this chapter covers types of knowledge, the definition of KM, as well an overview of knowledge processes. Based on the preceding chapters, Serdal Temel and Susanne Durst present in Chapter 4, "The Interplay between Open Innovation and Knowledge Management in SMEs", the core topic of the present book.

Having provided the book's theoretical background, in Part 2 — Research insights — empirical work is presented that shows the interplay in action.

The part commences with Chapter 5, "Knowledge Creation and Open Innovation in High-Technology SMEs", by Elsa Grimsdottir and Ingi Runar Edvardsson. The study shows how SMEs from Iceland deal with knowledge creation, knowledge sharing, and storage. Additionally, the study provides insights into how customers and other external stakeholders are involved in the innovation process. Different from other chapters, Chapter 6, "Knowledge Sharing and Open Innovation", by Ardalan Haghighi Talab, Victor Scholten, and Cees van Beers focuses more on the theoretical side of knowledge, the role of knowledge for firms in developing new ideas, and how knowledge plays a role in enhancing the competitiveness of companies. Chapter 7, "Comparing Open Innovation of Innovative Food SMEs with SMEs in the Seed and High-Tech Industries — An Analysis of 15 SMEs in the Netherlands", by Onno Omta, Frances Fortuin, and Niels Dijkman focuses on successful OI projects in three different sectors, namely food, plant breeding, and high tech. The authors highlight the important factors needed to successfully implement OI in different sectors. In Chapter 8, "ALITE: Open Innovation and Experimentation in a Small Learning Organization", by Joaquín Alegre, Francisco Romera, Ana García-Granero, and Anabel Fernández-Mesa, it is shown how OI and KM are undertaken in a successful, innovative, and small firm. It connects findings with OI and KM literature and highlights several implications for smaller companies. Haley Wing Chi Tsang and Rongbin W. B. Lee, in Chapter 9, "Mitigation of Knowledge Risks in Open Innovation", draw attention to four types of knowledge risk, namely knowledge loss, knowledge leakage, knowledge obsolescence, and knowledge shortage. Also, the authors present a case of knowledge risk assessment in a small firm using the four knowledge risks.

In Chapter 10, "Open Innovation and Knowledge Management in SMEs: What Comes Next?", Susanne Durst and Serdal Temel synthesize the evidence presented before and, based on this, list and discuss several promising research topics to further deepen our understanding of the interplay between OI and KM in SMEs.

3. Conclusion

We are very proud of having produced a book that targets readers from different levels, students to professors and staff to managers. We are convinced that all of them will find this book a useful aid during their daily work dedicated to enhancing the long-term success of small businesses. Finally, and yet importantly, we hope that this book will also encourage researchers to enter into more international collaborations to execute future academic projects.

Part 1

Introduction
to Main Concepts

Chapter 1

Small and Medium-sized Enterprises (SMEs)

Thomas Henschel* and Ilka Heinze[†]

**Hochschule für Technik und Wirtschaft Berlin,
Treskowallee 8, 10318 Berlin, Germany
[†]School of Management and Organizational Science,
Kaposvár University, P.O. Box 16, H-7400 Kaposvár,
Guba Sándor U. 40, Hungary*

In this chapter, we will introduce small and medium-sized enterprises (SMEs) by defining and discussing characteristics of SMEs in qualitative and quantitative terms. In doing so, this chapter takes an international perspective to account for regional and international differences. As SMEs are often owner-managed, individual attitudes to management and decision-making play an important role in management and governance issues. Therefore, major research findings that contribute to a better understanding of the complex dependencies of SMEs from their owners are presented. Finally, we will address recent challenges and discuss how SMEs can address them to identify and exploit business opportunities.

1. Introduction

The first chapter of this book aims to provide some general knowledge about how small and medium-sized enterprises (SMEs) can be defined, what makes them different from large enterprises, and what are the challenges for these enterprises.

Hence, the chapter is organized as follows. First, SMEs will be characterized by qualitative and quantitative criteria. Critical for a comprehensive understanding of the small businesses are the owners' motives as well as their approach in managing the firm. This will include their attitudes to risk and uncertainty and the financing behavior. Additionally, we will address megatrends that change our societies and hence also affect how SMEs are positioned and have been managed. In that connection, we will discuss recent challenges SMEs have to face and to find answers to, also with respect to the role of creator and innovator. Finally, the chapter will be rounded up with a short conclusion.

2. The Big Picture

Today, SMEs and entrepreneurs live in an age of change and opportunity. According to Burns (2016), there has been a shift in most economies away from manufacturing and toward the service sector where SMEs often flourish because of their ability to deliver a personalized, flexible, and tailor-made service approach at a local level. Start-ups have pioneered innovation in the IT sector and created new markets for these innovations. SMEs were at the forefront of developing mobile apps because the production costs were so low but the gains from selling it to the global market can be enormous. Furthermore, these technologies have facilitated the growth of self-employment and small businesses by easing communication and encouraging working from home and allowing smaller market segments to be served (Burns, 2016; Bridge and O'Neill, 2013).

Additionally, many new technologies (e.g. digital printing) have reduced fixed costs so that production can be more profitable in smaller and more flexible units. New technologies have also simplified the routes to market, small firms can sell to larger firms or directly to customers around the world without the expense of putting in place a distribution network. Nowadays, as large firms increasingly outsource non-core activities, the beneficiaries are often small firms (Burns, 2016). As we have moved from an industrial economy to a knowledge-based economy, the economies of scale have become less important as a form of competitive advantage (Burns, 2016).

These technological developments have affected markets; customers increasingly expect firms to address their particular needs. This means market niches are becoming slimmer and more competitive — which can be better served by SMEs that can get closer to their customers (Burns, 2016). As Haltiwanger *et al.* (2013) have shown that especially newly created firms, compared to established SMEs, are responsible for the job creation and growth in the new information age.

3. Characteristics of SMEs

3.1. *Qualitative characteristics*

Although researchers have been studying SMEs and how they are different from large organizations for many years, there is no universal approach to defining and researching SMEs nor their owners and managers (Gilmore *et al.*, 2013). The research to date has focused on how SMEs are created, grow, become successful or fail, and how they behave in an entrepreneurial sense.

SMEs are seen as a vibrant and innovative source of new ideas and have been the main source of new employment growth in many advanced economies. Looking back, we can now see that SMEs evolutionary capabilities were far more attuned to survival in a dynamic global economy subject to many significant economic shocks over the last 40 years (Gilmore *et al.*, 2013).

Small businesses are often defined by what they lack, namely, capital and human resources, management structures, and access to international markets. As confirmed by research and literature,

SMEs operate and do business in a different way from large firms. In small firms, the managerial roles and hence the overall decision-making rest with one person, the owner, whose personality, experiences, and knowledge clearly influence the management processes in the firm (McGregor and Tweed, 2002). As the international literature has revealed, these owner-managers show a lack of knowledge in management and planning practices (Woods and Joyce, 2003).

Small firms tend to have fewer layers of management and more people-focused working practices (Turner and Ledwith, 2016). Turner *et al.* (2010) found that micro firms had just one business unit, whereas larger firms had more, with more layers of management. In micro and small firms, employees work in multidisciplinary teams, with employees multitasking, able to perform several different functions, whereas in medium-sized firms employees work as specialists, performing just one function (Turner and Ledwith, 2016). Turner *et al.* (2010) provide an overview how the organizational and team structure differs by company size (see Table 1).

According to Turner and Ledwith (2016), medium-sized firms need more formal practices to coordinate the work of specialists working separately, whereas micro and small firms need more people-focused procedures to facilitate the working of people in multidisciplinary teams. Agile methods were often adopted in smaller companies. Nguyen and Bryant (2004) also found that larger

Table 1.   Organizational and Team Structures by Size of Company

Size of firm	Business units	Management layer	Nature of work	Nature of procedures
Micro	One	One (Entrepreneur)	Multitasking	People-focused
Small	Several	Two (Board, Team Leads)	Multitasking	People-focused
Medium	Several	Three (Board, Management, Team Leads)	Specialists	Formal

Source: Adapted from Turner *et al.* (2010).

firms were adopting more formal procedures than smaller ones. They suggested the reason was that larger firms face more internal uncertainty, whereas smaller firms face more external uncertainty and so need to be more agile (Nguyen and Bryant, 2004).

Brettel *et al.* (2010) suggested that SMEs follow a lifecycle model: as they grow, they need to change their organizational and management structures and ways of working. The owner is present in the enterprise as an entrepreneur. He is, directly and indirectly, liable for all decisions so that his entrepreneurial risk, is linked with the loss of wealth. The owner, therefore, has a personal as well as a professional interest in all procedures and decisions involving the company. But again, SMEs can often reach a size and complexity which require the owner to delegate decision-making to his employees.

Matching business processes to the needs of the organization can improve performance (Li *et al.*, 2013). As Perren and Grant (2001) confirm, informal management and leadership practices are most effective in newly founded businesses, but there is a need for greater formality and planning as the SME grows. They suggest the entrepreneur's fear of delegation may have a detrimental effect. Barbero *et al.* (2011) identified a significant barrier to the growth of SMEs: the owner-manager's ability to establish appropriate organizational models and business planning systems when the company develops.

As Fletscher and Harris (2002) have also observed, directors express the desire for an increased level of specific practical advice on implementing strategic planning to be taught in further training courses for entrepreneurs. Woods and Joyce (2003) have also established that owner-managers have less strategic planning skills than other managers. It is not that owner-managers view these techniques more skeptically but rather that they simply have less knowledge of the methods. One explanation is certainly that the other managers were often previously employed in larger companies and so had already come into contact with appropriate techniques. Woods and Joyce (2003) confirm that, as company size increases, the owner-managers begin to take on other managers to provide support for the top management. They also confirm that a greater utilization of strategic methods could be seen than in the companies surveyed.

Richbell *et al.* (2006) draw on the results of Woods and Joyce (2003) and confirm that the owner-managers characteristics can have a significant influence on the business planning activities in small firms. In particular, the level of education and previous work experience in a large firm immediately before setting up their firm and running firms in sectors outside their previous experience have a significant influence on the attitudes on planning activities and practices.

Business planning is hallmarked by the interaction between various subsystems, the degree of integration of their links and by the time horizon. Perry (2001) discovered that the critical size above which a systematic planning in the form of a master budget begins to make sense is from 5 to 15 employees. Below this level, detailed written planning makes little sense, and it cannot positively influence the potential to insolvency. However, if the company employs more than 15 employees, detailed planning has a clear positive effect on the likelihood of insolvency. Perry (2001) further determined that SMEs are either good planners or they are non-planners — there is no intermediate group between these two extremes.

Gibson and Cassar (2002) state that the age and size of a company have a substantial influence on the quality of planning as size increases, the responsibility for business planning shifts from the company management alone to the lower levels (accounting function). The level of training and knowledge also has a positive effect on successful planning.

As the literature indicates, SMEs show a strong capacity for innovation, but often they lack the necessary resources and knowledge to manage the whole innovation project by themselves (Marcelino-Sadaba *et al.*, 2014). To overcome this hurdle, SMEs can adopt an open approach to innovation, which means making use of corporate networks by tapping into partners' resource networks and making extensive use of their manufacturing facilities, distribution channels, and customer databases (Xia and Roper, 2016).

To summarize, SMEs tend to have a simple rather than a complex organizational structure and thereby avoid problems like duality, functional barriers, and overlap (O'Regan *et al.*, 2005). Well-performing SMEs often make effective use of existing resources and outsourcing. Through that, they keep a low hierarchy level and quick decision-making. In most SMEs, there is a high concentration of ownership with no separation of ownership from control (Neville, 2011). One can often find an overlap between ownership and the management of the firm. The owner is the central figure and involved in the day-to-day operations of the firm, and the social relationships are characterized by trust, cooperation, and stability (Zaheer and Venkatraman, 1995). These social relationships, in particular, the trust in employees, can act as compensation for strong levels of control stability (Zaheer and Venkatraman, 1995). It is further argued that the social relationships are responsible for the low turnover rates, which in turn leads to close working atmospheres and smooth operations in SMEs. Conversely, the danger of organizational inertia or clinging to the past — assuming that what worked in the past will work continuously — might be high (Pfeffer and Salancik, 1978). With regard to external support from consultants or business advisers, the literature suggests that SMEs continue to be reserved toward external expertise (Smallbone *et al.*, 1995).

3.2. *Quantitative characteristics*

According to Gilmore *et al.* (2013), SMEs globally account for up to 99% of all businesses, depending on what definition is used to describe an SME. Around the globe, there are many definitions in use to describe and define SMEs. While occasionally issues of ownership and control are used, other approaches use sales turnover, balance sheet total, profitability, and net worth; however, most official statistics focus on the number of people employed. There is also a group of business variously defined as micro or very small firms, i.e. employing one to ten people, which sometimes are subsumed within the SME categories or singled out. In terms of number of businesses, this group of businesses makes a significant contribution to national economies. Another strong feature is that the relative proportions of firms in each size category (micro, small, and medium-sized firms) have remained constant over the long term in Australia, China, Europe, and USA (Schaper *et al.*, 2008).

Workable definitions for quantitative criteria primarily focus on annual turnover and/or the number of employees. Often, a certain criterion of legal independence is also included (Curran and Blackburn, 2001; De, 2005). Why is it so important to look at the quantitative criteria for SMEs? If a firm wishes to be designated a small business for government programs such as contracting or receiving investment grants (e.g. for knowledge management and innovation projects), then it must meet the size standards (Gilmore *et al.*, 2013). Table 2 shows how the European Union utilizes the definition to group SMEs.

Table 2.   Small and Medium-sized Enterprises: EU Subclasses

Subclass	Number of employees	Annual turnover (million Euros)	Balance sheet total (million Euros)
Micro firm	<10	≤2	≤2
Small firm	<50	≤10	≤10
Medium-sized firm	<250	≤50	≤43

Source: Commission of the European Communities (2008).

To belong to one of the classes, i.e. micro, small and medium-sized, a firm must fulfill the following conditions:

The number of employees lies below the respective threshold in Table 2. Furthermore, at least one of the thresholds for annual turnover and balance sheet total is met. An SME may choose to meet either the annual turnover criterion or the balance sheet total; it does not have to meet both and can exceed one of the two and still be considered an SME.

The "legal independence criterion" must be fulfilled: A maximum of 25% is owned by one or more companies which themselves do not match the threshold conditions of Table 2. The above mentioned definition has been valid since 2008 and is updated in terms of annual turnover and balance sheet total at longer intervals of time (Commission of the European Communities, 2008).

In the European Union, SMEs create entrepreneurial spirit and innovation which is essential to promote competitiveness and employment. They are the major source of jobs (European Commission, 2015). SMEs generate 66.9% of employment in the European Union, employing over 90 million people (Eurostat, 2015). About 92% of firms in the euro area are micro firms, 7% are small firms, 1% are medium-sized firms, and only 0.2% are large firms (European Central Bank, 2013). Finding customers and access to finance remain the dominant concerns for euro-area SMEs. SMEs report a marginal deterioration in the perceived availability of bank loans (European Central Bank, 2013).

From an international perspective, there are major differences in the meaning of the criterion "number of employees". In the United States of America, a small business is defined as being an independent business having fewer than 500 employees (see Gilmore *et al.*, 2013; van der Horst *et al.*, 2005; Dana, 2006). The United States International Trade Commission (2010) provides the classification for SMEs as shown in Table 3.

Table 3. Definition of SMEs in North America

Subclass	Number of employees
Micro firm	0–20
Small firm	20–100
Medium-sized firm	100–500

Source: United States International Trade Commission (2010).

This is another clear indication of the problems which exist in defining thresholds, even for the quantitative criteria. According to the United States International Trade Commission in the USA, in 2009, there were a total of 27.5 million SMEs, which account for half of all private sector employees at 59.9 million jobs.

In China, SMEs are classified into many categories in line with the sector that their main business and operation belong. In the manufacturing sector, for example, SMEs refer to enterprises where the number of staff is fewer than 2,000 and whose annual revenues are under Chinese RMB 300 million (about US$ 35m), or total assets are under RMB 400 million (about US$ 46m). In the construction sector, SMEs refer to enterprises with full-time employees not exceeding 3,000, or annual sales not exceeding RMB 300 million, or the total value of assets not exceeding RMB 400 million (National Bureau of Statistics of China, 2013).

Ongoing reforms and opening-up policies have created and maintained a fertile environment for the development and growth of SMEs in China. It was estimated that SMEs contributed to over 68% of China's export. This is a much higher proportion than any country in the OECD (Hall, 2002). The failure rate among Chinese SMEs is very high. Around 68% of SMEs failed in their first five years (Barrow, 1997). SMEs face more governmental policy restrictions and uncertainty than large firms (Tang *et al.*, 2007).

In Australia, for example, the two most common ways of defining an SME are based on annual turnover, number of employees, or some combination of both of these measures. For statistical purposes, the Australian Bureau of Statistics (2011) defines a small firm as having 0–19 employees. Micro firms are small business employing 0–4 employees. A medium-sized firm is defined as 20–199, and large as 200 or more employees. It is important to note, that these definitions are based on headcount and not on a full-time equivalent measure as is the case for other SME definitions. In Australia in 2009 there were a total of 2,051,085 businesses, of which SMEs accounted for 47.2% of total industry employment at 4.8 million jobs (Australian Bureau of Statistics, 2011).

But apart from constituting the overwhelming majority of all enterprises, SMEs have a high value in other national economic functions. For example, during periods of high unemployment, the employment function of SMEs becomes one of the main supporting columns of the national economy. Over 80% of the dual training of qualified workers is carried out by SMEs as well. Moreover, because of their flat structures and the resulting flexibility and speed of decision-making, SMEs are extremely innovative and capable of growth. Further, the diversity of the sectors in which SMEs are active represents an opposite pole to the regional mono-structures (De, 2005).

This discussion has revealed that while there is no universal definition of an SME, the reason why SMEs are the focus of public and academic attention is more straightforward. Economically, SMEs contribute to job creation, value creation, innovation, investment, and exporting across many countries at different stages of development

(Gilmore *et al.*, 2013). The most established criteria for defining an SMEs is the number of full-time employees followed by the annual sales turnover. Especially for receiving government subsidies or state funding, it is important for an SME to check the local quantitative criteria dimensions. From a statistical point of view, it is the only way to make meaningful comparisons of the economic activities of SMEs.

3.3. *Interaction between quantitative and qualitative criteria*

Following the international literature, the quantitative and qualitative characteristics of SMEs are well researched and discussed. However, as Becker and Ulrich (2009) state, this may be a too narrow conception, especially when addressing family businesses. Also, Reinemann (2011) admits that a factual classification is difficult in many cases, e.g. in situations where a family-owned company is led by an employed management team.

To differentiate between enterprises based on the discussed quantitative and qualitative criteria, Reinemann (2011) presented a typology of company categories to be identified by the criteria. The typology is shown in Figure 1.

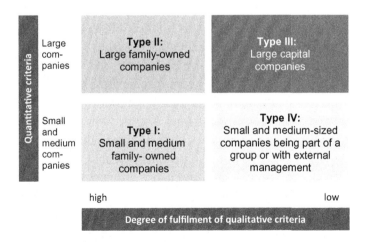

Figure 1. Typology of Companies
Source: Adapted from Reinemann (2011).

Hence, as Figure 1 illustrates, quantitative as well as qualitative criteria should not be interpreted as stand-alone factors but rather used in an integrative way to categorize or analyze SMEs in an accurate manner and better take into consideration the heterogeneity of that type of firms.

4. Small Business Management

We now leave the field of defining an SME in qualitative and quantitative terms and take a turn to discuss the important issues of management behavior and governance, finance, and risk.

4.1. *Management behavior and governance*

SMEs face a high risk of insolvency and many firms struggle to grow as they had planned; these issues are frequently caused by management errors and weakness in company structure, and they also encounter difficulties when trying to raise finance, a problem that has increased since the financial crises (Crossan and Henschel, 2012; Almus, 2004; Herbane, 2010; Paulet *et al.*, 2014). Many of these failures can be mitigated by the introduction of robust governance structures that would provide better planning and management structures (Banham and He, 2010), thus making SMEs less likely to fail and more likely to be able to access finance. However, little research has been carried out in the field of governance of SMEs. This is mostly due to the challenges researchers are faced with when trying to conceptualize the theory of governance in the context of SMEs.

The range of challenges is shaped by the fact that corporate governance research is multidimensional and evolves not only around organizational structure questions such as the facilitation of internal control (advisory boards) but also process-oriented questions such as how processes are implemented to ensure efficiency of existing controls (Gibson, 2009).

The other challenge identified by Gibson (2009) emphasizes the broadness of the governance topic: Governance is addressed in the context of the organization (institutional, ownership structure and lifecycle stages) as well as outside the boundaries of the organization (e.g. boards structure, stakeholder capital theories, other internal governance mechanisms such as reporting systems, executive remunerations, etc.).

Many researchers point out that SMEs depend on their owners, who are frequently also a manager (Brunninge *et al.*, 2007; Segaro, 2010; Solange and Perelli, 2013; Calabrò and Mussolino, 2011; Meiseberg and Ehrmann, 2013; Coulson-Thomas, 2007). There seems to be a common understanding that the success of the SME is dependent on the owner-manager's commitment and behavior Brunninge *et al.*, 2007; Segaro, 2010). Banham and He (2010) mention that the organizational size and the overlap of management and ownership add complexity to governance in the SME context. On the other hand, SMEs are highly flexible in adapting to change and there is no typical principal-agency issue which often occurs when the governance theories are applied to PLCs (Solange and Perelli, 2013).

Coulson-Thomas (2007) also highlights the dilemma between management control and empowerment as one of the major issues in the corporate governance debate. While the major task of governance systems is to exercise control, large corporations also need to motivate their managers to act more like entrepreneurs in order to realize all business opportunities (Coulson-Thomas, 2007). This issue is limited within the SMEs, but there are also arguments suggesting the owner-manager of an SME may not appreciate controls imposed by governance structures (Gibson, 2009). Also, Banham and He (2010) warn that too much control might cause SMEs to lose their flexibility, which is one of their major advantages.

Brunninge *et al.* (2007) analyze the effect that management and ownership structure have on the strategic direction of SMEs. They conclude that closely held firms have little success in strategic planning compared to those companies bringing in outside directors.

In a recent study, Durst and Henschel (2014) investigated the governance practices of SMEs with a particular emphasis on how governance can influence or mitigate the firm's ability to change. One important finding is that SMEs see corporate governance more as a concept for managing the internal and external relationships with the various stakeholders than as a control concept. The findings from the empirical study indicate that the respondents follow a relational approach. The firms involved put an emphasis on informal governance systems, which may be explained by a low staff turnover, which may, in turn, increase the chance of developing trust among the organization members. The existence of a good team apparently compensates for more formal (contractual) approaches (Mustakallio *et al.*, 2002).

Employees are regarded as a critical component for the firm's development which is in line with recent research (O'Donnell, 2013). Additionally, the low staff turnover might act as motivation for the employees to identify more strongly with the firm. It may also generate a stronger willingness to engage in firm issues. Regarding the particular role the employees play in terms of the firm's organizational development, the empirical results clarify that the managing directors/owner-manager continuously involve their staff in the decision-making process, thereby reducing the burden of the owner/director being the sole decision maker within the firm to some extent (Deakins *et al.*, 2000). This approach helps those who manage and direct such firms to gain access to different perspectives on firm issues, to test the suitability of ideas, and to build support for planned initiatives.

4.2. *Financing the business*

SMEs' sources of finance conform to the "pecking order" theory, which means internal finance from the entrepreneur's personal savings is used before external finances — principally in the form of bank debt followed by equity from business angels and venture capitalists (Burns, 2016; Fraser, 2009). The major internal source is personal savings from the owner, and loans or gifts from family or friends (Fraser, 2009). Many entrepreneurs, particularly at the start-up phase, try to avoid using money at all by borrowing or using other people's assets wherever possible — they follow the so-called "bootstrapping" approach. To make the bootstrapping work, the entrepreneur needs to tap into as wide a network of contacts as possible (Burns, 2016). They also use their personal credit cards, often repaying and recycling balances on a month-by-month basis.

As the literature shows, banks are the major source of external funding for SMEs. Besides that, private equity and venture capital are other important sources of external finances for SMEs. Only a small percentage of SMEs uses grants or subsidies (Fraser, 2009). There is also an overreliance on overdraft facilities from their banks, which makes their business more vulnerable and put the owner-managers of such firms at high personal risk of going bankrupt if their business fails (Geppert and Martens, 2008).

Due to the new capital regulations for banks (Basel II and Basel III), the rating of SMEs has become a common procedure in every country. In contrast to the past, where mutual trust and personal relationships and networking have helped to get the necessary financing, banks are now more formal and assess the credit risks of the SME in terms of enterprise performance and management systems (Geppert and Martens, 2008). As the literature reveals, this external monitoring by the lending banks has produced a learning effect in SMEs, which now have improved their management and accounting systems and the communication with the lending bank (Geppert and Martens, 2008; Haag and Henschel, 2016). A sound management and provision of prospective financial information will be very important to get access to external finance at acceptable terms and costs.

One typical problem for SMEs and entrepreneurs in the financing process is information opacity. SMEs often have to face restricted credit access due to problems in proving their creditworthiness to potential lenders (Berger and Udell, 1998). Many SMEs have no audited financial statements (Beck *et al.*, 2010). For that reason, they can hardly be monitored by rating agencies. Furthermore, SMEs and start-ups have no or little credit history. Therefore, it is difficult to assess the trustworthiness and the competence of an SME's management (Armstrong *et al.*, 2014). One instrument that is considered to be helpful in bridging the gap of insufficient information about a potential borrower is collateral. Collateral is seen as an effective means to mitigate these information asymmetries (Berger and Udell, 1990).

However, SMEs and star-ups often suffer from a lack of collateral (Berger and Udell, 1998). Here, the provision of a guarantee from a Credit Guarantee Scheme can help SMEs to get the necessary bank financing. The provision of a guarantee from a Credit Guarantee Scheme that acts as collateral for the lending bank can bridge this gap and therefore mitigate financial distress by SMEs and start-ups (Haag and Henschel, 2016).

The main advantage of the Credit Guarantee Scheme is that the provision of a guarantee puts lenders and borrowers in a situation to learn about each other over time. Suppose that the provision of the guarantee is the precondition for providing credit to a firm, the existence of a guarantee scheme is crucial for initiating learning. Banks that otherwise would not have provided a loan will now have the opportunity to learn about the creditworthiness and the risk of a borrower. In the same way, borrowers that otherwise would have been perceived as too risky and would not have received a loan get the opportunity to build up a repayment reputation (Haag and Henschel, 2016). According to the existing literature, the learning process is expected to result in a mitigation of information asymmetries between the SMEs and the bank and the "graduation" from SMEs with a guarantee to SMEs without one. As a result, an SME does not need a guarantee again when applying for another loan later on (Vogel and Adams, 1997).

To lessen the consequences for SMEs' access to finance, they should further increase their attractiveness as a prospective borrower and should make use of financial products that are independent from Basel regulations. The critical factors for increasing the attractiveness as a prospective borrower are:

- Improvement of the internal or external rating.
- The amount and type of collateral.
- Denomination of the loan among several lending banks.
- Development of a proactive relationship with the lending bank.

A good starting point for the development of a proactive relationship with the lending bank is the improvement of the financial communication. This means the preparation of a regular financial reporting package and addressing research & development activities and investment plans. This will lead to a reduction of information asymmetries and allow better analysis of risks and opportunities of the borrower, which in turn will reduce the screening and monitoring costs for the bank. Table 4 illustrates a selection of financing instruments that are independent from Basel regulations.

Table 4. Financial Sources which are Independent from Basel II Regulations

Standard financing	Grants or subsidized bank loans	New financing instruments
• Venture capital	• Support from public sources in the form of guarantees	• Debt securities issued (special segment on the stock market for SME debt securities)
• Private equity	• Reduced interest rate loans	
• Subordinated loans		
• Mezzanine financing		
• Leasing		
• Factoring		

Source: Adapted from Schmitt (2011).

4.3. *Attitudes to risk and uncertainty*

One of the most challenging questions is: how do successful SMEs manage their businesses? Here, the key is their very different approach to deal with risk and uncertainty. Their firm is a social entity built around personal relationships and around one person, the owner-manager (Burns, 2016).

A successful SME is good at developing relationships with customers, staff, suppliers, and all the other stakeholders in the business. This ability to generate strong personal relationships helps them to develop the partnerships and networks that are necessary for their business survival. These relationships are at the core of

how SMEs deal with risks and uncertainty. While SMEs are pre-
pared to take risks, they always want to keep them to a minimum.
Their network of personal relationships can work as an early warn-
ing system and alert them to risks and new opportunities as well.
It is a major source of knowledge and information (Burns, 2016;
Sparrow and Bentley, 2000).

As literature reveals, SMEs approach decision-making differently
than larger firms (Hang and Wang, 2012). According to Burns (2016),
they tend to adopt an incremental approach that is often seen as short
term. However, this limiting commitment is an approach that helps to
mitigate risk in an uncertain environment. SMEs tend to keep capital
investment and fixed costs as low as possible. They tend to commit
costs only after the opportunity has proved to be sound, and even
then only commit limited resources — the resources they can afford to
lose (O'Regan *et al.*, 2005). Another way how SMEs mitigate risk is
"compartmentalizing" of risks, which means separating out business
ventures into separate legal entities so that the failure of one does not
endanger the survival of the whole business (Burns, 2016).

Henschel and Durst (2016) did a cross-country investigation of
the attitudes of SME managers to risk and uncertainty, which con-
firms some of the theoretical observations by Burns (2016). SME
owners/managers take a different strategy for managing the risks
depending on the risk category they are looking at. SMEs attempt to
make a more comprehensive risk assessment than just a single-stage
approach. This could be due to the following reason: in contrast to
large companies, SMEs generally have only one risk strategy, namely,
that of bearing the risk themselves (risk taking). They only take out
standard insurance cover for damage resulting from fire, water, loss
in output, and interruption to operations. Otherwise, the risks
are more comprehensively assessed in terms of established/routine
variables in the business sector, in which the company is active, i.e.
in terms of supplier, customer, technology, and the internal business
processes. In terms of uncertainty in the external environment,
empirical findings revealed that SMEs face the highest uncertainty in
predicting the changes in legal regulations, in determining the buying
patterns of customers, and in assessing the strategies of competitors
(Henschel and Durst, 2016).

5. Recent Trends in the Context of SMEs

In the previous section, we focused on internal factors and took a resource-based view to exploring SMEs and their success factors. Understanding these factors is the first important step to successfully develop and pursue entrepreneurial activities. However, there are also external factors that largely influence entrepreneurial activities, and hence the success of SMEs.

To round up our introduction into entrepreneurship and SMEs, we will turn to take a look at recent developments such as megatrends: transformative global forces that have a huge impact on businesses, economies, industries, the global society, and individuals (European Cluster Observatory, 2015). Megatrends are often regarded as phenomena of a very wide nature, with no direct impact on our daily life. However, nowadays, disrupting inventions spread much quicker than they did 50 years ago. It took the radio broadcasters 38 years to reach 50 million users, TV only 13 years, the internet did it in four years, and Facebook in two years (Ovaskainen and Tinnilä, 2013). These figures show that megatrends are increasingly affecting small businesses and highlight the importance for SMEs to be alert to changes in their environment. Otherwise, these enterprises are running the risk of missing market opportunities and losing out against their competitors. Hence, also for SMEs, there is an increasing need to identify and analyze megatrends in regard to their business.

Megatrends are identified largely with the support of worldwide input from many researchers, scholars, and businesses (European Cluster Observatory, 2015; World Intellectual Property Organization, 2015, World Economic Forum, 2015). One of the most recent concepts in this area was introduced by Ernst and Young (EY) in their report "Megatrends 2015 — Making sense of a world in motion" (Ernst and Young, 2015). Figure 2 summarizes the identified factors and illustrates the single importance of each megatrend as well as the close relations between them:

When talking about *Digital Future*, the growing demand for anytime anywhere access to information technology is disrupting all areas of life across all industries and in all geographies. New opportunities arise for enterprises to take advantage of the "Internet of

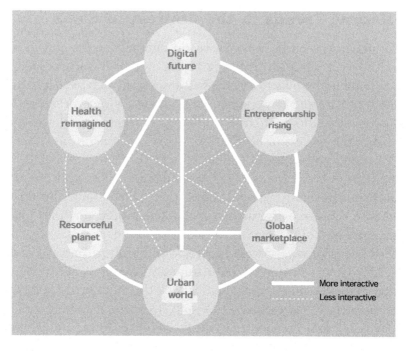

Figure 2.   Megatrends and Their Interactions
Source: Ernst and Young (2015).

Things" to enter new markets or transform existing products. However, digitalization also represents significant challenges, i.e. new competition, changing customer behavior, increasing transparency, data privacy, and cybersecurity threats (Nambisan, 2016; Li *et al.*, 2009; Ernst and Young, 2015). Especially, SMEs are hesitant to take advantage of digital disruption: a recent study carried out by PwC reveals that although 90% of German SMEs assess digitalization as the recent predominant topic, only 5% take action and look forward to starting digitalization in their own business (PwC, 2016).

Increasingly, technology is also changing the way we work. Enterprises and individuals who can seize the opportunities offered by digitalization can hugely benefit, whereas all others will likely lose quick a lot. Entrepreneurial activity is at the core of economic growth by providing income and employment for themselves as well as others and creates innovative products or services. The megatrend of *entrepreneurship rising* focuses on the growth of "high-impact" entrepreneurship that was once largely confined to mature markets and is now seen also as an important driver of economies in rapid-growth markets. Also, the face of entrepreneurship is changing: more entrepreneurs are either of young age and/or female and many of the start-ups are digital from the beginning. Both the public and the private sector play an important role in creating an entrepreneurial ecosystem. That and access to funding (which remains the primary obstacle for entrepreneurs) are the essential factors to promote entrepreneurial success (Ernst and Young, 2015).

Globalization will remain an increasing force with some new features to deal with. On the one hand, the gap between "mature" and "rapid-growth" countries continues to shrink. Also, there are new "emerging nations" that will draw global attention. Asia is likely to surface as a major hub in rapid-growth markets where innovation will increasingly take place. On a global scale, workforce diversity will increase as a weapon to fight with in the "war for talent" to secure competitive advantage. Interdependences between the economies of the world through trade, investments, and financial systems will drive the need for global policy coordination among nations. However, domestic interests will compete with global integration and lead to trade and currency protectionism, sanctions to achieve political aims, and anti-globalization protests. Hence, we will experience the strengthening of nationalistic, religious, and ethnic movements all over the world (World Economic Forum, 2015).

As number and size of cities are growing across the world, the phenomenon of an *urban world* has to be addressed. Especially, the rapid urbanization in emerging markets (Levy and Banerjee, 2008) and continued urbanization in mature markets will result in an increasing amount of the world's population living in cities, from 54% today to 66% in 2050. To secure the economic benefits of urbanization, effective planning and sustained investment in infrastructure is required from policy makers and the private sector.

The global demand for natural renewable and non-renewable resources is driven by factors such as population growth, economic development, and consumers. The megatrend *resourceful planet* addresses finiteness of the world's supply of non renewable resources by developing new technologies to access hard-to-reach and valuable oil, gas, and strategic mineral reserves. At the same time, natural resources must be more effectively managed, as protecting and restoring the planet is crucial for our future. Sustainable approaches are requested to balance economic growth and protection of natural resources (Bos-Brouwers, 2010; Ernst and Young, 2015).

The necessity to *reimagine* our approach to *health* is based on the effects of demographic change, rising incomes in rapid-growth markets, and an imminent lifestyle-related chronic disease epidemic (Williams and Snow, 2012). Hence, health care systems are under increasing cost pressure. On the other hand, big data and new mobile health technologies are enablers for real-time information creation and analysis that lead to a fundamentally different approach: focusing on the management of health, with more focus on healthy behaviors, prevention, and real-time care, instead of the traditional delivery of health care in terms of "sick care" (Ernst and Young, 2015).

To summarize, megatrends are offering opportunities and are risk-threats at the same time. Based on their characteristics such as flexibility and flat hierarchy, SMEs can benefit especially from analyzing the megatrends and acting in a proactive manner. It is worth observing these trends and moving along with them in our world of motion to ensure that SME's find creative spaces where innovation will happen. Furthermore, megatrends also lead to more permeable boundaries between a firm and its environment; hence, innovations can flow easily inward and outward — a clear indication for SMEs to get involved with the paradigm of open innovation (OI).

6. Conclusion

The aim of the first chapter was to introduce the readers to the manifold aspects of SMEs and their core drivers. Therefore, we first painted the big picture by addressing recent challenges and opportunities for SMEs in a broad and high-level manner. The second section addressed qualitative and quantitative characteristics of SMEs as well as the interaction between these characteristics.

In nearly any organization nowadays, the people behind the enterprise are one of the most important success factors. However, in SMEs, the founder or the manager plays an even more significant role for prosperity. Thus, our third section aimed to provide some insights into management behavior and governance issues of small businesses.

For a more detailed understanding of recent developments, (in the fourth section), we pointed out alternatives for financing an SME and offered some insights from current research focusing attitudes toward risk and uncertainty. With our fifth section, we took a turn to look at external challenges and opportunities that are defined as global megatrends. With our discussion, we aimed to close the circle back to the beginning of our chapter and provide our reader with some detailed information regarding the age of change and opportunity SMEs today live in.

References

Almus, M. (2004). The shadow of death — An empirical analysis of the pre-exit performance of new German firms. *Small Business Economics*, 23(3), pp. 189–201.

Armstrong, C., Craig, B., Jackson, W. and Thomson, J. (2014). The moderating influence of financial market development on the relationship between loan guarantees for SMEs and local market employment rates. *Journal of Small Business Management*, 52(1), pp. 126–140.

Australian Bureau of Statistics (2011). *Small Business in Australia 2011*, Canberra, Australian Bureau of Statistics.

Banham, H. and He, Y. (2010). SME governance: Converging definitions and expanding expectations. *International Business & Economics Research Journal*, 9(2), pp. 77.

Barbero, J., Casillas, J. and Feldman, H. (2011). Managerial capabilities and paths to growth as determinants of high-growth small and medium-sized enterprises. *International Small Business Journal*, 29(6), pp. 671–694.

Barrow, C. (1997). *Small Business*. Renmin University Publishing Company: Beijing.

Beck, T., Klapper, L and Mendoza, J. (2010). The typology of partial credit guarantee funds around the world. *Journal of Financial Stability*, 6(1), pp. 10–25.

Becker, W. and Ulrich, P. (2009). Mittelstand, KMU und Familienunternehmen in der Betriebswirtschaftslehre. *Wirtschaftswissenschaftliches Studium*, 1, pp. 2–7.

Berger, A. and Udell, G. (1990). Collateral, loan quality, and bank risk. *Journal of Monetary Economics*, 25(21) pp. 21–42.

Berger, A. and Udell, G. (1998). The economics of small business finance: The roles of private equity and debt markets on the financial growth cycle. *Journal of Banking and Finance*, 22(6–8), pp. 613–673.

Bos-Brouwers, H. (2010) Corporate sustainability and innovation in SMEs: Evidence of themes and activities in practice. *Business Strategy and the Environment*, 19(7), pp. 417–435.

Brettel, M., Engelen, A. and Voll, L. (2010). Letting Go to Grow — Empirical Findings on a Hearsay. *Journal of Small Business Management*, 48(4), pp. 552–579.

Bridge, S. and O'Neill, K. (2013). *Understanding Enterprise: Entrepreneurship and Small Business*, 4th edn. Palgrave Macmillan: London.

Brunninge, O., Nordqvist, M. and Wiklund, J. (2007). Corporate Governance and strategic change in SMEs: the effects of ownership, board composition and top management teams. *Small Business Economics*, 29(3), pp. 295–308.

Burns, P. (2016). *Entrepreneurship and Small Business*, 4th edn. Palgrave: London.

Calabrò, A. and Mussolino, D. (2011). How do boards of directors contribute to family SME export intensity? The role of formal and informal governance mechanisms. *Journal of Management & Governance*, 17(2), pp. 363–403.

Commission of the European Communities (2008). Commission recommendation concerning the definition of micro, small and medium-sized enterprises. *Official Journal of the European Union*, L124, pp. 36–41.

Coulson-Thomas, C. (2007). SME directors and boards: The contribution of directors and boards to the growth and development of small and medium-sized enterprises (SMEs). *International Journal of Business Governance and Ethics*, 3(3), p. 250.

Crossan, K. and Henschel, T. (2012). An holistic model of corporate governance for SMEs. *Journal of Management and Financial Sciences*, 5(8), pp. 54–73.

Curran, J. and Blackburn, R. (2001). *Researching the Small Enterprise*. London, Thousand Oaks, New Delhi: Sage Publications.

Dana, L. (2006). *Entrepreneurship and SMEs in the Euro-Zone. Towards a Theory of Symbiotic Entrepreneurship*, Imperial College Press: London.

De, D. (2005). *Entrepreneurship. Gründung und Wachstum von kleinen und mittleren Unternehmen*. Pearson Education: Munich.

Deakins, D., O'Neill, E. and Mileham, P. (2000). The role and influence of external directors in small entrepreneurial companies: Some evidence on VC and non-VC appointed external directors, *Venture Capital*, 2(2), pp. 111–127.

Durst, S. and Henschel, T. (2014). Governance in small firms — A country comparison of current practices. *International Journal of Entrepreneurship and Small Business*, 21(1), pp. 16–32.

Ernst and Young (2015). Megatrends 2015: Making sense of a world in motion. Available at: http://www.ey.com/Publication/vwLUAssets/ey-megatrends-report-2015/$FILE/ey-megatrends-report-2015.pdf (accessed 9 January 2017).

European Cluster Observatory (2015). European Cluster Trends. Executive Summary, European Commission: Brussels.

Eurostat (2015). Key Figures on European Business with a Special Feature on SMEs [online]. Available at: http://epp.eurostat.ec.europa.eu/cache/ITY_OFFPUB/KS-ET-15-001/EN/KS-ET-15-001-EN.PDF (accessed 13 May 2017).

European Central Bank (2013). Survey on the access to finance of small and medium-sized enterprises in the euro area, Frankfurt am Main, Germany.

European Commission (2011). *The New SME Definition: User Guide and Model Declaration*. Enterprise and Industry Publications, European Union Publications Office.

Fletscher, M. and Harris, S. (2002). Seven aspects of strategy formation: Exploring the value of planning. *International Small Business Journal*, 20(3), pp. 297–314.

Fraser, S. (2009). How Have SME Finances Been Affected by the Credit Crisis? BERR/ESRC Seminar, March.

Geppert, M. and Martens, B. (2008). Corporate financing, management and organization in SMEs: An Anglo-German comparison. In: K. Blum and R. Schmidt (Eds.), *Change in SMEs Towards a New European Capitalism*? Palgrave: New York, pp. 58–76.

Gibson, B. and Cassar, G. (2002). Planning behavior variables in small firms. *Journal of Small Business Management*, 40(3), pp. 171–186.

Gibson, B., (2009). A research framework for exploring corporate governance in SMEs. *Conference Proceedings International Council for Small Business*, Seoul, South Korea, pp. 1–12.

Gilmore, A., McAuley, A., Gallagher, D., Massiera, P. and Gamble, J. (2013). Researching SME/entrepreneurial research. *Journal of Research in Marketing and Entrepreneurship*, 15(2), pp. 87–100.

Haag, A. and Henschel, T. (2016). SME lending relationships: A learning perspective. *International Journal of Entrepreneurship and Innovation*, 17(3), pp. 184–193.

Hall, C. (2002). Entrepreneurship densities in APEC and Europe: How many entrepreneurs should there be in China, or other developing countries? *Small Enterprise Research*, 10(1), pp. 3–15.

Haltiwanger, J., Jarmin, R. and Miranda, J. (2013). Who creates jobs? Small versus large versus young. *Review of Economics and Statistics*, 95(2), pp. 347–361.

Hang, X. and Wang, C. (2012). Strategic decision-making in small and medium-sized enterprises: Evidence from Australia, *International Journal of Business Studies: A Publication of the Faculty of Business Administration, Edith Cowan University*, **20**(1), p. 91.

Henschel, T. and Durst, S. (2016). Risk management in Scottish, Chinese and German small and medium-sized enterprises: A country comparison. *International Journal of Entrepreneurship and Small Business*, **29**(1), pp. 112–132.

Herbane, B. (2010). Small business research: Time for a crisis-based view. *International Small Business Journal*, **28**(1), pp. 43–46.

Levy and Banerjee (2008). Urban entrepreneurs, ICTs, and emerging theories: A new direction for development communication. *Asian Journal of Communication*, **18**(4), pp. 304–317.

Li, J., Merenda, M. and Venkatachalam, A. (2009). Business process digitalization and new product development: An empirical study of small and medium-sized manufacturers. *International Journal of e-Business Research*, **5**(1), pp. 49–64.

Li, W., Veliyath, R. and Tan, J. (2013). Network characteristics and firm performance: An examination of the relationships in the context of a cluster. *Journal of Small Business Management*, **51**(1), pp. 1–22.

Marcelino-Sádaba, S., Perez-Ezcurdia, A., Echeverria Lazcano, A. and Villanueva, P. (2014). Project risk management methodology for small firms. *International Journal of Project Management*, **32**(2), pp. 327–340.

McGregor, J. and Tweed, D. (2002). Profiling a new generation of female small business owners in New Zealand: Networking. mentoring and growth. *Gender, Work & Organizations*, **9**(4), pp. 420–438.

Meiseberg, B. and Ehrmann, T. (2013). Tendency to network of small and medium-sized enterprises: Combining organizational economics and resource-based perspectives. *Managerial and Decision Economics*, **34**(3), pp. 238–300.

Mustakallio, M., Autio, E. and Zahra, S. A. (2002). Relational and contractual governance in family firms: Effects on strategic decision making. *Family Business Review*, **15**(3), pp. 205–222.

Nambisan, S. (2016). Digital entrepreneurship: Toward a digital technology perspective of entrepreneurship, entrepreneurship: Theory and practice. Doi: 10.1111/etap.12254.

National Bureau of Statistics of China (2013). Yearly Data. Available at: http://www.stats.gov.cn/english/stasticaldata/yearlydata/ (accessed 18 January 2016).

Neville, M. (2011). The role of boards in small and medium-sized firms. *Corporate Governance*, **11**(5), pp. 527–540.

Nguyen, T. and Bryant, S. (2004). A study of the human resource management practices in small and medium-sized enterprises in Vietnam. *International Small Business Journal*, **22**(6), pp. 595–616.

O'Donnell, A. (2013). The contribution of networking to small firm marketing. *Journal of Small Business Management*, **52**(1), pp. 164–187.

O'Regan, N., Sims, M. and Ghobadian, A. (2005). High performance: Ownership and decision-making in SMEs. *Management Decision*, **43**(3), 382–396.

Ovaskainen, M. and Tinnilä, M. (2013). Megatrends in electronic business: An analysis of the impacts on SMEs. *Modern Entrepreneurship and E-Business Innovations*, IGI Global: Hershey, USA, pp. 12–27.

Paulet, E., Parnaudeau, M. and Abdessemed, T. (2014). The SME struggle for financing: a clampdown in European banks post-crisis. *Journal of Business Strategy*, **35**(2), pp. 36–45.

Perren, L. and Grant, P. (2001). The evolution of management accounting routines in small business: A social construction perspective. *Management Accounting Research*, **11**(4), pp. 391–411.

Perry, S. C. (2001). The relationship between written business plans and the failure of small businesses in the U.S. *Journal of Small Business Management*, **39**(3), pp. 201–208.

Pfeffer, J. and Salancik, G. R. (1978). *The External Control of Organizations. A Resource Dependence Perspective*, Harper & Row: New York.

PricewaterhouseCoopers (PWC) (2016). Die Neujahrswünsche des deutschen Mittelstandes Januar 2017. Available at https://www.pwc.de/de/ mittelstand/ assets/neujahrsbefragung-mittelstand-2017.pdf (accessed 9 January 2017).

Reinemann, H. (2011). *Mittelstandsmanagement*, Schäfer-Poeschel: Stuttgart.

Richbell, S., Watts, D. and Wardle, P. (2006). Owner-managers and business planning in the small firm. *International Small Business Journal*, **24**(5), pp. 496–514.

Schaper, M., Dana, L., Anderson, R. and Moroz, P. (2008). Distribution of firms by size: Observations and evidence from selected countries. *International Journal of Entrepreneurship and Innovation Management*, **8**(6), 718–726.

Schmitt, C. (2011). Finanzierungsstrategien mittelständischer Unternehmen vor dem Hintergrund von Basel III (Finance strategies for SMEs in the light of Basel III). *Betriebs-Berater*, **2**, pp. 105–109.

Segaro, E. (2010). Internationalization of family SMEs: The impact of ownership, governance, and top management team. *Journal of Management & Governance*, **16**(1), pp. 147–169.

Smallbone, D., Leigh, R. and North, D. (1995). The characteristics and strategies of high growth SMEs. *International Journal of Entrepreneurial Behaviour & Research*, **1**(3), pp. 44–62.

Solange, C. and Perelli, S. (2013). Threats to board stability: Understanding SME director behavior. *International Journal of Disclosure and Governance*, **10**, pp. 175–191.

Sparrow, J. and Bentley, P. (2000). Decision tendencies of entrepreneurs and small business risk management practices. *Risk Management: An International Journal*, **2**(1), pp. 17–26.

Tang, J., Tang, Z., Zhang, Y. and Li, Q. (2007). The impact of entrepreneurial orientation and ownership type on firm performance in the emerging region of China. *Journal of Developmental Entrepreneurship*, 12(04), pp. 383–397.

Turner, R. and Ledwith, A. (2016). Project management in small to medium-sized enterprises: fitting the practices to the needs of the firms to deliver benefit. *Journal of Small Business Management*, in press. DOI: 10.1111/jsbm.12265.

Turner, R., Ledwith, A. and Kelly, J. (2010). Project management in small to medium-sized enterprises: matching processes to the nature of the firm. *International Journal of Project Management*, Special Issue IRNOP IX 28, pp. 744–755.

United States International Trade Commission (2010). *Small and Medium-sized Enterprises*. US International Trade Commission: Washington.

Van der Horst, R., King-Kauanui, S. and Duffy, S. (2005). *Keystones of Entrepreneurship Knowledge*. Blackwell Publishing: Malden, USA, Oxford, UK.

Vogel, R. and Adams, D. (1997). Costs and benefits of loan guarantee programs. *The Financier*, 4(1&2), pp. 22–29.

Williams, S. and Snow, D. (2012). Promoting health in small and medium-sized enterprises. *Journal of Small Business and Enterprise Development*, 19(4), pp. 929–744.

Woods, A. and Joyce, P. (2003). Owner-managers and the practice of strategic management. *International Small Business Journal*, 21(2), pp. 181–195.

World Economic Forum (2015). Deep Shift. *Technology Tipping Points and Societal Impact*. World Economic Forum: New York.

World Intellectual Property Organization (2015). *The Global Innovation Index 2015*. World Intellectual Property Organization: Geneva.

Xia, T. and Roper, S. (2016). Unpacking open innovation: Absorptive capacity, exploratory and exploitative openness, and the growth of entrepreneurial biopharmaceutical firms. *Journal of Small Business Management*, 54(3), pp. 931–952.

Zaheer, A. and Venkatraman, N. (1995). Relational governance as an interorganizational strategy: An empirical test of the role of trust in economic exchange. *Strategic Management Journal*, 16(5), pp. 373–392.

Chapter 2

The Concept of Open Innovation

Ilker Murat Ar

Department of Business Administration,
Karadeniz Technical University, Trabzon, Turkey
ilkerar@ktu.edu.tr

Innovation activities in the global economies are becoming more interrelated and open in nature. So, firms want to enter into more collaborative relationships to exploit innovation. This trend shapes a new approach called as "Open Innovation (OI)". It involves forming collaborative relationships with other organizations as the basis for achieving competitive advantage through the development of new or improved products and services. This chapter mainly describes the general framework of OI. In this context, it defines the OI term and presents the scope of OI. It also contributes the benefits and risks of OI. The effects of OI may not be the same at all firms because it is a multi-dimensional concept. Thus, the same output may not be reached at the end of the same OI process for all organizations. For this reason, attention should be paid to the organizational and environmental characteristics in the planning of the process.

1. Introduction to Open Innovation (OI)

At the beginning of the 21st century, more organizations moved toward collaborating with each other to enhance their competitive advantage. This cooperation approach has also affected the innovation process. Thus, innovation processes and activities have become important for interaction and cooperation.

Innovation activities in the global economies have become more interrelated and open in nature. The open attitude considers the organization as a nonbounded entity which is in interaction with its surroundings. This approach emphasizes the rationality of the organizational processes and the exchange between the organization and the environment (Abouzeedan and Hedner, 2012). So, the nature of the innovation model has changed from linear to nonlinear (Kline and Rosenberg, 1986). The nonlinear innovation model basically focuses on the learning and exploration processes within and between firms (Teirlinck and Spithoven, 2008).

Applying the input of outsiders can improve internal innovation processes and expand the utilization of current capabilities. Thus, innovation cooperation activities are considered an efficient means for industrial organization of Research and Development (R&D) and innovation processes (Yoon and Song, 2014). Chesbrough (2003c) posited that firms in the 21st century are more likely to be successful by entering into collaborative relationships with other organizations when seeking to exploit innovation.

2. Emergence of Open Innovation

Not many years ago, firms used to rely almost entirely upon their internal resources when conducting R&D, and, typically, only firms that had adequate internal resources could obtain revenue through their own innovations (Hossain et al., 2016). According to Chesbrough (2003a), firms have traditionally managed their R&D activities as an internal process, relying mostly only on their internal capabilities and skills. He argues that internal R&D is no longer the invaluable strategic asset that it used to be due to a fundamental shift in how companies generate new ideas and bring them to the market (Chesbrough, 2003b, 2003c).

Because useful knowledge is no longer concentrated in a few large organizations, it becomes necessary to open the R&D models of organizations. The potential for obtaining knowledge and technology from outside a firm's boundaries has significantly increased (Inauen and Schenker-Wicki, 2011). As a result of this trend, enterprises can no longer afford to innovate on their own, but rather need to engage in alternative innovation practices (van de Vrande *et al.*, 2009).

Chesbrough (2003c) stated that firms in the 21st century are more likely to be successful by engaging in "Open Innovation (OI)". This involves forming collaborative relationships with other organizations as the basis for achieving competitive advantage through the development of new or improved products and services. The OI model has centered on the R&D process in relation to the inflows and outflows of knowledge to accelerate internal and market innovation (Chesbrough, 2006a).

Consequently, OI has received substantial business attention as a means of providing firms in hyper-competitive environments with the ability to create a stream of new products and services (Almirall *et al.*, 2014). OI has been an emergent concept in innovation studies and a major trend in practice, attracting wider attention from academics, policymakers, and practitioners (Fu and Xiong, 2011). Today, the concept of OI has become a paradigm that connects research from various disciplines.

3. What is Open Innovation and What is not?

There are various definitions of OI in the related literature. The definition of Chesbrough, who first proposed the team OI, is the most widely accepted. Chesbrough (2003b) describes it as the integration of knowledge and technology from multiple sources to develop and create new products and services. According to the definition, OI stresses the importance of capturing external knowledge or technology and converting it into innovative products and services (Chesbrough, 2003c).

Chesbrough's (2003b) paradigm was revised three years later (Chesbrough, 2006b) as the use of inflows and outflows of knowledge to accelerate internal innovation and to expand the markets for external use of innovation. Thus, the OI concept has been considered mainly as the relationship between various institutions for innovation. Today, it was extended to define (Chesbrough and Bogers, 2014) as an innovation process managed by knowledge flows across organizational boundaries in line with the organization's business model.

What OI really is, is still a great discussion among the researchers and practitioners. However, the OI idea assumes that corporate innovation activities are more like an open system than the traditional vertically integrated model (West *et al.*, 2014). The OI concept can be considered as an antithesis to the traditional vertical integrated innovation paradigm where products are developed internally (Schroll and Mild, 2011). It emphasizes the sharing of knowledge within and among organizations (Abouzeedan and Hedner, 2012).

In the concept of OI, firms can use external knowledge, together with their own, to create new products or services. In this line of thought, R&D is seen as an open system (Duarte and Sarkar, 2011). In other words, OI suggests that firms should combine external and internal ideas and technologies as effective pathways to market when advancing and commercializing technologies (Wynarczyk *et al.*, 2013).

Chesbrough (2011) extended the OI approach by introducing the concept of open service innovation. He argues that adopting the open service innovation approach is imperative, especially for western firms. He also provided a framework for the open service innovation concept, which consists of four fundamental activities:

- thinking of a business as an open service business,
- co-creating innovations,
- using OI to accelerate and deepen service innovations, and
- transforming the whole business model with the help of the open service innovation approach.

4. Closed vs. Open Innovation

Traditionally, large firms relied on internal R&D to create new products and services. In many industries, large internal R&D labs were a strategic asset and represented a considerable entry barrier for potential rivals (van de Vrande *et al.*, 2009). This process by which large firms discover, develop, and commercialize technologies internally has been labeled as a closed innovation model (Chesbrough, 2003c).

In the closed innovation model, firms relied on the assumption that innovation processes needed to be controlled by the organization (Elmquist *et al.*, 2009). The closed innovation model is reaching its limits as a result of the increasing mobility of knowledge and highly skilled employees, rapid alternations in consumption and production functions, and the shortening of product lifecycles. In addition, the latest advances in the commercialization of technology and intellectual property (IP) strengthen the shift from a closed towards an open model (Inauen and Schenker-Wicki, 2011).

In contrast to the traditional closed innovation model, Open Innovation (OI) describes a core concept of enterprises breaking through their previously closed borders to take in more innovative ideas from the external environment while sharing unused innovative ideas with other organizations (Huang *et al.*, 2015). Furthermore, driver factors (van de Vrande *et al.*, 2009; Geum *et al.*, 2013) from closed to OI model can be seen in Figure 1.

There is a remarkable finding when comparing the closed innovation and OI models in terms of their impact on the innovation process. According to the results of Inauen and Schenker-Wicki's (2012)

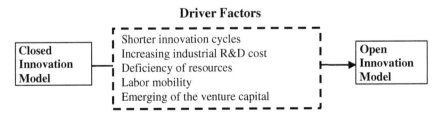

Figure 1.   Driver Factors from Closed to Open Innovation Model

study, companies that emphasize OI are more likely to create radical innovations. Companies pursuing closed innovation are more likely to exhibit a higher incremental product innovation performance.

5. The Scope of Open Innovation

OI suggests that enterprises not only can but also should utilize external concepts just as they use internal concepts (Huang *et al.*, 2015). Thus, the nature of the OI model makes it easy for the firms to adapt their business model in favor of R&D activities and technical changes that take place outside the firm (Abouzeedan and Hedner, 2012). OI can be viewed not just as collaborative innovation with competitors or suppliers, but also with users (Geum *et al.*, 2013). Therefore, the scope of OI ranges from the direction of knowledge flows (outside–in or inside–out), to the forms of openness (alliances, joint ventures, networks, etc.), and the parties involved (suppliers, users, competitors, communities).

OI is the result of successful relations with outside entities, such as other firms, suppliers, lead users, competitors, consultants, commercial laboratories, R&D institutes, universities, opinion leaders, public research centers, customers, and even groups of product users as sources of innovations (Duarte and Sarkar, 2011).

In fact, after reviewing the relevant literature, key dimensions of OI approach can be classified into three general dimensions as organizational readiness, collaborative capabilities, and absorptive capacity (Hafkesbrink and Schroll, 2010; Khosropour *et al.*, 2015):

Organizational Readiness: This dimension pays attention to cultural dimensions and organizational atmosphere, appropriate structure and process, change and renewal, and technological enhancement for application of such an approach in the organization. OI requires the following approaches:

- Flexible organizations border to environment.
- Easy communication between organization's employees and people outside of the organization.

- Free flow of information between organization and environment.
- Dynamic capabilities for change and renewal.
- Organization's ability for construction, merger, and reforming.
- Organizational learning concept.

Collaborative capabilities is at the heart of the OI discourse and can be considered as the organizational merger and levering elements for creating organization's ability and capacity for OI. It includes three functions as internal cooperation, networking competency, and outside–inside and inside–outside cooperation.

Internal cooperation function consists of cooperation for increasing inter-field technology and knowledge interchanges inside structural borders.

Networking competency function includes the organization's ability and chief capacity for creating, managing, completing, maintaining, and concluding in innovation network.

Outside–inside and inside–outside cooperation function indicate the internal and external flow of technology and knowledge for internal innovation.

Absorptive capacity is a feature of an organization that follows OI and includes the following competencies:

- Identification of technological opportunities.
- Elicitation and assimilation (including the ability to recognize internal and external knowledge and technological capabilities).
- Understanding and transforming (including the ability to absorb, adjust, and merge external knowledge and technology to internal product development).
- Sharing, dissemination, and exploitation (including the ability to determine the knowledge value in market's direction).

As it has been stated above, theoretical background to the OI concept stems from learning theories, dynamic capabilities theory, and absorptive capacity, all of which are related to notions of knowledge (Geum *et al.*, 2013).

6. Types of Open Innovation Model

According to Chesbrough (2012), there are mainly two kinds of OI: outside–in and inside–out. Firms may open up their OI processes in these two dimensions (Lichtenthaler and Ernst, 2007).

Outside–in OI refers to inside knowledge acquisition and to leveraging the discoveries of others (Chesbrough and Crowther, 2006). It refers to the acquisition of external technology in open exploration processes (Fu and Xiong, 2011). Outside–in OI is the internal use of external knowledge from external partners. In this way, firms can reinforce their competence by integrating other actors into the internal innovation process.

Studies have defined the types of outside–in OI with different perspectives. Some examples of the outside–in OI types are as follows (Gassmann and Enkel, 2004; Spithoven *et al.*, 2010; Abulrub and Lee, 2012):

- technology in-licensing
- acquisition
- joint development
- joint venture
- earlier supplier integration
- customer co-development (involvement)
- external knowledge sourcing
- contract R&D (outsourcing)
- in-licensing
- buying patents.

Alternatively, inside-out OI refers to the external exploitation of internal knowledge. Firms can carry out inside-out OI activities, such as technology licensing; thus, they can make profits by bringing ideas, patents, and other forms of Intellectual Property (IP) rights to the market (Lichtenthaler, 2008) to open up a company's innovation process to the external environment (Hossain, 2013). This describes the inside-out transfer of technology in open exploitation processes (Enkel *et al.*, 2009) and also suggests that firms can look for external organizations with business models that are suited to commercializing a technology exclusively or are additional to its internal application (Chesbrough and Crowther, 2006). Abulrub and Lee (2012) listed the inside–out OI types as selling, licensing-out, spin-off, and open source.

Apart from these two main classifications of OI, some researchers propose combined or coupled OI when both outside–in and inside–out OI processes take place simultaneously (Enkel *et al.*, 2009; Gassmann *et al.*, 2010; Veugelers *et al.*, 2010). Gassmann and Enkel (2004) have defined coupled OI as the phenomenon in which both outside–in and inside–out OI coexist through partnerships, collaborations, alliances, joint ventures, etc. It is reasonable to assume that a collaboration may lead to different results compared to the mere simultaneous existence of outside–in and inside–out OI (Greco *et al.*, 2015). Greco *et al.* (2015) found that process innovation is more likely to benefit from coupled OI activities rather than outside–in activities. It should be noted that an integrated management system is necessary to support both outside–in and inside–out OI (Brunswicker and Ehrenmann, 2013).

7. The Benefits of Open Innovation

OI provides access to new knowledge, permitting the evolution of new strategies more appropriate for responding to turbulent conditions that exist in world markets (Chesbrough, 2007). There are many advantages to being gained from using OI. The most important aspect of involvement in OI is to access new sources of external knowledge that will enhance the new innovation activities (Lichtenthaler and Lichtenthaler, 2009). Many of these benefits are listed below (Niehaves, 2010; Almirall *et al.*, 2014; McCormack *et al.*, 2015):

- increased revenues
- cost reduction
- customer involvement
- up-to-date product ranges.

According to Usman and Vanhaverbeke (2017), startups benefit from OI in many ways such as the following:

• It can commercialize its technology without investing in complementary assets.
• It keeps the option to serve niche markets.
• The royalty income allows it to invest in R&D for new technologies.

Results of the empirical research by Theyel (2012) pointed out that a strong interrelationship between OI practices with customers and suppliers throughout the firm's value chain affect the product and process innovation performance activities.

The general business performance will be higher among firms involved in OI. Hossain and Kauranen (2016) found that adopting OI by small and medium-sized enterprises (SMEs) improves their overall innovation performance. Similarly, Inauen and Schenker-Wicki (2011) indicated that openness toward customers, suppliers, and universities has a significant positive impact on the different innovation performance measures. Lichtenthaler (2008) also concluded that the degree of openness seems to rise with the degree of emphasis on radical innovation. Rajala *et al.*'s (2012) case highlighted that an ambidextrous approach that combines market orientation with the principles of OI increases profitability and enhances innovation capability.

There still remains an important void in the literature; namely, empirical validation of claims that OI enhances financial performance (Gianiodis *et al.*, 2010; Caputo *et al.*, 2016) and business performance (Chaston and Scott, 2012; Scott and Chaston, 2013). Huang *et al.* (2010) proposed that OI leads to business growth by permitting organizations to leverage more ideas from a variety of external sources. The results obtained from Wynarczyk (2013) showed that a significantly higher proportion of OI firms were involved in exports.

8. Open Innovation Strategies

OI is a well-documented innovation strategy which sees companies utilize outside knowledge to enhance their capabilities or allow

Table 1.   Classification of the OI Actions

External OI actions	
Outside–in actions	Internal use of external knowledge
Inside–out actions	External exploitation of internal knowledge
Coupled actions	Collaboration by means of partnerships, collaborations, alliances, joint ventures
Internal OI actions	
Internal OI actions	Actions promoted within a company in order to improve innovation performance in an OI perspective

Source: Greco *et al.* (2015).

outside partners or independent actors to share or buy their unused IP (McCormack *et al.*, 2015). Chesbrough (2007) noted that not all companies utilize the same approach to OI. Christensen *et al.* (2005) concluded that OI is influenced by a number of different factors such as (i) the position of a firm in the market system, (ii) the position of a firm's products or services on the product life-cycle, and (iii) the scale of added value available through the introduction of new production technologies.

Classification of the OI actions is shown in Table 1. It consists of four categories, the first three being representative of external OI actions and the fourth of internal one.

Schuhmacher *et al.* (2013) identified and characterized four new types of open innovators based on their analysis of the R&D models of 13 multinational companies. According to them, open innovator types are knowledge creator, knowledge integrator, knowledge translator, and knowledge leverage (Table 2).

9. The Risks and Challenges of Open Innovation

Managing the network of innovation partners takes a central place in an OI environment and is crucial for the success of the firms (Usman and Vanhaverbeke, 2017). In this point, a central concern in an OI strategy is how the generated value can be captured and how

Table 2.   Open Innovator Types

Type	Definition
Knowledge creator	It is defined as an outside–in preference in innovation management combined with a lower level of externally acquired R&D projects when compared with the industry standard.
Knowledge integrator	It describes the preference of using externally generated innovation in a model that predominantly relies on internal resources and know-how.
Knowledge translator	It is defined as a preference to use resources and knowledge that come from the outside of the company to accelerate internally generated innovation.
Knowledge leverager	It describes a focus toward externally generated innovation in combination with a predominantly extroverted innovation management.

Source: Schuhmacher *et al.* (2013).

potential risks can be managed and minimized (Siakas and Siakas, 2016). Therefore, many researchers believe that OI could be harmful to the firm (Keupp and Gassmann, 2009).

The literature on OI has focused more extensively on the benefits than on the costs, disadvantages, limitations, and risks that need to be emphasized so that companies can prepare accordingly (Siakas and Siakas, 2016). The challenges of OI were identified by Siakas and Siakas (2016) as in Table 3.

Firms developing OI applications should pay attention in protecting their organizational knowledge. Islam (2012) states that OI can have a negative impact on an organization's competitive advantage and its long-term sustainability. Moreover, as highlighted by Lichtenthaler (2011), if a company shares its knowledge externally, it exposes its core competencies to competitors, thus creating vulnerability. Therefore, knowledge sharing is considered the main risk of OI (Bigliardi and Galati, 2016). Moreover, many firms often choose not to implement OI in order to avoid such vulnerability and not lose control on their proprietary knowledge (Bigliardi and Galati, 2013).

Table 3.   The Challenges of OI

Challenge	Definition
Lack of control	Openness implies an inherent lack of control both regarding the processes and the potential results.
Difficulties to manage incoming innovations	Integrating ideas, insights, concepts, and solutions from OI initiatives into established new product development processes is a significant challenge.
Misappropriation of ideas	Competitors and others may misappropriate the openly exposed business idea.
Protection of intellectual property right (IPR)	The complexity of IPR and fear of infringements may be a barrier for companies to engage in OIs.
Reduction of openness	At some point, returns of openness may be diminished due to poor maintenance of an open attitude.
Human resource challenges	How to improve employee engagement and empowerment.
Culture of sharing	Sharing information without and trusting stakeholders.
Information and communication technology (ICT) literacy	Not all people are confident users of ICTs.

10. Conclusion

Organizations are more likely to be successful by entering into collaborative relationships with their environments. So, they can no longer afford to rely entirely on their own internal R&D efforts, but rather need to engage in alternative cooperation practices to create new products and services. The most important reasons for this trend, called OI, are increasing industrial R&D cost and deficiency of resources and shorter innovation cycles.

OI has been an emergent concept in innovation studies and a major trend in practice attracting wider attention from academicians, policymakers, and practitioners. The effects of OI may not be the same in all firms because it is a multi-dimensional concept that can be implemented in many different ways. Thus, the same output may not be reached at the end of the same OI process for all organizations. For this reason, it should be paid to the organizational characteristics such as size, industry type, age, and ownership in the planning of the process. External environmental characteristics also affect the OI performance.

It is necessary to pay attention to the risks of innovation such as lack of control and IP protection. Managing the OI partners takes a central place and is crucial for the success of the organization. With regard to this, organizations should carefully plan many critical issues such as level of openness, context dependency, quality of knowledge to be shared, and IP sharing.

OI is a dynamic process, not a clear-cut concept. It comes in many forms and cases. Therefore, OI frameworks and implementation process should be rigorously planned and strategically structured from a tactical point of view. Otherwise, it may not be possible to achieve the expected benefits of OI.

References

Abouzeedan, A. and Hedner, T. (2012). Organization structure theories and open innovation paradigm. *World Journal of Science, Technology and Sustainable Development*, 9(1), pp. 6–27.

Abulrub, A.-H. G. and Lee, J. (2012). Open innovation management: Challenges and prospects. *Procedia-Social and Behavioral Sciences*, 41, pp. 130–138.

Almirall, E., Lee, M. and Majchrzak, A. (2014), Open innovation requires integrated competition-community ecosystems: Lessons learned from civic open innovation. *Business Horizons*, 57, pp. 391–400.

Bigliardi, B. and Galati, F. (2013). Models of adoption of open innovation within the food industry. *Trends in Food Science & Technology*, 30, pp. 16–26.

Bigliardi, B. and Galati, F. (2016). Open innovation and incorporation between academia and food industry. In: Galanakis, C. (Ed.). *Innovation Strategies in the Food Industry*, Academic Press, pp. 19–39.

Brunswicker, S. and Ehrenmann, F. (2013). Managing open innovation in SMEs: A good practice example of a German software firm. *International Journal of Industrial Engineering and Management*, 4(1), pp. 33–41.

Caputo, M., Lamberti, E., Cammarano, A. and Michelino, F. (2016). Exploring the impact of open innovation on firm performances. *Management Decision*, 54(7), pp. 1788–1812.

Chaston, I. and Scott, G. J. (2012). Entrepreneurship and open innovation in an emerging economy. *Management Decision*, 50(7), pp. 1161–1177.

Chesbrough, H. (2003a). The logic of open innovation: Managing intellectual property. *CA Management Review*, **45**(3), pp. 33–58.

Chesbrough, H. W. (2003b). *Open Innovation: The New Imperative for Creating and Profiting from Technology*, Harvard Business School Press, Boston, MA.

Chesbrough, H. W. (2003c). The era of open innovation. *Sloan Management Review*, **44**(3), pp. 35–41.

Chesbrough, H. (2006a). *Open Business Models: How to Thrive in the New Innovative Landscape*, Harvard Business School Publishing, Cambridge, MA.

Chesbrough, H. (2006b). Open Innovation: A New Paradigm for Understanding Industrial Innovation. In: H. Chesbrough, W. Vanhaverbeke, and J. West (Eds.). *Open Innovation: Researching a New Paradigm*. Oxford: Oxford University Press, pp. 1–12.

Chesbrough, H. W. (2007). Why companies should have open business models. *Sloan Management Review*, **48**(2), pp. 22–28.

Chesbrough, H. (2011). The case for open services innovation: The commodity trap. *CA Management Review*, **53**(3), pp. 5–20.

Chesbrough, H. (2012). Open innovation: Where we've been and where we're going. *Research-Technology Management*, **55**(4), pp. 20–27.

Chesbrough, H. and Crowther, A. K. (2006). Beyond high-tech: Early adopters of open innovation in other industries. *R&D Management*, **36**(3), pp. 229–236.

Chesbrough, H. and Bogers, M. (2014). Explicating open innovation: Clarifying an emerging paradigm for understanding innovation. In: H. Chesbrough, W. Vanhaverbeke, and J. West (Eds.). *New Frontiers in Open Innovation*. Oxford: Oxford University Press, pp. 3–28.

Christensen, J. F., Olesen, M. H. and Kjaer, J. S. (2005). The industrial dynamics of open innovation-evidence from the transformation of consumer electronics. *Research Policy*, **34**(10), pp. 1533–1549.

Duarte, V. and Sarkar, S. (2011). Separating the wheat from the chaff — a taxonomy of open innovation. *European Journal of Innovation Management*, **14**(4), pp. 435–459.

Elmquist, M., Fredberg, T. and Ollila, S. (2009). Exploring the field of open innovation. *European Journal of Innovation Management*, **12**(3), pp. 326–345.

Enkel, E., Gassmann, O. and Chesbrough, H. (2009). Open R&D and open innovation: Exploring the phenomenon. *R&D Management*, **39**(4), pp. 311–316.

Fu, X. and Xiong, H. (2011). Open innovation in China: Policies and practices. *Journal of Science and Technology Policy in China*, **2**(3), pp. 196–218.

Gassmann, O. and Enkel, E. (2004). Towards a Theory of open innovation: Three core process archetypes. *The R&D Management Conference*, Lisbon, Portugal.

Gassmann, O., Enkel, E. and Chesbrough, H. (2010). The future of open innovation. *R&D Management*, **40**(3), pp. 213–221.

Geum, Y., Kim, J. Son, C. and Park, Y. (2009). Development of dual technology roadmap (TRM) for open innovation: Structure and typology. *Journal of Engineering and Technology Management*, **30**, pp. 309–325.

Gianiodis, P., Ellis, S. C. and Secchi, E. (2010). Advancing a typology of open innovation. *International Journal of Innovation Management*, 14(4), pp. 531–572.

Greco, M., Grimaldi, M. and Cricelli, L. (2015). Open innovation actions and innovation performance: A literature review of European empirical evidence. *European Journal of Innovation Management*, 18(2), pp. 150–171.

Hafkesbrink, J. and Schroll, M. (2010). Organizational competences for open innovation in small and medium sized enterprises of the digital economy, http://www.innowise.eu/sites/default/files/pubs/Organizational%20Competences%20for%20Open%20Innovation%202010.pdf (accessed 15 February 2017).

Hossain, M. (2013). Open innovation: So far and a way forward. *World Journal of Science, Technology and Sustainable Development*, 10(1), pp. 30–41.

Hossain, M. and Kauranen, I. (2016). Open innovation in SMEs: A systematic literature review. *Journal of Strategy and Management*, 9(1), pp. 58–73.

Hossain, M., Islam, K. M. Z., Abu Sayeed, M. and Kauranen, I. (2016). A comprehensive review of open innovation literature. *Journal of Science & Technology Policy Management*, 7(1), pp. 2–25.

Huang, T., Wang, W. C., Yun, W., Tseng, C. and Lee, C. (2010). Managing technology transfer in open innovation: The case study in Taiwan. *Modern Applied Science*, 4(1), pp. 2–11.

Huang, H-C., Lai, M-C. and Huang, W-W. (2015). Resource complementarity, transformative capacity, and inbound open innovation. *Journal of Business & Industrial Marketing*, 30(7), pp. 842–854.

Inauen, M. and Schenker-Wicki, A. (2011). The impact of outside–in open innovation on innovation performance. *European Journal of Innovation Management*, 14(4), pp. 496–520.

Inauen, M. and Schenker-Wicki, A. (2012). Fostering radical innovations with open innovation. *European Journal of Innovation Management*, 15(2), pp. 212–231.

Islam, A. M. (2012). Methods of open innovation knowledge sharing risk reduction: A case study. *International Journal of e-Education, e-Business, e-Management and e-Learning*, 2(4), pp. 294–297.

Keupp, M. M. and Gassmann, O. (2009). Determinants and archetype users of open innovation. *R&D Management*, 39, pp. 331–341.

Khosropour, H., Feizi, K., Tabaeean, K. and Taheri, Z. (2015). The effect of open innovation on technology intelligence in aviation industry of Iran. *Science, Technology & Society*, 20(1), pp. 89–113.

Kline, S. and Rosenberg, N. (1986). An overview of innovation. In: Landau, R. and Rosenberg, N. (Eds). *The Positive Sum Strategy: Harnessing Technology for Economic Growth*, National Academy Press, Washington, DC, pp. 275–305.

Lichtenthaler, U. (2008). Open innovation in practice: An analysis of strategic approaches to technology transactions. *IEEE Transactions on Engineering Management*, 55(1), pp. 148–157.

Lichtenthaler, U. and Ernst, H. (2007). External technology commercialization in large firms: Results of a quantitative benchmarking study. *R&D Management*, 37(5), pp. 383–97.

Lichtenthaler, U. and Lichtenthaler, E. (2009). A capability based framework for open innovation: Complementing absorptive capacity. *Journal of Management Studies*, 46(8), pp. 1315–1338.

Lichtenthaler, U. (2011). Is open innovation a field of study or a communication barrier to theory development? A contribution to the current debate. *Technovation*, 31, pp. 138–139.

McCormack, B., Fallon, E. F. and Cormican, K. *et al.*, (2015), An analysis of open innovation practices in the medical technology sector in Ireland. *Procedia Manufacturing*, 3, pp. 503–509.

Niehaves, B. (2010). Open process innovation: The impact of personnel resource scarcity on the involvement of customers and consultants in public sector BPM. *Business Process Management Journal*, 16(3), pp. 377–393.

Rajala, R., Westerlund, M. and Möller, K. (2012). Strategic flexibility in open innovation-designing business models for open source software. *European Journal of Marketing*, 46(10), pp. 1368–1388.

Schroll, A. and Mild, A. (2011). Open innovation modes and the role of internal R&D An empirical study on open innovation adoption in Europe. *European Journal of Innovation Management*, 14(4), pp. 475–495.

Schuhmacher, A., Trill, H. and Gassmann, O. (2013). Models for open innovation in the pharmaceutical industry. *Drug Discovery Today*, 18(23, 24), pp. 1133–1137.

Scott, G. J. and Chaston, I. (2013). Open innovation in an emerging economy. *Management Research Review*, 36(10), pp. 1024–1036.

Siakas, D. and Siakas, K. (2016). *User Orientation through Open Innovation and Customer Integration*. In: C. Kreiner *et al.* (Eds.), EuroSPI 2016, CCIS 633, Springer, pp. 325–341.

Spithoven, A., Clarysse, B. and Knockaert, M. (2010). Building absorptive capacity to organize inbound open innovation in traditional industries. *Technovation*, 30(2), pp. 130–141.

Teirlinck, P. and Spithoven, A. (2008). The spatial organization of innovation: Open innovation, external knowledge relations and urban structure. *Regional Studies*, 42(5), pp. 689–704.

Theyel, N. (2012). Extending open innovation throughout the value chain by small and medium-sized manufacturers. *International Small Business Journal*, 31(3), pp. 256–274.

Usman, M. and Vanhaverbeke, W. (2017). How start-ups successfully organize and manage open innovation with large companies. *European Journal of Innovation Management*, 20(1), pp. 171–186.

van de Vrande, V., de Jong, J. P. J., Vanhaverbeke, W. and de Rochemont, M. (2009). Open innovation in SMEs: Trends, motives and management challenges. *Technovation*, **29**, pp. 423–437.

Veugelers, M., Bury, J. and Viaene, S. (2010). Linking technology intelligence to open innovation. *Technological Forecasting & Social Change*, **77**(2), pp. 335–343.

West, J., Salter, A., Vanhaverbeke W. and Chesbrough, H. (2014). Open innovation: The next decade. *Research Policy*, **43**, pp. 805–811.

Wynarczyk, P., Piperopoulos, P. and McAdam, M. (2013). Open innovation in small and medium-sized enterprises: An overview. *International Small Business Journal*, **31**(3), pp. 240–255.

Wynarczyk, P. (2013). Open innovation in SMEs: A dynamic approach to modern entrepreneurship in the twenty-first century. *Journal of Small Business and Enterprise Development*, **20**(2), pp. 258–278.

Yoon, B. and Song, B. (2014). A systematic approach of partner selection for open innovation. *Industrial Management & Data Systems*, **114**(7), pp. 1068–1093.

Chapter 3

Knowledge Management

Helio Aisenberg Ferenhof

*Post-Graduation Program in Information
and Communication Technologies,
Federal University of Santa Catarina (UFSC), Campus Araranguá,
Campus Reitor João David Ferreira, Florianópolis,
SC 88040-900, Brazil*

This chapter presents what knowledge is, what types of knowledge are there, what knowledge management (KM) is about, and finally how knowledge is created and shared. What can be learned from this chapter? Knowledge is the most important asset an organization has! It is inherent in people and forms the organizational intellectual capital. It is hard to share, acquire, and store if knowledge is in the tacit format because of that, it should be converted into explicit knowledge. There is a way of dealing with knowledge — KM — that tries to "get the best out of it". To do effective KM, there are components, standards, and processes. They must be understood by and incorporated in the organization, so that knowledge can be extracted from people's mind and be internalized into the company as organizational knowledge. Doing that will make possible the development of goods, services, business processes, and systems.

1. Introduction

In a globally competitive market, the basis for competitiveness, in other words, competitive advantage, is geared more and more toward the creation and assimilation of knowledge (Porter, 1993). Knowledge is the asset with the highest value that a company can have, and thus it constitutes the main source of competitiveness (Davenport and Prusak, 1998; Nonaka and Takeuchi, 1997). With embedded knowledge, it is possible to innovate the business processes, services, assets, and systems inherent in the organization. To achieve this purpose, knowledge management (KM) has become a fundamental part of making the knowledge flow, permeating the whole company.

KM is founded on the idea that an organization's most precious resource is the people's knowledge. Thus, the extent to which an organization performs well will depend, among other things, on how effectively its people can create new knowledge, share knowledge around the organization, and use that knowledge to the best effect (Servin and De Brun, 2005).

Given the briefing context, the main idea of this chapter is to present what is knowledge, what are the types of knowledge, what is organizational knowledge, what is KM, what are the KM components and process, and finally how to create and share knowledge.

2. What is Knowledge?

There are several definitions of knowledge, depending on the perspective that you see knowledge from, i.e. your background and the discipline used to understand it. This chapter starts with the definition of Aranha and Martins (1993), who view knowledge as the thought that results from the relation that is established between the subject that knows and the object to be known. Based on this statement, it makes clear that knowledge institutes the act of knowing as an association established between the known world and the perceiver's consciousness. Besides this "philosophic" definition, Davenport and Prusak (1998, p. 6) define knowledge aligned with the business context, they state that "knowledge is a fluid mixture of condensed experience, values, contextual information and experienced insight, which provides a framework for evaluating and embedding new experiences and information". They also say that it has its origin and is applied in the minds of connoisseurs. This means that knowledge is attached to people. But from another perspective, knowledge is also "embedded in the physical goods, the organizational procedures and in the rules and routines that the organization adopts" (Ichijo and Nonaka, 2006, p. 135).

In summary, knowledge is the most valuable asset that an organization may have (Davenport and Prusak, 1998). Its applications/uses include the transformation of ideas into products (goods or services) by a company; the creation, implementation, and improvement of a process; and the generation and application of technology. Given such importance, which is inherent to the people of the organization, knowledge must be identified, explained, and socialized to improve the knowledge of the organization.

3. Types of Knowledge

Normally knowledge can be divided into tacit and explicit, and the ways to deal with it are slightly different.

Tacit knowledge is the personal knowledge embedded in individual experience and intangible factors that refer to one's value systems, beliefs, and perspectives. Because of this subjective nature, it is difficult to transmit (Ichijo and Nonaka, 2006; Nonaka and Takeuchi, 1997). It consists of many components, for instance, assumptions, beliefs, experience, ground intelligence, intuition, judgment, truth, and values. The tacit component is predominantly developed by a trial and error process in practice (Tiwana, 2002). In synthesis is the knowledge which is comprehended inside a knower's mind. For instance, walking. You know how to do it, you can repeat the task of a walk, but you cannot express easily, in words or writing, the instructions of how to walk. Corroborating that, Choo (2006, p. 136) states that "tacit knowledge may be linked to knowing that is in our action, 'implicit in our patterns of actions and in our feel for the stuff with which we are dealing'". And "knowing-in-action" still according to Choo (2006), is defined by Schön (1983) with three properties:

(1) There are actions, recognitions, and judgments which we know how to carry out spontaneously; we do not have to think about them prior to or during their performance.

(2) We are often unaware of having learned to do these things; we simply find ourselves doing them.

(3) In some cases, we were once aware of the understandings which were subsequently internalized in our feeling for the stuff of action. In other cases, we may never have been aware of them. In both cases, however, we are usually unable to describe the knowing which our action reveals (Schön, 1983, p. 54).

Explicit knowledge is one that can be articulated in formal language through drawings, writing, mathematical expressions, etc. It is easily transmitted between individuals and is capable of being stored and processed by computers (Nonaka and Takeuchi, 1997). This means that it can be expressed directly by knowledge representations. According to Tiwana (2002, p. 45), "Is that component of knowledge that can be codified and transmitted in a systematic and formal language: documents, databases, webs, emails, charts, etc."

Explicit knowledge is essential to develop organizational knowledge. The specification about how to do things like rules, policies, and directives, which is a significant part of an organization's operational knowledge, are results of explicit knowledge. Also, it encodes previous learning, generating lessons learned. The procedures, actions, activities, solutions, and methods that went right or wrong can be registered and formalized as rules to avoid knowledge waste by reinvention. Moreover, explicit knowledge assists in the management of distinct functions and activities in the organization. Furthermore, its usage permits the organization to project its professional skill and technical wisdom, therefore presenting a self-image of accountability, competence, and legitimacy (Choo, 2006).

When talking about the distinction between tacit and explicit knowledge, normally the main discussion is made on knowledge transferability and the mechanisms that accomplish this transfer. Tacit knowledge is revealed by its application. On the other hand,

Table 1. Comparing Tacit and Explicit Knowledge

Characteristics	Tacit	Explicit
Nature	Personal, context-specific	Can be codified and explicated
Formalization	Difficult to formalize, record, encode, or articulate	Can be codified and transmitted in a systematic and formal language
Development process	Developed through a process of trial and error encountered in practice	Developed thought explication of tacit understanding and interpretation of information
Location	Stored in the heads of people	Stored in documents, databases, Web pages, e-mails, charts, etc.
Conversion process	Converted to explicit thought externalization that is often driven by metaphors and analogy	
IT support	Hard to manage, share, or support with IT	Well supported by existing IT
Medium needed	Needs rich communication medium	Can be transferred through conventional electronic channels

Source: Tiwana (2002).

explicit knowledge is revealed by its communication (Choo, 2006). For a better understanding, a comparison is presented in Table 1.

There are other ways of classifying knowledge (individual, collective, etc.) that depend on the theoretical background it is being assigned to. The classifications used here are aligned with management/engineering.

4. Organizational Knowledge

Organizational knowledge, according to Nonaka *et al.* (2000), is an organization's ability to create new knowledge, share it, disseminate it internally, and incorporate it into business processes, goods, services, and systems, transforming individual and organizational knowledge. Expanding the understanding, Choo (2006) defines organizational knowledge as a set of collective property processes of information use, in which people create common meanings, develop new knowledge, and use it for taking action. And according to Trkman and Desouza (2012, p.3), "organizational knowledge is generated from the combination of knowledge that exists within individuals, processes, and their interactions". It can take the form of intellectual assets, for instance: blueprints, computer programs, drawings, memo plans, procedures, and sketches (Choo, 2006). "Organizational knowledge creation is a never-ending process that upgrades itself continuously" (Ichijo and Nonaka, 2006, p. 279).

The aim of KM is centered in developing ways (methods, procedures, tools, etc.) to understand what is in people's mind and keep this "thing", which is called knowledge, within the organization, named organizational knowledge.

5. Definition of Knowledge Management

Companies are not structurally prepared to deal with knowledge. They usually are not prepared to absorb and transform the tacit knowledge contained in people into explicit knowledge. This unpreparedness can be offset by KM (Carlos Bou-Llusar and Segarra-Ciprés, 2006).

KM is defined as a collective expression of a group of processes and practices used in organizations to increase their value, improving the efficiency of generation and application of their intellectual capital (Marr et al., 2003). It signifies the usage/application of people's/employee's/human capital's knowledge, skills, abilities, and attitudes in an organized way to reach company goals. At this point, it is worth highlighting that the objective of KM is not necessarily to manage all knowledge, but just the ones that are most important to the organization. Also, KM helps guarantee that people have the knowledge they need, where they need it and when they need it (Servin and De Brun, 2005). Summarizing, KM is the management of activities and processes that promote knowledge to increase competitiveness, through better use and creation of individual and collective knowledge sources (CEN, 2004). Having a more holistic view, KM consists of four main activities: (1) creating — organizations should be knowledge-creative, should create new knowledge that adds value to be ahead of rivals; (2) sharing — As soon the new knowledge is created, it must be shared inside the whole organization; (3) protecting — the organization's knowledge asset is hidden; and (4) discarding — organizations should get rid of knowledge that is outdated, promoting new knowledge creation. It is undeniable that without discarding outdated knowledge, the one that does not add more value to the company, it is difficult to create new ones, that add value (Ichijo and Nonaka, 2006).

6. Components of Knowledge Management

A widely used approach is to understand/think of KM in terms of three components, i.e. people, process, and technology (Servin and De Brun, 2005).

(1) People are the most important component, as KM is first and foremost a people issue. The organizational culture is intrinsic to people. The process and technology are developed and used by people. They are the "master spring" that make the organization exist, coexist, develop, and maintain the organizational knowledge.

(2) Process is the structure that the organization establishes, evaluates and reestablishes in order to support people in creating, sharing, and using knowledge.

(3) Technology is a vital enabler of KM. It can assist in providing the right information at the time that is needed to those who need it. The technology must fit the organizational process and people, not the contrary.

These three components can be seen as legs of a three-legged stool, if one is cut-off, then the stool will collapse (Servin and De Brun, 2005).

7. Knowledge Management Processes

How can KM be structured? To answer this question, this chapter took as its basis the work entitled "Practical Knowledge Management: A Model That Works" of Probst (1998), which aimed to define standards for a KM concept, and founded on these standards to build a model that is meant to work in practice.

The resulting model defined five standards that must be followed: (1) compatibility; (2) problem orientation; (3) comprehensibility; (4) action orientation; and (5) appropriate instruments, as can be seen in Table 2.

With these standards in mind, it is good to remember that KM's aim, in this case, is a practical one: to improve organizational capabilities through better use of knowledge, be it individual or collective/organizational.

Table 2.   KM Concepts Standards

Standard	Description
Compatibility	In order to make effective KM, it is required that the organization have and share a common language, fitting with the concepts that already exist in the organization, such as business process reengineering, total quality management, project management, lean thinking, design thinking, etc.
Problem orientation	KM must address real problems, meaning focus on solutions to an organization's practical issues. It must not be permitted to remain just in theory.
Comprehensibility	The organization must create KM terms and ideas that are readily comprehended across the organization and relevant to its success.
Action orientation	Managers must evaluate the impact of their instruments on the organizational knowledge base, and this should lead to focused action.
Appropriate instruments	Focused intermediations need to be proven/tested instruments. The final aim of the KM concept's final aim is to deliver a collection of such instruments. However, the tools itself are less important than their skillful use.

Source: Based on Probst (1998).

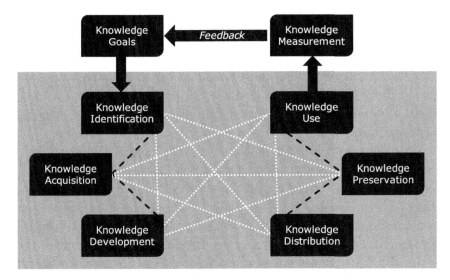

Figure 1. The Building Blocks of KM
Source: Probst (1998).

Probst (1998, p. 19) structured his model as building blocks of KM, which "represent activities that are directly knowledge-related". The five standards, mentioned above, are the conceptual basis for the model. Moreover, it is composed of an inner and outer cycle. The inner cycle comprises the identification, acquisition, development, distribution, preservation, and knowledge use building blocks. The outer cycle comprises the activities to establish the goal and how to measure. Additionally, the model provides a feedback loop for iteration. The objective is to focus on goal-oriented interventions, acting with relevant information that came from measuring the measurable variables established previously. Figure 1 displays the model.

It is important to highlight that "many knowledge problems occur because organizations neglect one or more of these building blocks and thus interrupts the knowledge cycle" (Probst, 1998, p. 19). It is also relevant to underline that the building blocks are interdependent; this means that KM activities should never be conducted in separation from each other.

In order to understand the model better, each building block is described in the sequence as follows:

Knowledge Goals — defines and creates the preconditions for an effective KM. It establishes the strategic and operational aim, meaning the desirable competence portfolio for putting what was planned into action now and in the future and also determining the way of turning it into reality.

Knowledge Identification — creates the essential internal and external transparency to support the employees in their knowledge-seeking activities. The main objective of these building blocks is to know how to locate "the knowledge". This is done by answering two questions: Where is the knowledge needed? And, how to access it, when needed? In order to do this, the company should make use of knowledge mapping tools and also create an organizational knowledge base.

Knowledge Acquisition — It is the company's ability to build up all the know-how they need for market success by themselves. Companies should sense what is needed to stay in the market and/ or acquire more market share. Four channels for acquisition are presented in the model: (1) Knowledge held by other firms, contracting new people can build companies' knowledge competence fast; (2) stakeholders' knowledge, get ideas to create/improve products. Involving the consumers from the beginning of product development process can assist in information gathering; (3) experts' knowledge, an interesting way of boosting the staff's knowledge; and (4) knowledge products, software, patents can stimulate new ideas.

Knowledge Development — Comprises all management activities which are premeditated to create new internal or external knowledge at both the individual and the collective level.

Knowledge Distribution — It is the act of making available the usable knowledge when it is needed by the person that needs it and then making it accessible to the whole company. For this, it is assumed that the company has already identified knowledge and has the technical support of a knowledge base, like information systems, groupware, forums, wikis, and other computer-supported tools for cooperative works, in order to take action. With that in mind, the efficient knowledge distribution can generate time and quality advantages and also directly increase costumers' satisfaction.

Knowledge Preservation — Once knowledge has been developed or acquired, it must be wisely preserved. If the company does not pay attention to this, organizational amnesia will probably occur as a result of not registering lessons learned, destruction of informal networks, and loss of valuable expertise. Companies must identify valuable knowledge and regularly incorporate this as organizational knowledge, adding them into daily routines, procedures, people's mind, and into the organizational knowledge database.

Knowledge Use — This involves daily effective use of the organizational knowledge in the production process. The potential knowledge user must see a real advantage of KM and change their mindset to have a proactive attitude to follow the process, adopting this new behavior to use knowledge in the organization.

Knowledge Measurement — The company's biggest challenge is to evaluate and measure the organizational knowledge. Knowledge and capabilities can hardly be tracked to a single influencing variable. However, knowledge measurement holds considerable latent value; e.g. when proving the impact of taking the right decision, a precise decision is based on knowledge. Also, it assists in making the right investments decisions on training the human capital, leveling and/or elevating the structural capital, and assisting in building/maintaining the relational capital.

8. How to Create or Share Knowledge?

Knowledge can be created or transferred, according to Nonaka and Takeuchi's (1997) perspective, by four modes, explained in detail below. The first letter of each mode forms an anagram that comprises the model name, SECI model (Figure 2).

Socialization (Tacit-to-Tacit) is based on social interaction, the act of sharing experiences and thus constructing tacit knowledge. Tacit knowledge is obtained through the interaction of imitation, observation, and practice.

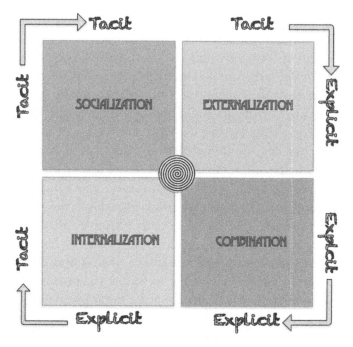

Figure 2.   Knowledge Creation Spiral (SECI Model)
Source: Based on Nonaka and Takeuchi (1997).

Externalization (Tacit-to-Explicit) is the act of transforming what is known in such a way that it can be represented in an understandable and shareable form. For instance, written documents, hypotheses, images, concepts, processes, metaphors, and models.

Combination (Explicit-to-Explicit) is the act of combining different types of explicit knowledge. Explicit knowledge could be acquired inside and outside the organization. This combination could also generate new knowledge.

Internalization (Explicit-to-Tacit) is the act of converting explicit knowledge into tacit knowledge; it happens when knowledge becomes part of an individual's knowledge. It is closely related to learning by doing.

As the human being and the organization are a "living being", while they exist, they continue to learn. Thus, the process after internalization continues in many iterations as they learn new things.

This continued improvement of knowing is represented in the SECI model by the metaphor of knowledge creation spiral.

9. Concluding Remarks

What could be learned from this chapter? Knowledge is the most important asset an organization has! It is inherent to people; it composes the organizational intellectual capital. It is difficult to share, acquire, and store knowledge if it is in the tacit form. Because of this, it should be converted to explicit knowledge.

There is a way of dealing with knowledge, and KM is the discipline that deals with knowledge in order to "get the best out of it". The main focus of KM is to increase an organization's value, improving the efficiency in generating and maintaining the intellectual capital and seeking to acquire or maintain market share.

To do effective KM, components, standards, and processes must be understood and incorporated by the organizations so that knowledge can be extracted from people's mind and be internalized into the company as organizational knowledge. Doing that, it is possible to incorporate knowledge to develop goods, services, business processes, and systems, and also create new knowledge to share and disseminate and internally and externally.

References

Aranha, M. L. A. and Martins, M. H. P. (1993). *Filosofando: Introdução à Filosofia*. São Paulo: Moderna.

Carlos B.-L., Juan and Segarra-Ciprés, M. (2006). Strategic knowledge transfer and its implications for competitive advantage: An integrative conceptual framework. *Journal of Knowledge Management*, 10(4), pp. 100–112.

CEN (2004). Comité Européen De Normalisation: European Guide to Good Practice in Knowledge Management CWA 14924. Retrieved 09/30, 2004, from ftp://cenftp1.cenorm.be/PUBLIC/CWAs/e-Europe/KM/CWA14924-04-2004-Mar.pdf

Choo, C. W. (2006). The Knowing Organization: How Organizations use Information to Construct Meaning, Create Knowledge and Make Decisions (2nd ed.), Vol. 16, Oxford University Press. DOI:10.1093/acprof:oso/9780195176780.001.0001

Davenport, T. H. and Prusak, L. (1998). Conhecimento empresarial. Rio de Janeiro. Campus. Francisco, USA, Morgan Kaufmann.

Ichijo, K. and Nonaka, I. (2006). *Knowledge Creation and Management: New Challenges for Managers*: Oxford University Press.

Marr, B., Gupta, O., Pike, S. and Roos, G. (2003). Intellectual capital and KM effectiveness. *Management Decision*, **41**(8), pp. 771–781.

Nonaka, I. and Takeuchi, H. (1997). Criação de conhecimento na empresa: como as empresas japonesas geram a dinâmica da inovação, Rio de Janeiro Campus, 16, p. 360.

Nonaka, I., Toyama, R. and Konno, N. (2000). SECI, Ba and leadership: A unified model of dynamic knowledge creation. *Long Range Planning*, **33**(1), pp. 5–34.

Porter, M. E. (1993). *A Vantagem Competitiva das Nações*. Rio de Janeiro: Campus.

Probst, G. J. B. (1998). *Practical Knowledge Management: A Model that Works*. Prism-Cambridge Massachusetts, pp. 17–30.

Schön, D. A. (1983). *The Reflective Practitioner: How Professionals Think in Action*, Vol. 5126, Basic books.

Servin, G. and De Brun, C. (2005). *ABC of Knowledge Management*. NHS National Library for Health: Specialist Library.

Tiwana, A. (2002). *The Knowledge Management Toolkit: Orchestrating IT, Strategy, and Knowledge Platforms*. Pearson Education India.

Trkman, P. and Desouza, K. C. (2012). Knowledge risks in organizational networks: An exploratory framework. *The Journal of Strategic Information Systems*, **21**(1), pp. 1–17.

Chapter 4

The Interplay between Open Innovation and Knowledge Management in SMEs

Serdal Temel* and Susanne Durst†

*Ege University, Erzene Mahallesi, Gençlik Caddesi,
35040 Boronova, İzmir, Turkey
†University of Skövde Högskolevägen 1, 54128, Skövde, Sweden
and Universidad del Pacífico, Lima, Peru

In this chapter, the interplay between open innovation (OI) and knowledge management (KM) in small and medium-sized enterprises (SMEs) is addressed. More precisely, the three OI archetypes, which are the outside–in and inside–out processes, and coupled process, are used to show this interplay. It is shown how SMEs can benefit from applying these three archetypes and what are the preconditions for applying them in the best way.

1. Introduction

We all know that innovation does not work without knowledge; this holds true for open innovation (OI) as well. According to Du Plessis

(2007), innovation is "the creation of new knowledge and ideas to facilitate new business outcomes, aimed at improving internal business processes and structures and to create market-driven products and services" (p. 21). Therefore, a firm's capacity to continuously create new knowledge can be regarded as a determining factor for its competitiveness. This refers to all approaches to innovation. Knowledge creation and updating take place internally and externally. Given both the internal limitations as well as external business challenges, organizations should be more outward-looking than they were in the past (Durst *et al.*, 2015; Majchrzak *et al.*, 2004).

In the previous chapters, the topics of knowledge management (KM), OI, and small and medium-sized enterprises (SMEs) have been presented in isolation; therefore, the aim of this chapter is to bring them together to address the book's main intention. More precisely, the aim of this chapter is to show the interplay between OI and KM in SMEs.

The chapter is structured as follows. In the next section, important domains relevant to the study are introduced briefly. This is followed by an introduction to the three OI archetypes. Then, the three archetypes in application will be illustrated, taking into consideration KM and SMEs. In the concluding section, some implications and future research directions will be addressed.

2. Short Recap of Key Terms

Before we start demonstrating the interplay between OI and KM in SMEs, in this section we briefly recap the main essence of the three main concepts to set the frame.

2.1. SMEs

The term SMEs refers to micro, small and medium-sized firms, and according to the European Commission these firms can be classified as micro, small or medium-sized depending on the number of employees, annual turnover, and balance sheet totals (Commission of the European Communities, 2005). Referring to the number of employees, a company with fewer than 250 employees is considered to be an

SME. More precisely, an organization with fewer than 10 employees is a micro firm, that with between 10 and 49 employees is considered to be a small firm, and one with between 50 and 249 employees is a medium-sized firm. Considering this broad range, comparisons between the different sub-types of SMEs are rather difficult, if not impossible. For example, given the larger number of employees in medium-sized firms, the use of more formal approaches and systems regarding firm management is rather likely (Cakar and Ertürk, 2010). In addition, one can assume that the influence of the owner-managers' is reduced, which in turn will lead to a decision-making that is more decentralized (Culkin and Smith, 2000). This brief discussion clarifies that when SMEs are addressed, it is important to consider the issue of heterogeneity (Curran and Blackburn, 2001).

2.2. *Open innovation*

Chesbrough defines OI as "the use of purposive inflows and out-flows of knowledge to accelerate internal innovation, and expand the markets for external use of innovation, respectively" (2006a, p. 1). This stresses that organizations should put even greater emphasis on collaboration and networking (Vanhaverbeke, 2006). In contrast to earlier concepts discussed in the academic literature, the OI paradigm regards internal and external knowledge as being of equivalent quality.

2.3. *Knowledge management*

"Knowledge management serves as an organizational infrastructure that captures and leverages existing information and knowledge assets of the organization, facilitates information and knowledge dissemination across boundaries, and integrates the information and knowledge into day-to-day business processes" (Liebowitz and Beckman, 1998, p. 20). Because of the SMEs' specific characteristics such as smallness, flexibility, and informal atmosphere, KM is conducted differently in comparison to larger businesses (e.g. Durst and Edvardsson, 2012; Durst and Wilhelm, 2012), which, however, underlines that they do KM (Hutchinson and Quintas, 2008). Chesbrough and Bogers (2016, p. 17) define OI as a "flows of knowledge; a distributed innovation process based on purposively managed knowledge flows across organizational boundaries, using pecuniary and non-pecuniary mechanisms in line with the organization's business model".

To illustrate the interplay between OI and KM in SMEs, we take advantage of the three OI archetypes proposed by Gassmann and Enkel (2004), which are outside–in and inside–out processes, and coupled process.

3. Open Innovation Archetypes

The idea of this section is to briefly introduce the three archetypes.

3.1. *Inside–out process*

The inside–out process creates revenues by transferring internal knowledge, know-how, and technologies which have been developed or improved by the company to the outside. Thus, this type of OI allows companies to maximize the economic benefit from their know-how and technologies in collaboration with external partners through licensing and commercialization (Lichtenthaler, 2007; Kutvonen and Torkkeli, 2008; Hafkesbrink and Schroll, 2010; Hafkesbrink and Kirkels, 2016) (see Figure 1).

According to Chesbrough (2003, 2006b), the sale and licensing of companies' own technologies to other market actors are not standard practice. Gassmann and Enkel (2006) discuss how companies practice different "inside–out" processes to externalize internal knowledge and invention to the society. Based on R&D projects, companies may develop different types of inventions and file patent applications — even without having evaluated their potential commercial value (Nerkar, 2007). The licensing out of technologies to other market actors creates an additional stream of revenue, which could be used not only to cover the R&D costs but also for other business activities. Recent studies (e.g. Fosfuri, 2006; Walter, 2012) have shown that some companies practice out-licensing of their inventions to generate more income. This approach helps those companies to prioritize their "strategic" partners.

Inside-Out Process

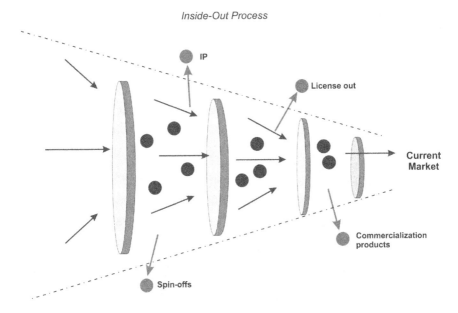

Figure 1. The Inside–out Process

There are, however, many barriers that prevent companies from out-licensing their inventions (Rivette and Kline, 2000). These barriers can come from inside the company, such as the lack of confidence, lack of intellectual property (IP) management capacity, and fear of being deceived by the partner, but also from outside the company, an example could be a missing established ecosystem. Because of these barriers, the potential of out-licencing technologies into the economy has not been fully implemented (Gambardella *et al.*, 2007).

Those companies practicing out-licensing become better aware of IP issues, which motivates them to seek better protection for their IP assets. It may lead to a better market position with regard to their competitors. Furthermore, out-licensing can also enhance the social status of companies since they may become the dominant technology power in their markets or industry, and this can motivate them to patent all their technologies to extend their market position even further (Srivastava and Wang, 2015). Apart from the positive impact of out-licensing, it can also have negative effects, e.g. on the companies' market share (Fosfuri, 2006; Walter, 2012) or the companies' profit (Arora and Fosfuri, 2003).

Gambardella *et al.* (2007) assumed that the market for technology could be larger (close to 70%) when some of the obstacles are overcome — although often this is easier said than done. An obstacle that often prevents firms from out-licensing technologies is that they have difficulty in anticipating the potential value (Chesbrough and Rosenbloom, 2002). For instance, firms may be over-committed regarding the investment of resources in order to offer products even though another organization may be better equipped in commercializing these products. Chesbrough and Rosenbloom's (2002) analysis of Xerox illustrates how the combined market capitalization of spin-offs and other external commercialization subsequently overtook the value of Xerox. This underlines the need for a deliberate strategy. Lichtenthaler and Ernst (2007) suggest that while many firms are open to licensing technologies, they lack a conscious strategy for bringing this into practice. Lichtenthaler (2009), for instance, discussed how a combination of strategic planning and content characteristics (e.g. availability of skills to see the customer needs and latent markets) shapes a firm's potential of benefiting from out-licensing.

In many technology-driven environments, patents provide firms an opportunity to overcome disclosure problems (Arrow, 1962). In general, and even more so specifically, inside–out open innovation requires that buyers and sellers reach an agreement so that appropriability regimes allow the sellers to disclose information. It is assumed that intellectual property right (IPR) is important for trading innovation (West, 2006). Understanding the disclosure paradox calls attention to the means of appropriability in OI and how firms attempt to be open yet are able to appropriate commercial returns from their innovative efforts. To overcome this paradox, firms often require that inventors have a formal IPR in place before they work together.

3.2. *Outside–in process*

The outside–in process enhances a company's competitiveness through the integration of consumer, competitors, suppliers, as well as research

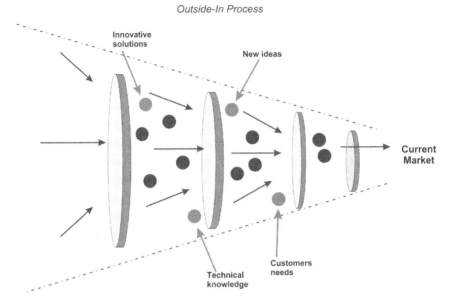

Figure 2.   The Outside–in Process

centers and universities (Gassmann and Enkel, 2006) (see Figure 2). This type of OI refers to companies that cooperate with external part- ners such as suppliers, customers, and competitors to access new ideas, knowledge, and expertise for innovation. This process is not limited to the mentioned actors but also refers to other channels such as social media, fairs, and the licensing of new technologies into the companies. If companies can access better ideas, knowledge, or other inputs from outside for enhancing the quality of the final product, then they will use these options instead of developing them internally (Laursen and Salter, 2006). However, absorbing external ideas and benefiting from them requires significantly different skills (Fritsch and Lukas, 2001), e.g. an ability to sense, value, assimilate, and apply new knowledge. These skills are viewed as a prerequisite for sourcing inno- vation from external sources (Hossain and Kauranen, 2016). If companies do not have these skills and capacities, then they may embrace the disadvantages instead of the advantages the outside–in option is offering (e.g. West and Gallagher, 2006).

Integrating external partners such as customers, consumers, competitors, and research centers into the internal innovation process is not a recent issue. It has proved to have a positive impact on company's competencies and competitiveness (Wagner, 2002). For instance, the supplier can increase the quality of the final product by providing better and innovative solutions. Suppliers can also identify technical problems and inconsistency at earlier stages, and by informing companies it helps in reducing technical and financial risks of projects (Dröge *et al.*, 2000; Boutellier and Wagner, 2003). Consequently, welcoming outside knowledge from suppliers into innovation process positively affects the receiving companies and creates a long-lasting collaboration between them.

Integrating customers' needs and preferences into the final product is considered as an important strategy for company success (Trott and Hartmann, 2009). This integration can happen in the innovation process but also at an earlier stage. For instance, Henkel runs "focus groups" involving customers to identify the customers' actual needs and to list their priorities, whereas DuPont prefers to integrate customers into their R&D activities at the project level so that they can integrate the customers' real needs at an early stage which can help companies be first in the market. Thus, in such a situation companies use customers as co-creators of competence (Enkel *et al.*, 2009).

Universities and research centers represent other sources used by companies in the outside–in approach (Belderbos *et al.*, 2004; Liefner *et al.*, 2006; Temel *et al.*, 2013). The technical knowledge and expertise, and the technical infrastructures such as laboratories and equipment, are important inputs for the companies' R&D and innovation projects. Having access to well-educated and trained students of different fields is another contribution of universities to companies. Access to these resources can give companies the opportunity to develop a better competitive standing.

However, outside–in processes need to be managed carefully, and companies should act as "knowledge hunters", because the receipt of inadequate or even wrong information or knowledge being used in R&D and innovation projects may cause serious problems in the company. Thus, companies should be careful in the process of selecting partners or information/knowledge. Another problem that may occur in outside–in scenarios is the so-called "not invented here" syndrome (Katz and Allen, 1982), which refers to internal staff not welcoming new ideas from outside the company. This means, in turn, that companies need to be ready for the outside–in process before they start implementing it.

3.3. *Coupled process*

The coupled process refers to the value creation with external partners through synergies, cooperation, and joint ventures by both internalizing external knowledge and externalizing internal knowledge (see Figure 3). Thus, companies that implement the coupled process are trying to take advantage of both the outside–in and the inside–out processes, and in this way develop value-added products, processes, or know-how.

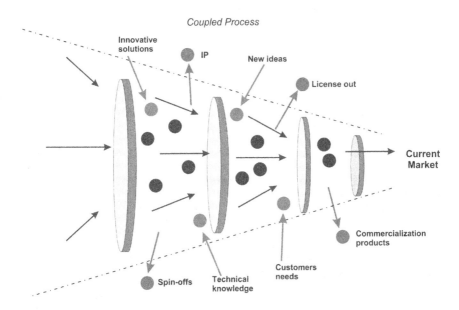

Figure 3. The Coupled Process

The implementation of the coupled process requires more skills than the other two archetypes. Companies need to have a set of skills to make possible the implementation of both options. This means that these companies would be able to bring ideas to market, out-license or sell their technologies, and benefit from the contribution of their external partners. Relationship capacity and relationship management can be named as core skills for the coupled process (Dyer and Sing, 1998; Johnson and Sohi, 2003). Indeed, companies should have the capacity to easily create and maintain reliable and long-standing relationships and to manage these relationships to gain a long-term benefit, which may result in competitive advantage as well. Therefore, the main success factor for the coupled process is finding the right balance between giving and taking. The successful implementation of such an OI option allows companies to reduce the cost of innovation.

For companies, however, it is very difficult to develop all the necessary skills and implement a coupled process. Some reasons might be that the company's core business is not appropriate for a coupled process, or the companies priorities are different. For instance, ICT companies mainly implement inside–out process, while automobile companies prefer the implementation of outside–in processes to reduce the costs and produce better and high-in-demand automobiles (Ili, 2010).

Having provided a general introduction to the three archetypes, in the next section we provide examples of how SMEs could take advantage of the three different options.

4. Illustration of the Three Archetypes in Application

4.1. *Inside–out process*

Many SMEs know the situation that there are more tasks to be done than people available to do these tasks (Durst, 2012). This may lead to a sort of understanding that it would make sense to delegate certain projects and tasks to the outside. Indeed, this business practice, which is known as outsourcing of business functions, is widely used by organizations regardless of size (Mudambi and Tallman, 2010). While outsourcing might often be applied to reduce costs (Edvardsson and Durst, 2014), the inside–out type of OI emphasizes the collaboration between partners. Thus, even though the starting points of outsourcing and OI are different, the outsourcing strategy may be further developed and turned into an inside–out process. For example, a small firm could establish collaboration with a service provider, which is based on the idea that the latter drives the innovation work. This work could result in continuous improvements in the small firm, for example, of the systems already in place.

SMEs may also sell or rent their IPs. Even though SMEs register fewer IPs because of high costs and administrative burden (Robert Huggins Associates, 2005, van de Vrande *et al.*, 2009), there are smaller firms who are creating some additional streams of revenue through their IPs, which provides additional scope for other business operations.

The examples of inside–out OI are very common in IT sectors. Many software companies' license their developed software to other companies in different sectors, and this helps both sides to be more competitive in the market. For instance, the processor was developed and mainly used in IT sector. However, now it has a variety of uses in almost all industries including automotive industries. This kind of inside–out open innovation helps companies generate more income as well as helps companies use their investment more efficiently and cover millions of dollars' investment.

The inside–out process is also helping companies to focus on their niche business and not try to do other's expertise. For instance, a spin-off company based in Turkey developed a brand new wound healing bandage for diabetic wound diseases. Although the spin-off has the technological capacity for product development, the lack of packaging skills and expertise with regard to the pharmaceutical industry were the challenging issues. In order to solve this problem, the spin-off collaborated with another spin-off company for proper packaging. Although this inside–out collaboration did not create additional income for the spin-off, this was the best way to introduce the product into the market.

4.2. *Outside–in process*

Given the situation that SMEs need to collaborate in order to overcome any form of source constraints and the fact that they actually are good networkers, and take advantage of a number of different external actors and sources (Durst *et al.*, 2013), realization of the outside–in process is found in SMEs. SMEs collaborate to get access to new knowledge and appear to take a targeted approach. For example, SMEs may be opening to the outside to realize new product introductions (Wynarczyk *et al.*, 2013). Or they may turn to suppliers in order to update their technical knowledge (Durst *et al.*, 2013). SMEs may also collaborate with universities and research institutions to have access to recent knowledge or to jointly develop new knowledge (Bengtsson, 2016). SMEs can also buy or rent licenses to have access to recent knowledge and thus strengthen and/or develop their market position (van de Vrande *et al.*, 2009).

Many smaller companies are very outward-looking and benefit from external partners' capacities and know-how to develop better products and thereby reduce both R&D and production cost. Instead of setting up their own laboratories, smaller companies use university infrastructure. They also collaborate with university staff to have access to recent knowledge.

A spin-off company called Bionorm based in Turkey and established with the purpose of producing pharmaceutical component from endemic herbs growing in Turkey proceeded as follows. At the beginning, instead of setting up laboratories, buying expensive equipment, and hiring well-paid engineers, the company collaborated with the Bioengineering Department of Ege University and used all their laboratories and equipment. It also collaborated with the researchers whenever needed. As a result, the start-up developed one of the most value-added products in Turkey and moved from the university's technopark to a bigger industrial zone. Thus, by using the outside–in approach, the start-up company benefited from external resources and converted it into economic growth.

4.3. *Coupled process*

As described above, realization of the coupled process will hardly be possible without the commitment from all actors in the small firm, but still it is possible. For example, the small firm could enter into a research partnership with a university or a research institute; in such a partnership, the focus would be on combining extant resources and competencies to make possible both outside–in and inside–out activities. An example of an outside–in process could be that the small firm gets access to a research infrastructure that enables the performance of clinical trials, whereas an example of an inside–out process could be that the university (its researchers) gets insights into business skills and competencies (entrepreneurial skills) which will help extend the existing knowledge base and result in more market-oriented solutions. This might be of interest for universities of applied sciences or regionally focused universities in particular. Another example of the coupled process could be that the smaller firm enters a so-called OI arena that involves a number of different actors (e.g. university, companies, policymakers (municipality), society) who collaborate to address complex issues a single actor cannot master alone, for example, efforts dedicated to the issues of mobility, housing, or climate.

5. Conclusion

The motive behind this chapter was to bring together the three key terms of the book, namely KM, OI, and SMEs to establish the basis for the second part of the book: research insights. Thereby, the authors took advantage of the three OI archetypes and described them in general before possible options for implementation in the SME context were illustrated.

As it has been discussed, OI is one of the strategic methods for small business to enhance their innovation output. Recent publications and professional experiences promote OI as a "nostrum". However, this is not a magic tool that can work in every company. Different archetypes of OI require different skills as well as the right strategy. Therefore, mainly small businesses should carefully plan their objective and should choose the right archetypes of OI.

Furthermore, the implication of OI may not be as easy as it is told. There are different internal and external parameters for companies to practice OI such as sector, size, absorption capacity, innovation project experiences, and innovation culture in companies. Therefore, these parameters should be considered by the smaller companies before they decide on an innovation archetype. For making better decisions, companies need to understand both the pros and the cons of each type of OI and, based on this, select the most promising one.

In the following chapters, recent insights into the actual implementation of the interplay between OI and KM in SMEs will be presented.

References

Arora, A. and Fosfuri, A. (2003). Licensing the market for technology. *Journal of Economic Behavior and Organization*, 52(2), pp. 277–295.

Arrow, K. (1962). The economics implications of learning by doing. *Review of Economic Studies*, 29, pp. 155–173.

Belderbos, R., Carree, M. and Lokshin, B. (2004). Cooperative R&D and firm performance. *Research Policy*, 33(10), pp. 1477–1492.

Bengtsson, L. (2016). Universitetsforskning och öppen innovation. In Öppen Innovation — i teori och praktik. N. Lakemond and F. Tell. Studentlitteratur, pp. 75–93.

Boutellier, R. and Wagner, S. M. (2003). Sourcing concepts: Matching product architecture, task interface, supplier competence and supplier relationship. In *Business Engineering*, Springer Berlin Heidelberg, pp. 223–248.

Cakar, N. D. and Ertürk, A. (2010). Comparing innovation capability of small and medium-sized enterprises: Examining the effects of organizational culture and empowerment. *Journal of Small Business Management*, 48(3), pp. 325–359.

Chesbrough, H. (2003). *Open Innovation: The New Imperative for Creating and Profiting from Technology*. Harvard Business School Press, Boston, MA.

Chesbrough, H. (2006a). Open innovation: A new paradigm for understanding industrial innovation. In: H. Chesbrough, W. Vanhaverbeke and J. West (Eds.), *Open Innovation: Researching a New Paradigm*. Oxford: Oxford University Press, pp. 1–12.

Chesbrough, H. W. (2006b). *Open Innovation: The New Imperative for Creating and Profiting from Technology.* Harvard Business Press, Boston, MA.

Chesbrough, H. and Bogers, M. (2016). Explicating open innovation: Clarifying an emerging paradigm for understanding innovation. In: H. Chesbrough, W. Vanhaverbeke and J. West (Eds.), *New Frontiers in Open Innovation.* Oxford: Oxford University Press, pp. 3–28.

Chesbrough, H. and Rosenbloom, R. S. (2002). The role of the business model in capturing value from innovation: Evidence from Xerox Corporation's technology spin-off companies. *Industrial and corporate change,* 11(3), pp. 529–555.

Commission of the European Communities (2005). Commission recommendation concerning the definition of micro, small and medium-sized enterprises. *Official Journal of the European Union,* L124, pp. 36–41.

Culkin, N. and Smith, D. (2000). An emotional business: A guide to understanding the motivations of small business decision takers. *Qualitative Market Research: An International Journal,* 3(3), pp. 145–157.

Curran, J. and Blackburn, R. A. (2001). *Researching the Small Enterprise.* Sage, London.

Dröge, C., Jayaram, J. and Vickery, S. K. (2000). The ability to minimize the timing of new product development and introduction: An examination of antecedent factors in the North American automobile supplier industry. *Journal of Product Innovation Management,* 17(1), pp. 24–40.

Du Plessis, M. (2007). The role of knowledge management in innovation. *Journal of Knowledge Management,* 11(4), pp. 20–29.

Durst, S. (2012). Innovation and intellectual capital (risk) management in small and medium-sized enterprises. *International Journal of Transitions and Innovation Systems,* 2(3/4), pp. 233–246.

Durst, S. and Edvardsson, I. R. (2012). Knowledge management in SMEs: A literature review. *Journal of Knowledge Management,* 16(6), pp. 879–903.

Durst, S. and Wilhelm, S. (2012). Knowledge management and succession planning in SMEs. *Journal of Knowledge Management,* 16(4), pp. 637–649.

Durst, S., Edvardsson, I. R. and Bruns, G. (2013). Knowledge creation in small building and construction firms. *Journal of Innovation Management,* 1(1), pp. 125–142.

Durst, S., Edvardsson, I. R. and Bruns, G. (2015). Sustainable organisations and knowledge process outsourcing: Conditions for success. *International Journal of Knowledge and Learning,* 10(2), 110–123.

Dyer, J. H. and Singh, H. (1998). The relational view: Cooperative strategy and sources of interorganizational competitive advantage. *Academy of Management Review,* 23(4), pp. 660–679.

Edvardsson, I. R. and Durst, S. (2014). Outsourcing of knowledge processes: A literature review. *Journal of Knowledge Management,* 18(4), pp. 795–811.

Enkel, E., Gassmann, O. and Chesbrough, H. (2009). Open R&D and Open Innovation: Exploring the phenomenon. *R&D Management*, 39(4), pp. 311–316.

Fosfuri, A. (2006). The licensing dilemma: Understanding the determinants of the rate of technology licensing. *Strategic Management Journal*, 27(12), pp. 1141–1158.

Fritsch, M. and Lukas, R. (2001). Who cooperates on R&D? *Research Policy*, 30(2), 297–312.

Gambardella, A., Giuri, P. and Luzzi, A. (2007). The market for patents in Europe. *Research Policy*, 36(8), pp. 1163–1183.

Gassmann, O. and Enkel, E. (2006). Open innovation. *Zeitschrift Führung + Organisation*, 75(3), pp. 132–138.

Gassmann, O. and Enkel, E. (2004). Towards a Theory of Open Innovation: Three Core Process Archetypes. *R&D Management Conference (RADMA)* 2004, 07-09.07.2004, Lisbon, Portugal.

Hafkesbrink, J. and Kirkels, Y. (2016). Open Innovation in SMEs. In: A.-L. Mention, A. P. Nagel, J. Hafkesbrink and J. Dabrowska (Eds.), *Innovation and Education Reloaded; Nurturing Skills for the Future*. Finland: Open Innovation Network-OI, pp. 281–301.

Hafkesbrink, J. and Schroll, M. (2010). Organizational competences for OI in small and medium sized enterprises of the digital economy. In: J. Hafkesbrink, H.-U. Hoppe and J. Schlichter (Eds.), *Competence Management for OI — Tools and IT-support to Unlock the Potential of OI*. Lohmar: Josef Eul Verlag, pp. 21–52.

Hossain, M. and Kauranen, I. (2016). Open innovation in SMEs: A systematic literature review. *Journal of Strategy and Management*, 9(1), pp. 58–73.

Hutchinson, V. and Quintas, P. (2008). Do SMEs do knowledge management? Or simply manage what they know? *International Small Business Journal*, 26(2), pp. 131–154.

Ili, S., Albers, A. and Miller, S. (2010). Open innovation in the automotive industry. *R&D Management*, 40(3), pp. 246–255.

Johnson, J. L. and Sohi, R. S. (2003). The development of interfirm partnering competence: Platforms for learning, learning activities, and consequences of learning. *Journal of Business Research*, 56(9), pp. 757–766.

Katz, R. and Allen, T. J. (1982). Investigating the Not Invented Here (NIH) syndrome: A look at the performance, tenure, and communication patterns of 50 R&D Project Groups. *R&D Management*, 12(1), pp. 7–20.

Kutvonen, A. and Torkkeli, M. (2008). External Exploitation of Technology: A Literature Review on Precommercialization Activities. In Proceedings of the 1st ISPIM Innovation Symposium, Singapore, pp. 14–17.

Laursen, K. and Salter, A. (2006). Open for innovation: The role of openness in explaining innovation performance among UK manufacturing firms. *Strategic Management Journal*, 27(2), pp. 131–150.

Lichtenthaler, U. (2009). Absorptive capacity, environmental turbulence, and the complementarity of organizational learning processes. *Academy of Management Journal*, 52(4), pp. 822–846.

Lichtenthaler, U. (2008). Externally commercializing technology assets: An examination of different process stage. *Journal of Business Venturing*, 23, pp. 317–330.

Lichtenthaler, U. and Ernst, H. (2007). External technology commercialization in large firms: results of a quantitative benchmarking study. *R&D Management*, 37(5), pp. 383–397.

Liebowitz, J. and Beckman, T. (1998). *Knowledge Organisations: What Every Manager should Know*. St. Luice Press, Boca Raton, FL.

Liefner, I., Hennemann, S. and Xin, L. (2006). Cooperation in the innovation process in developing countries: Empirical evidence from Zhongguancun, Beijing. *Environment and Planning A*, 38(1), pp. 111–130.

Majchrzak, A., Cooper, L. P. and Neece, O. E. (2004). Knowledge reuse for innovation. *Management Science*, 50(2), pp. 174–188.

Mudambi, S. M. and Tallman, S. (2010). Make, Buy or Ally? Theoretical perspectives on knowledge process outsourcing through alliances. *Journal of Management Studies*, 47(8), pp. 1433–1456.

Nerkar, A. T. U. L. (2007). The folly of rewarding patents and expecting FDA approved drugs: Experience and innovation in the pharmaceutical industry. Kenan-Flagler Business School, University of North Carolina at Chapel Hill.

Rivette, K. G. and Kline, D. (2000). *Rembrandts in the Attic: Unlocking the Hidden Value of Patents*, Harvard Business School Press, Boston, MA.

Robert Huggins Associates (2005) Conceptualising and Framing Intellectual Assets from a SME Perspective. Positioning report for the study on investigating the feasibility of a Scottish intellectual assets scoreboard and benchmarking tool. Available from: <http://www.ia-centre.org.uk/members_area/?blnhere=1> (accessed 28 February 2007).

Srivastava, M. K. and Wang, T. (2015). When does selling make you wiser? Impact of licensing on Chinese firms' patenting propensity. *The Journal of Technology Transfer*, 40(4), pp. 602–628.

Temel, S., Scholten, V., Akdeniz, R. C., Fortuin, F. and Omta, O. (2013). University–industry collaboration in Turkish SMEs: Investigation of a U-shaped relationship. *The International Journal of Entrepreneurship and Innovation*, 14(2), pp. 103–115.

Trott, P. and Hartmann, D. A. P. (2009). Why "open innovation" is old wine in new bottles. *International Journal of Innovation Management*, 13(04), pp. 715–736.

Van de Vrande, V., De Jong, J. P., Vanhaverbeke, W. and De Rochemont, M. (2009). Open innovation in SMEs: Trends, motives and management challenges. *Technovation*, 29(6), pp. 423–437.

Vanhaverbeke, W. (2006). The Interorganizational Context of Open Innovation. In: H. Chesbrough, W. Vanhaverbeke and J. West (Eds.), *Open Innovation: Researching a New Paradigm*. Oxford: Oxford University Press, pp. 205–219.

Wagner, J. (2002). The Impact of Risk Aversion, Role Models, and the Regional Milieu on the Transition from Unemployment to Self-Employment: Empirical Evidence for Germany. IZA Discussion Paper No. 468. Available at SSRN: https://ssrn.com/abstract=310341

Walter, J. (2012). The influence of firm and industry characteristics on returns from technology licensing deals: Evidence from the US computer and pharmaceutical sectors. *R&D Management*, 42(5), pp. 435–454.

West, J. (2006). Does appropriability enable or retard open innovation. In: H. Chesbrough, W. Vanhaverbeke and J. West (Eds.), *Open Innovation: Researching a New Paradigm*. Oxford: Oxford University Press, pp. 109–133.

West, J. and Gallagher, S. (2006). Patterns of open innovation in open source software. In H. Chesbrough, W. Vanhaverbeke and J. West (Eds.), *Open Innovation: Researching a New Paradigm*. Oxford: Oxford University Press, pp. 235–281.

Wynarczyk, P., Piperopoulos, P. and McAdam, M. (2013). Open innovation in small and medium-sized enterprises: An overview. *International Small Business Journal*, 31(3), pp. 240–255.

Part 2

Research Insights

Chapter 5

Knowledge Creation and Open Innovation in High-Technology SMEs

Elsa Grimsdottir and Ingi Runar Edvardsson

School of Business, University of Iceland, Gimli, 101 Reykjavík, Iceland

The aim of this chapter is to present findings on knowledge creation and open innovation (OI) in small and medium-sized enterprises (SMEs) in Iceland. The main focus is on how these SMEs deal with knowledge creation, knowledge sharing and storage, and how customers and other external stakeholders are involved in the innovation process. The research consists of three case studies in knowledge-intensive enterprises in Iceland. Semi-structured interviews were taken with managers and key employees who deal with knowledge creation processes and innovation.

In all the three companies, the knowledge creation process is similar: Groups of employees work on the development of new solutions by experimenting and sharing knowledge through brainstorming and discussing ideas, which can be described as collaborative learning. Knowledge sharing is mainly through personalization strategy, although the product development process tends to be intensively documented. Customers and external stakeholders are rarely consulted until the testing of software programs at the end of the process. The findings are in accordance with other findings that high-tech companies tend to prefer inside-out strategies of open innovation. The findings are also in line with earlier studies which show that SMEs use OI more often in the later stages of the innovation process.

1. Introduction

In order to develop their innovation capabilities, firms need to invest more resources to constantly create new knowledge so they can build new products, services, or procedures. In this respect, the relationship between knowledge management and corporate innovation has been the focus of numerous studies, most of which assume that knowledge creation is a fundamental predictor of innovation (Miller and Morris, 1999; Nonaka, 1991; Nonaka and Takeuchi, 1995; Sankowska, 2013; Wang and Wang, 2012).

New knowledge can generally come to light from new ideas or by emergent internal or external needs. New ideas are often transferred to organizations through suppliers, professionals, consultants, or research literature (external influences), or they stem from internal creativity and inventions. New knowledge also originates from needs and pressures from customers, competition, legislation, and so on (external forces), or it may arise from perceived problems and opportunities identified by the members of the organization (Daft, 2007; Hughes *et al.*, 2009; Sparrow, 2005). Improving brand value and attaching importance to customer satisfaction also fosters knowledge creation (Ueki *et al.*, 2011). Traditionally, innovation was seen to take place within a single company; companies managed innovation mainly by utilizing their own knowledge, R&D capacity, and technology to create new products in their own laboratories (Lee *et al.*, 2010; Wynarczyk, 2013). Open Innovation (OI), in contrast, refers to the inflow of knowledge from both internal and external sources to enhance innovation and expand markets for the use of new devices. According to Chiaroni *et al.* (2011), OI is about exploiting knowledge generated inside and outside the firm to exploit and develop innovation. Implementing OI means, therefore, to use knowledge management (KM) systems able to foster the dissemination and sharing of knowledge within the firm, and between the firm and external environment.

KM is about developing, sharing, and applying knowledge within the organization to gain and sustain a competitive advantage (Davenport and Prusak, 1998; Edvardsson, 2009; Jashapara, 2011; Lichtenthaler and Lichtenthaler, 2009). The KM literature has focused on internal processes, such as knowledge transfer, knowledge sharing culture, organizational learning, ICT, etc., in order to enhance productivity and sales, lower cost, or increase innovation and quality. KM has been extensively studied. However, there is a tendency to focus on large businesses and neglect SMEs (Durst and Edvardsson, 2012; McAdam and Reid, 2001).

The KM process can be divided into capturing or documenting knowledge; packing (cleaning, formatting, and indexing) knowledge for reuse; distributing knowledge; and reusing knowledge (Markus, 2001). In all of these steps, new knowledge and opportunities may emerge when individuals and groups sense problems in the process. The main focus of the chapter is on the knowledge creation process and OI; hence, other aspects of the KM process will not be dealt with further.

Knowledge creation is defined as a continuous process in which the knowledge created by groups or individuals becomes available and amplified within the organization's knowledge system (Von Krogh *et al.*, 2012). Only limited expertise seems to exist, however, on knowledge creation in SMEs (Durst and Edvardsson, 2012). Considering the importance of knowledge creation to SMEs, this situation can be assessed as unsatisfactory.

In light of the current situation of limited knowledge on OI and KM in SMEs, this chapter aims to present findings on OI and KM in SMEs in Iceland. Three case studies on small and medium-sized companies will be presented in order to answer the questions: (1) how do firms deal with knowledge creation, knowledge sharing, and storage and (2) how are customers and other external stakeholders involved in the innovation process?

The chapter is organized in the following manner: The theoretical framework is presented in the next section, followed by a methodological section. Findings are then presented and, finally, conclusions.

2. Theoretical Framework

2.1. *Knowledge management*

KM is, as already noted, about developing, sharing, and applying knowledge within the organization to gain and sustain a competitive advantage (Davenport and Prusak, 1998; Edvardsson, 2009; Jashapara, 2011; Lichtenthaler and Lichtenthaler, 2009). KM has been widely used by firms and organizations in order to improve decision-making, product innovation, productivity, and profits (Edvardsson, 2006).

Hansen *et al.* (1999) argue that there are basically two strategies for managing knowledge. They term these strategies "codification" and "personalization". The former refers to the codification of explicit knowledge which is formal and objective and can be expressed in words, numbers, and specifications. Such knowledge tends to be stored in databases where it can be accessed and readily used by anyone in the company. Such organizations invest heavily in ICT for projects like intranets, data warehousing and data mining, knowledge mapping (identifying where the knowledge is located in the firm), and electronic libraries. This increases effectiveness and growth (Hansen *et al.*, 1999, p. 110): "The reuse of knowledge saves work, reduces communications costs, and allows a company to take on more projects". It is thus closely related to exploitative learning, which tends to refine existing capabilities and technologies, forces thorough standardization and routinization, and is risk-averse (Clegg and Clarke, 1999). Personalization refers to the personal development of tacit knowledge, based on insights, intuition, and personal skills, for solving complex problems. Such knowledge is mainly shared through direct person-to-person contacts. Dialogues, learning histories, and communities of practice are among the techniques that have to be used in order to facilitate tacit knowledge sharing. It is based on the logic of "expert economics", which is, used primarily to solve unique problems where rich, tacit personal knowledge is needed, such as in strategy consulting. Personalization and explorative learning are closely related, where explorative learning is associated with complex search, basic research, innovation, risk-taking, and more relaxed controls. The stress is on flexibility, investment in learning, and the creation of new capabilities (Clegg and Clarke, 1999).

2.2. *Knowledge creation*

Knowledge creations have been measured as a process, output, and outcome (Mitchell and Boyle, 2010). The process perspective assesses the steps or activities undertaken to create new knowledge, such as the use of metaphors to externalize knowledge. As an output, knowledge creation is measured in terms of an immediate product of the knowledge creation process, usually reflecting a significant enrichment of existing knowledge, such as the representation of a spoken idea. Knowledge creation as an outcome is measured in terms of a value-adding object, for instance, a new service, a changed routine, or a product prototype. Here, the link with innovation is quite prevalent.

Knowledge can be created through different processes. According to Nonaka and Konno (1998) and Nonaka *et al.* (2000), the interaction between tacit and explicit knowledge via socialization, externalization, combination and internalization (SECI), leads to the creation of new knowledge.

The link between learning and knowledge creation is quite strong in the literature, and so these are often used as synonyms. Kolb (1984) argues that learning is the process of creating knowledge, where knowledge is generated by grasping and transforming experience. Argyris (1999) sees organizational learning as a process of detecting and correcting errors. This would comprise a proper diagnosis of the error's cause, along with its correction, so that organizations can learn from experience and implement suitable actions intended to prevent a repetition of these errors. In this context, according to Allard (2003), this often leads to identifying a need that requires new knowledge to be created to answer the need. According to Nonaka and Takeuchi (1995), knowledge creation involves interaction between two kinds of learning: obtaining know-how to solve specific problems based upon existing premises, and establishing new premises to override existing ones. Ueki *et al.* (2011) stress that providing employees with challenging initiatives and systematically applying comprehensive human resource development practices, such as cross-functional projects, job rotation, career development, group training, and e-learning, can contribute to the stimulation of knowledge creation in organizations. An organization's success and ability to innovate and develop new routines is tied to its capacity for higher-order learning, while lower-order learning potentially limits knowledge creation and ways of working. Lower-order learning is engaging with the demands of the internal or external environment by using current organizational practices. Higher-order learning goes beyond adaptation by questioning current assumptions and developing new insights that may lead to new practices and routines (Spicer and Sadler-Smith, 2006). According to Garvin (1993), learning organizations are skilled at creating new knowledge by systematic problem solving, experimenting with new approaches, learning from experiences, and sharing knowledge. Employees should be encouraged by managers to ask questions, challenge, engage in collaborative problem solving, learn, and be inquisitive for successful knowledge creation. This has led to an increased interest in the role of managers in this process (Thompson and Heron, 2005). According to Berraies *et al.* (2014), managers provide the knowledge vision and promote the spiral of knowledge creation; they must adopt the best leadership style that motivates and empowers employees.

Collaborative learning is thought to be one of the key factors for successful knowledge creation since it allows employees to access diverse sources of knowledge. The knowledge emerges through discussions, active dialogues among employees working in groups to achieve a shared understanding. The groups enhance the critical thinking by questioning existing solutions and assumptions and by creating new ones (Hedlund, 1994; Jakubik, 2008; Nejatian *et al.*, 2013). Collaboration is mostly planned and directed through organizational structures and processes. Yet, knowledge creation often involves spontaneous collaboration between individuals and teams where individuals with different skills and abilities recognize a project and believe it to be important for their work or interests (Nonaka and Takeuchi, 1995). Teamwork has been proven to be an economic way to create new knowledge and to provide foundations for intelligent working procedures and learning among employees (Awad and Ghaziri, 2004; Szarka *et al.*, 2004).

2.3. *Knowledge creation in SMEs*

Many smaller firms have a flat structure and an organic, free-floating management style that encourages entrepreneurship and innovation. They tend to be informal, non-bureaucratic, and with few rules. Control tends to be based on the owner's personal supervision, and formal policies tend to be absent in SMEs (Daft, 2007). SMEs have certain advantages in comparison with large firms, as, for example, a lower number of employees and a higher degree of cooperation, simpler processes that facilitate the implementation of new ideas, a unified culture, simple structures, and direct communication with managers. Nonetheless, it is undeniable that SMEs experience restrictions, such as lack of financial, technical, and human resources, that may put the implementation of knowledge creation processes at risk. SMEs are less hierarchical, which means that managers are nearer to the operational functions and close to the point of delivery and likely to have a deeper and broader understanding of key knowledge-related issues (Wong and Aspinwall, 2004). The managers are often the owners who supervise every aspect of the firm. The decision-making chain is often shorter because of fewer layers of management and decision makers, and the ultimate power of control is limited to only one person (Culkin and Smith, 2000; Wong and Aspinwall, 2004).

As resources are scarce in SMEs, knowledge is likely to result from secondary data (e.g. trade journals, sector research, conferences, and professional journals) or from personal contacts. Knowledge acquisition activities in SMEs are concentrated in a few individuals, primarily managers, who have to divide their attention over several activities (Lowik *et al.*, 2012). In addition, as systematic knowledge search and creation will be more expensive compared to informal meetings with suppliers or customers, it is likely that the latter will be favored by SMEs (Cegarra-Navarro and Martínez-Conesa, 2007). Given the internal resource constraints many SMEs are exposed to, external knowledge sources may be assumed to have a critical role in terms of knowledge creation (Egbu *et al.*, 2005), as SMEs seem to look more outside the organization for new knowledge (Desouza and Awazu, 2006). A recent case study from Singapore showed that the SME owner, rather than the employees, was the key source and creator of knowledge and the sole driver of the KM processes. The enablers of a knowledge creation process rested largely on the owner's innovativeness, creativity, and ability to acquire knowledge of the industry (Wee and Chua, 2013). Durst *et al.* (2013) studied which knowledge creation activities are undertaken in small German firms operating in the construction industry. The findings demonstrate the influence of external knowledge sources on knowledge creation activities and the use of OI. Even though the managing directors take advantage of different external knowledge sources, they seem to emphasize informed knowledge sources. The study's findings advance the limited body of knowledge regarding knowledge creation in SMEs.

2.4. *Open innovation*

No consensus exists about how to define the concept "open innovation" (Chiaroni *et al.*, 2011). However, the definition by Chesbrough (2003, p. 15) has gained popularity, where he defines OI as "the use of purposive inflows and outflows of knowledge to accelerate internal innovation, and to expand the markets for external use of innovation, respectively". Three OI practices are commonly mentioned in the literature; outside–in process, inside–out process, and coupled processes. Wynarczyk (2013, pp. 260–261) explains these concepts in the following manner:

> The *"outside-in"* process is based on the assumption that the firm adds to its own knowledge-base through inter-firm linkages with suppliers, customers and/or collaboration with other external institutions (e.g. universities). The *"inside-out"* process refers to generating and accelerating profits by transferring innovative ideas to market through, for example, selling or licensing out intellectual property (IP). Enkel et al. (2009) argue that this form of open innovation enables firms to reap the benefits of their innovative ideas at an earlier stage rather than attempting to translate them into new products themselves. The *"coupled process"* refers to partnership or *"co-creation"* with (mainly) complementary partners through, for example, supply chain, clusters, alliances, co-operation, and joint ventures.

Former studies indicate that larger firms use OI more than smaller firms, although the latter have a lot to gain from OI as both their resources and market research are limited (Huizingh, 2011; Wynarczyk, 2013). OI practices in SMEs seem to be more common in the later innovation stages, especially at the commercialization stage. Employee characteristics may matter for OI, as the adoption of open source software supply strategies can be related to a university-educated workforce. OI seems, moreover, more likely in situations characterized by globalization, new business models, technological intensity, and turbulence (Huizingh, 2011). Chiaroni *et al.* (2011) argue that low-tech industries prefer outside–in strategies of OI, while inside–out strategies are far more common in high-tech companies. In addition, Vrande *et al.* (2009) found out that medium-sized firms are more involved in OI than smaller firms and that they utilize OI for market-related motives, or for keeping up with competitors. Small firms often lack the resources which are essential for transforming inventions into products or processes (Lee *et al.*, 2010). While SMEs' flexibility and specificity can be advantages in accelerating innovation, few SMEs have sufficient capacity to manage the whole innovation process by themselves, and this encourages them to collaborate with other firms (Edwards *et al.*, 2005). Lee *et al.* (2010) explored motives of SMEs to take on OI and the barriers managers experience in implementing it in the companies. The main barrier is related to the organizational and cultural issues that arise when SMEs start to interact and collaborate with external partners.

3. Methodology

Qualitative research is the approach used in this research, and the research design is a case study (Eisenhardt, 1989). A qualitative research design was chosen as we are dealing with a complicated and little-known phenomenon. A case study was selected as the research strategy because the knowledge creation process consists of iterative activities which make the case study a feasible approach. Given the background that knowledge creation in SMEs in Iceland is very limited, a case study approach allowed a more contextual assessment of social phenomena in real-life contexts (Yin, 1994), and the limited amount of prior research means that themes and patterns need to be identified rather than confirmed (Edmondson and McManus, 2007; Eisenhardt, 1989; Yin, 2009). This exploratory research consists of three case studies in SMEs in Iceland. Purposive sampling was used to select cases, and semi-structured interviews were conducted with managers and key employees involved in decision-making or dealing with the knowledge creation process. The reason behind purposeful sampling resides in selecting "information-rich" cases that provide an in-depth understanding of the phenomena under study (Patton, 2002).

Three to four interviews were conducted in each firm. The interviews were recorded and field notes were taken. Other documents relating to the firms, addressing relevant issues on knowledge creation, were also examined, as well as the firms' web pages. Data collection took place in April–October 2015. Interview duration was 60–90 minutes. Research diary, memos, documentations, and direct observation were also part of the data collection. Field note framework was developed and written in reports. The analytical process of data started alongside data collection in order to find emerging themes. After transcription and analysis of each interview, notes were read thoroughly line-by-line to see which codes and themes emerged from the data. Interviews were considered a good way to gather data, to gain a deep understanding of the knowledge creation process. Interviews often revealed key points difficult to reach by other methods, providing opportunities for further questions.

It is also relevant here that it often requires only a small amount of data or a small sample in order to achieve the information sufficient for the purpose of research (Braun and Clarke, 2013; Yin, 2009). Selection of cases is a vital aspect of building theory (Eisenhardt, 1989). Previous research on SMEs has shown that firm size does have an impact on formal strategy, decision-making, formalization, and KM practices (Edvardsson, 2009).

4. Findings

4.1. *Knowledge creation and open innovation in Company Alpha*

Company Alpha is a high-technology company, where software development is the core business activity. The company has received many awards for its products and innovations. Alpha is a leader in finance technology solutions, combining technological innovation and entrepreneurship. The products and solutions are used by institutions, companies, and consumers worldwide. The company is one of those that came out of the financial collapse of Iceland and is a fast-growing concern with around 100 employees. Alpha uses the Scrum development framework and most projects are implemented in teams. The management team consists of eight people, three of whom are the founders of the company. Company Alpha has participated in various competitions and conferences relating to innovation and received awards for its products. The majority of the employees have a university education, are 30–40 years of age, and have more than 10 years' work experience.

Knowledge creation within Company Alpha is mainly a group process, where the expertise of employees is the main resource, giving the company a leading edge. Managers rely strongly on employees for identifying new possibilities. "We work hard trying to find something new" one managers said. Employees have the flexibility to create and come up with new ideas; they must, however, make all decisions in cooperation with their team. Employees begin by selling the team their idea and then a decision is made on whether it should achieve a high ranking. Teams are the main company units, and support for these units, and their structure is of prime importance.

More precisely, new ideas come to light in connection with product development in the company, both from employees and from customers. According to one interviewee, there are often several hundred ideas on the table and about half of them could be of interest. New knowledge is mostly gained in connection with problem-solving. "The chances of solving a problem at the first attempt are minimal", according to one interviewee. Continuous learning takes place by doing a task repeatedly with new and varying methods. Most effort goes into simplifying tasks to such an extent that people begin to understand them. Making things simple takes a lot of time; employees work on a problem for a long time and then all of a sudden there is a "eureka" moment when someone realizes that the proposal for a solution was too complicated or that the task was developing into something quite different.

Teamwork is an important source of knowledge in the opinion of all respondents. Most projects in Company Alpha are implemented in teams. Teams enjoy considerable autonomy and they bear a high level of responsibility in the knowledge creation process. The teams are very independent and strong and actually operate as small individual start-up companies. The production process is extremely disciplined and employees use a roadmap to define and organize procedures. According to one interviewee, it is important to look at the whole process as new knowledge can be generated at all stages on the journey toward creating new products or service. Training and further education are mostly conducted within the company and, according to all of the interviewees, employees gain new knowledge from the specialists being brought to the company who then work closely with the employees on on-going projects. There are not many instances of employees going to courses or conferences external to the company.

External sources are not of great importance in the developmental process, but their feedback is essential in its later stages. Many ideas or comments from clients (individuals) reach the company every day. Also, courses for customers are held, thus engendering feedback about the company's products. One interviewee said: "I hardly ever go to a reception without taking out my phone and showing someone something or talking about it, so one always gets feedback". Representatives of client companies often voice their own opinions on product design. Another interviewee commented on this is in this way: "(often these are) ideas we have tried and that we know have not worked for us; so at times the interplay can be quite entertaining". The interviewee also mentioned that, in addition, ideas were put forward which were a bit outside the framework and which might or might not be feasible; a situation where possibilities are limited and there is a question of what the system can or cannot do and what is the most sensible route to take.

When new ideas in Company Alpha are promoted to development work, the whole team is called to a meeting and a design sprint is implemented in order to understand the problem and to create what are called "personas". According to the interviewees, this is extremely fast creative work. Meetings and brainstorming sessions with customers are widely used when new ideas are promoted to development work. When the process has reached the stage of testing a product, a group of users is brought in to test the innovation. As one interviewee stated:

> We take people who are completely 'cold', it could be people from the street, employees or their partners. In some instances, this testing is recorded by video and customer reactions to the product are monitored. This is, in fact, the way to create a kind of demo edition of the product; we then let someone use it and provide us with feedback.

The testing department has also sent out requests to people for assistance in testing a new product and for gathering opinions. The company is a leader in the market, so that competitors look to them for innovation. Interviewees emphasized that there is very significant competition in this sector, but mostly with foreign parties. The interviewees all had good contact networks in the field of enterprise when the company was founded and they have been maintained. This has a major impact on appointing employees, as well as gaining customers and access to the knowledge they need. According to interviewees, employees are very active in using their contact networks in order to increase their knowledge and to gain new customers which can, among other things, lead to a new service, strategy, or product.

Knowledge sharing activities within Company Alpha are mainly according to a personalization strategy. The shared space for employees to discuss projects is considered by the interviewees to provide the company with valuable new knowledge. For instance, Q&A meetings and Techtalk that is held twice a week during which an employee presents a project solution he is working on. Employees gather at these events and follow developments. To a large extent, knowledge sharing occurs due to conversations between employees and within groups. The teams all have their own organizational walls on which show their work. One interviewee said this was a good example of brainstorming between employees; there were a strong flow and continuous dissemination of knowledge throughout the entire day. The emphasis is on creativity, with employees encouraged to create and share new knowledge and with special Idea Days where employees present their ideas and solve problems they have long struggled with. Regular meetings are held with each team where employees go over the status and problems are discussed and larger meetings convened with all employees. One interviewee mentioned that in spite of all the communication paths to which employees have accesses, it is important to communicate face to face. As he described here:

> *Forwarding information can be difficult; I want people to talk to each other. You can enter whatever you like on Wiki and into any*

other system, but it does not ensure that someone is going to read it. So I would say, rather, just stand up and ask the people next to you; find out whether he has solved a similar problem ...

Employees use the intranet, email, blog, chat threads, Slack, Hangouts, Twitter, and Facebook to share knowledge and provide new solutions and ideas. Employees submit questions relating to problems that need to be solved and receive information from other employees who have encountered the same problems or they are referred to documentation that can prove useful. Twitter has been the main source of new knowledge for many of the company's employees, as one interviewee described: "I take the advice from people who are working in this sector. They put articles on the wall or their thoughts, on something that is innovative". Employees regularly try new media that facilitate their access to knowledge, and the interviewee added that: "The really important thing here is to have your finger on the pulse. Regardless of whether it is Twitter or SnapChat, to be an early adopter and use the best practice that we know others have used successfully".

Documentation and archiving of knowledge are conducted in a structured manner in Company Alpha. The publishing process demands that everything is documented. The gathering of knowledge from employees is mainly by a chain of experiments and tests by the employees in question. "It requires many diagrams and many pages that are written then discarded, and the whole process started again from scratch. Then we progress to testing and iterations in repeated cycles". According to an interviewee, all employees are expected to toe a very strict line and they have access to an inner network in which everything is registered. "Nevertheless, I would say that we can do better there". The company's inner network is where employees record interesting information. One interviewee described it more fully as follows:

So that if you find some article, presentation or something that has caught your interest, you just post it and then people may or may not have time to look at it. Also, we have an instrument to manage ideas so that all employees access these and post suggestions for some innovation and other members of employees can make their own choices.

The interviewees say that this is a web tool to which everyone has access and each and every one can go on it and contribute their ideas. Then other employees can comment on these and choose between the ideas. This is followed up, and a decision is made on whether or not the idea will be placed on the agenda for further development.

4.2. *Knowledge creation and open innovation in Company Beta*

Beta is a high technical software company with the latest technology in management software. The company has around 30 employees who are engineers, computer scientists, and programmers with a long history of work experience. Parts of the company use Scrum development framework, and development projects are implemented in teams. The management team consists of seven people. At Company Beta, work is continuously in progress in introducing innovations or improvements to existing products. The company is a market leader in Iceland.

Knowledge creation within Company Beta is mainly based on the employees' expertise, but new products are only taken on board when contracts have been signed with customers. On this, one interviewee said: "There are very creative employees here who provide ideas, but most new knowledge originates from problems that need to be solved. We are providing solutions for certain needs." Employees are very active in identifying new solutions and possibilities as they use the product at work. "Our culture is characterised by a high level of cooperation and thus by a high level of teamwork", claims one interviewee. He also mentions that this does not necessarily apply to the operation as a whole, but that it applies to the development process where all basic decisions are taken in accordance with Scrum, and which is characterized by a strong emphasis on teamwork. Furthermore, he says: "We also create teams to deal with certain tasks; we are, for example, looking at project management in our company and considering how we can improve it and make it more effective; in this connection, we are thinking of project-oriented teams". The company bases its thinking to a great extent on teamwork, which reflects the whole process concerning product development. According to one interviewee, the product is very complicated and multifaceted in that it stimulated employees to come up with new business ideas that can be sold to customers. Interviewees believe that the best way for employees to gain new knowledge is from working on the ongoing projects. There are not many instances of employees going to courses or conferences external to the company "the problem is that there is not much knowledge in this country about the tasks we are handling". The circumstance that new projects start only after signing contracts with customers has the consequences that ideas from employees are not encouraged. This is seen as demotivating among the employees, and they ask for more motivation to promote new business ideas.

External sources, such as constant communication with customers, are vital to the innovation process. Getting customers to test the software and thus work with company employees to prepare the marketing of a particular version is an important learning experience. There are several large updates every year, and feedback from customers is a vital aspect of this work. An interviewee says: "We are solving certain problems for our customers, often with their participation. We have meetings with customers and there is a lot of development cooperation". Customers bring ideas, queries, and requests, which more often than not end up as projects. One interviewee stated:

> *This is a little like being in a spider's web; there are customers everywhere and we are in the middle, and there is continuous communication between us. Knowledge is generated as a result of ideas (here), we are like a sponge, we absorb. Our employees have considerable knowledge and this is tightly interwoven...*

A customer purchases a solution which is then further developed. Thus, the product is not designed for specific customers but rather so that these solutions and additions can be used for other customers. The company is developing one particular product, and if there is further development for the customer, then it becomes part of the product. On this, one interviewee noted: "In the case of in-house ideas expected to be needed by the customer, we may wait for the need to arise with the customer". Testing, experimenting, and correcting errors in the software is very important, and customers are brought in to test equipment in the beta edition, thus working with employees in bringing the edition into use. In such a case, they are using all of the new functionalities where the objective is to remove errors that have developed in the testing.

One interviewee raises an interesting issue when he points out that the size of a customer company has a significant impact on the knowledge creation process. "We have this one extremely large customer and most new knowledge is created for this one company. This is because they are so specialized". Furthermore, the interviewee says they would gain more in terms of knowledge if they had many smaller customers and smaller projects, "but it is our reality today that we have been targeting larger customers because they obviously pay most. Money makes the world go around".

Company Beta does not have many competitors in Iceland, so this is not a significant factor "possibly one company which is in a comparable sector, but our paths never actually cross". Competition abroad is stiffer and quite different because there the company competes with firms specializing in these products, and employees learn a lot from chasing the market there. The company has participated in many partnership innovation projects through funds. One of the interviewees said these had not been successful enough to bring new ideas to their completion. There are plenty of ongoing projects paid for by customers, and therefore little financial flexibility exists to take on larger development projects. "It is important to have 'pilot' customers who are willing to work with us regarding development costs". He mentioned an example of a new idea that has been on the drawing board for two years without going further. The company joins various events involving associations and companies and participates in boards to strengthen its contact network. The knowledge gained through communication with contacts has led to new methods or products, according to the interviewees.

Knowledge sharing activities within Company Beta are not conducted in a systematic way and the employees access information and educational material on the Internet on their own initiative. They have flexibility but are not specifically encouraged to do so. The interviewees consider the lack of time as a hindrance; employees do not give themselves adequate time to share knowledge at formal presentations or meetings where there is an exchange of information. Meetings and brainstorming sessions with customers are used when new product development ideas are promoted. One interviewee touches upon the discussion on the gender gap, technical development, and methods of communication. He says there are at least two generations in the company, if not three, which has an impact on the use of knowledge management tools and the communication of information in the knowledge creation process. Brainstorming and mind mapping are widely used, especially within teams in the developmental stage, where managers and employees reflect on projects and products. Information walls (scrum task boards) are used that can be seen by all employees and are thought to be a good forum for employees to brainstorm. Regular meetings are held with each individual team where employees go over the current status and problems are discussed. Larger meetings are also convened with all employees. The service team, which works as a kind of "cross-border group", meets every morning and employees plan the tasks of the day; this is where project work is discussed and any problems people may be dealing with are focused upon. This is where employees can contribute on the basis of their knowledge and experience.

Documentation and archiving of knowledge could be more formal according to the interviewees. Information on projects is stored in databases. Employees use the company's computer system to a great extent, as it is also the company's main product. Considerable emphasis has been placed on developing an intranet to replace email messages between employees, which are currently used to a greater or lesser degree. "The problem is that not everyone reads the emails and it varies how carefully people read them and then they are deleted". Employees do not use any special systems to share or store knowledge, and there is no general discussion or awareness of this within the company:

> *There aren't really any ongoing incentives. We just somehow lack this culture ... a kind of incentive culture — people writing articles and having them published; just creating the habit and knowhow to write things down and present them. But people are gradually becoming aware that this must change. We must present and publish the knowledge that exists because there are people here who possess a lot of knowledge.*

There is, then, no formal strategy on knowledge sharing or documenting of knowledge. In reality, it is up to individuals to share their knowledge in teams and document it.

4.3. *Knowledge creation and open innovation in Company Delta*

Delta is a high-technology company that produces research equipment. Delta specializes in the design and manufacture of scientific equipment and is on the frontline in developing research products. The company has worked with scientists and research institutes worldwide, providing innovative solutions and equipment. Delta has been a leading developer and manufacturer in its sector for many years. The company has under 20 employees who all are well educated and have years of experience. The manager is also the owner and founder of the company.

Knowledge creation within Delta is a process where employees are the main experts in their field and considerable specialized knowledge lies behind new products. Ideas for new products often originate from employees who are making suggestions about what can be done with the technology they already have. As one interviewee describes, new knowledge also derives from various types of in-house creative work "sometimes we just do something that occurs to us". In some cases, the need for new knowledge is discovered from experiments or ideas that have not proved successful or in instances where the ideas are slightly restructured. Then a new idea can come to light. Ideas and knowledge behind the company' current products originate, to a large extent, from the company manager. As few employees work in the company, every idea of improvement is considered and not left on the table. One interviewee describes the process in the following manner:

> *When we are looking for ideas, we refuse to let anything stop us…*
> *we conduct experiments and we know that we will have problems.*
> *By being aware of the risks and by finding solutions we have*
> *succeeded in providing simple solutions to difficult problems.*
> *It really revolves around resolving matters in a simple manner…*

The work requires advanced specialization and knowledge that can only be gained in-house. All training and education for employees take place internally in the company. One interviewee states: "Our business is such that we are not getting any assistance within the country. If we were to bring someone in to advise us, then we would need to educate that person first. There is no one as far advanced as we are in this sector".

External sources are of great importance. The company is fulfilling the requirements of customers, but ideas can originate in-house as well as in communication with customers. On this, one interviewee comments, "We then ask them whether this is something they would like to use and if they say 'yes', we look for commitment". Dedication is an important factor as these are large projects involving a significant amount of development work. Not all ideas come to fruition, because the development takes an extremely long time, particularly if there is a significant leap from what they have been doing. Normally they begin with a few items of the product, even where the customer indicates that the project will be large, and the quantity of the product we manufacture then depends on sales. It is always assumed that it is not possible to guarantee that a large project will result from development work and that the company will recoup its development costs. The interviewees take an example of a product the company has long had their eye on, then suddenly the opportunity came through funds and partnerships with enterprises in other countries. "It is so difficult to pass such a big task if you do not have a springboard. It can take a minimum of two years to develop a product if it is completely new".

The company has recently been running a large project where one of the company's products was adapted to a piece of software being run by a customer. The customer consulted the company because they could not find a comparable product anywhere else. The negotiations relating to this project were concluded in such a way that the customer paid the development cost and, in return, received a certain quantity of the product. One interviewee mentions other projects where the company has cooperated with large businesses abroad. Interviewee 1 describes cooperation of this kind:

We received a request from a customer who was struggling with a certain problem. Their branch could not find a solution and we had the knowledge. They paid us to do a feasibility study and when we were ready, a protocol was conducted which was a great success. But then there was a certain collapse in the sector and the project had to be put on ice for the time being.

The interviewee also says that this process is really a "spinweb" since IP rights rest with both parties, which can be a complicated matter. The interviewee brings up an example where cooperation with another large company was attempted but did not work out. "They just tried to walk over us and I have known nothing like this for 15 years. They insisted on exclusive production rights and just wanted to throw us out so they are no longer our partners". As regards cooperation with other enterprises and customers in the area of product development, one of the interviewees makes the following point:

We have the knowledge and it is a matter of (two companies) finding each other to finance the project and it is, of course, the ideal solution to have a customer arrive from abroad so that we no longer have to worry about the money, we just go ahead.

Company Delta has had good cooperation with institutions on development work, but because of their current financial situation there is little cooperation at present as part of the sector has shrunk significantly. There is, therefore, no longer any basis for these contracts said the interviewee. Since the financial crisis in 2008, the company has been able to greatly increase its knowledge but finds it more difficult to negotiate long-term agreements with research institutions today, and this is a risk inherent in embarking on large development projects. The contact network is largely based on research institutions and companies, which used to serve an important role in creating new knowledge. Now, the company largely stands alone. The interviewee indicated that the company is indeed in competition to some degree, but that there are only a few other companies in the world that are working in this sector, "It is a very small world but it is vital to get products on the market at the right time. New products come both as a result of pressure from customers and because competitors are offering them", as one interviewee pointed out.

Knowledge sharing activities within Delta occur mostly when employees meet and discuss matters among themselves. There is less emphasis on communicating through computers or other KM tools. The interviewee says there is no need for an intranet: "This is very convenient for such a small company; very easy to walk around, discuss an issue and gather information." The employees work closely together and they can observe one another in their workspace. Sharing of knowledge mostly revolves around the manager asking the employees questions: how things worked and why they do not work. The interviewee further says:

People just meet and talk. I only use email as a memo, it's just for ideas and I have sometimes wanted to get an email covering something I have to do, then I can remember it. Emails are OK as are other systems like that, but I just want people to meet and this is what we emphasise. We have coffee breaks in the morning and afternoon, and people also meet at noon, and this is just, like, you and me.

Delta holds a meeting twice a month where employees discuss ongoing projects, but there are few other organized meetings. Should issues arise that need to be examined more deeply, a special meeting is called. Employees discuss the issues they have problems with and these problems are followed up with even two to three employees being sent to help with a problem.

Documentation and archiving of knowledge within Company Delta are rather informal. Information regarding the company's ongoing projects, project ideas, and projects under development can be obtained from an Excel document under the control of the managing director but accessible to employees. The manager collects all ideas and goes over them with those who have the best relevant knowledge within the company. Lately, however, the process has been more extensive with respect to development work. The interviewees are pleased with the flow of information within the company, although the presentation of information can always be improved; "sometimes people are very busy in their own little world and this may hinder information flow between departments". According to one interviewee, the company has been busy recently improving its databases. All employees can access recorded knowledge, "but not every employee has knowledge of everything, that is simply impossible." The interviewees say, however, that this might change because the company might embark on projects which demand a high degree of secrecy. In that case, the entire computer system will need to be updated in such a way that only those involved in a particular project can see data relating to that project. "This is just something the customer insists on and he will pay for it." One interviewee says there is no need for an internal web since the small size of the company makes it easy for employees to access information. It is a simple matter to stroll around, discuss things, and obtain information. As regards the recording and preservation of knowledge, the interviewee says:

> I have been building up the company and therefore I deliberately maintain double functions so that we don't get into trouble if someone leaves. We run this like an aircraft. There are two engines,

two control panels and if one goes wrong the other gets started up.
That's how I have tried to develop the business.

Knowledge sharing within Company Delta is largely based on personalization strategy. Documentation of knowledge is not extensive.

5. Discussions and Conclusions

The aim of the chapter was to present findings on OI and KM in SMEs in Iceland. Three case studies on small and medium-sized companies were presented in order to answer the questions: 1) how do firms deal with knowledge creation, knowledge sharing, and storage? 2) how are customers and other external stakeholders involved in the innovation process?

New knowledge in Company Alpha originates from new business ideas and problems that need to be solved. In Company Beta, new business ideas and problems are developed with customers, and innovation starts after an agreement has been signed. In Company Delta, the manager is the main driver of new business ideas. In all the three companies, the knowledge creation process is similar: Groups of employees work on the development of new solutions by experimenting and sharing knowledge through brainstorming and discussing ideas, which can be described as collaborative learning. Knowledge sharing is mainly through personalization strategy, although the product development process tends to be intensively documented.

The companies Alpha and Beta both focus on one main product, "software", where customers are most likely to be involved when updates are on the agenda or custom-built solutions developed in cooperation with customers. Thus, customers' suggestions or requirements regarding improved products or innovations and how the companies go about this are of vital importance as catalysts for new knowledge within the companies. The employees have accumulated a great deal of specialist knowledge and expertise with regard to the companies' products. Consequently, the companies rarely embark on development projects in cooperation with other parties or seek external knowledge at the stage of product development. In Company Delta, customers are involved in the original stage, and in some instances other firms take part in developing products. Customers and external stakeholders are rarely consulted when the projects have started, until the testing of software programs at the end of the process. Although their feedback is important, it is only limited in the knowledge creation process in general. All the companies have, accordingly, some features of an inside-out innovation model, while Company Delta has some signs of coupled processes (Lee *et al.*, 2010; Wynarczyk, 2013).

The three case companies share many characteristics of SMEs: they do not have a formal strategy on knowledge management and knowledge sharing and storage (Durst and Edvardsson, 2012; McAdam and Reid, 2001). Knowledge creation and innovation is a learning process in the companies. They come close to the findings of Garvin (1993) who argues that new knowledge is created in organizations by systematic problem-solving, experimenting with new approaches, learning from experience, and sharing knowledge. Collaborative learning is also prevalent in the three cases, with new knowledge emerging through critical discussions and active dialogue among employees working in groups to achieve a shared understanding (Hedlund, 1994; Jakubik, 2008).

The findings regarding the three companies are in accordance with the arguments of Chiaroni *et al.* (2011) where they state that high-tech companies tend to prefer inside-out strategies of OI, while low-tech companies prefer outside–in strategies. The findings are also in line with earlier studies which show that SMEs use OI more often in the later stages of the innovation process (Vrande *et al.*, 2009).

These three cases give us an insight into what knowledge-intensive SMEs in Iceland are dealing with regarding OI and knowledge creation. There is a lot to be learned from these cases, and they indicate areas for further examination and research. First, there are various aspects which influence the possibilities that companies have to use and introduce innovation in their operations. Aspects such as company structure and cultural challenges are influencing factors here. As for the managerial challenges, Lee *et al.* (2010) found that organizational and cultural issues are the key barriers to implementing OI in SMEs.

Secondly, there is the difference in size of companies and their varying approaches to OI. Two of the larger companies, Alpha and Beta, have a lot in common with regards to the role of customers in the process. Their employees continuously communicate with customers and have an open channel to enlist their participation in forming the product. Conclusions indicate that larger companies have greater resources to deal with OI, with respect to customer participation. According to Lee *et al.* (2010) and Vrande *et al.* (2009), SMEs often lack the resources to be able to leverage OI. At Delta, which is also the smallest company, communications with customers are different, as has been previously stated, and the company seeks more to cooperate with larger customers.

Finally, the cases illustrate the importance of knowledge storage and KM for the OI process in the firms. Knowledge sharing is the essence of OI, both within and between firms, and KM systems can enhance such processes (Chiaroni *et al.*, 2011).

In future research, it would be interesting to examine more closely the characteristics of OI in knowledge-intensive SMEs generally, and also to compare them with other kinds of firms. Also, a cross-national research on OI in SMEs would be essential to reveal cultural and societal effects on the innovation process.

References

Awad, E. M. and Ghaziri, H. M. (2004). *Knowledge Management*. New Jersey, Pearson Education.

Allard, S. (2003). Knowledge Creation. In: C. W. Holsappe (Ed.) *Handbook of Knowledge Management*, vol. 1, pp. 367–379.

Argyris, C. (1999). *On Organizational Learning*. 2nd ed., Malden: Blackwell, Addison Wesley.

Berraies, S., Chaher, M. and Yahia, K. B. (2014). Knowledge management enablers, knowledge creation process and innovation performance: An empirical study in tunisian information and communication technologies sector. *Business Management and Strategy*, 5, pp. 1–26.

Braun, V. and Clarke, V. (2013). *Successful Qualitative Research: A Practical Guide for Beginners*. Sage.

Cegarra-Navarro, J. G. and Martínez-Conesa, E. A. (2007). E-business through knowledge management in Spanish telecommunications companies. *International Journal of Manpower,* **28,** pp. 298–314.

Chesbrough, H. (2003). *Open Innovation: The New Imperative for Creating and Profiting from Technology.* Harvard Business School Press, Boston, MA.

Chiaroni, D., Chiesa, V. and Frattini, F. (2011). The open innovation journey: How firms dynamically implement the emerging innovation management paradigm. *Technovation,* **31,** pp. 34–43.

Clegg, S., and Clarke, T. (1999). Intelligent Organizations? In: SR Clegg, E. Ibarra-Colado and L. Bueono-Rodriquez (Eds.) *Global Management: Universal Theories and Local Realities,* pp. 177–201. London: Sage

Culkin, N. and Smith, D. (2000). An emotional business: A guide to understanding the motivations of small business decision takers. *Qualitative Market Research: An International Journal,* **3,** pp. 145–157.

Daft, R. F. (2007). *Understanding the Theory and Design of Organizations.* Mason: Thomson South-Western.

Davenport, T. H. and Prusak, L. (1998). *Working Knowledge: How Organizations Manage What They Know.* Harvard Business Press.

Desouza, K. C. and Awazu, Y. (2006). Knowledge management at SMEs: Five peculiarities. *Journal of Knowledge Management,* **10,** pp. 32–43.

Durst, S. and Edvardsson, I. R. (2012). Knowledge management in SMEs: A literature review. *Journal of Knowledge Management,* **16,** pp. 879–903.

Durst, S., Edvardsson, I. R. and Bruns, G. (2013). Knowledge creation in small building and construction firms. *Journal of Innovation Management,* **1,** pp. 125–142.

Edmondson, A. C. and McManus, S. E. (2007). Methodological fit in management research. *Academy of Management Review* **32,** pp.1155–1179.

Edvardsson, I. R. (2006). Knowledge Management and SMEs: The case of Icelandic firms. *Knowledge Management Research & Practice,* **4,** pp. 275–282.

Edvardsson, I. R. (2009). Is knowledge management losing ground? Developments among Icelandic SMEs. *Knowledge Management Research & Practice,* **7,** pp. 91–99.

Edwards, T., Delbridge, R., and Munday, M. (2005). Understanding innovation in small and medium-sized enterprises: A process manifest. *Technovation,* 25(10), pp. 1119–1127.

Egbu, C. O., Hari, S. and Renukappa, S. H. (2005). Knowledge management for sustainable competitiveness in small and medium surveying practices. *Structural Survey,* **23,** pp. 7–21.

Eisenhardt, K. M. (1989). Building theories from case study research. *Academy of Management Review,* 14(4), pp. 532–550.

Enkel, E., Gassmann, O. and Chesbrough, H. (2009). Open R&D and open innovation: Exploring the phenomenon. *R&D Management,* **39,** pp. 311–316.

Garvin, D. A. (1993). Building a learning organization. *Harvard Business Review,* **71,** pp. 78–91.

Hansen, M. T., Nohria, N. and Tierney, T. (1999). What's your strategy for managing knowledge? *Harvard Business Review*, 77, pp. 106–116.

Hedlund, G. (1994). A model of knowledge management and the N-form Corporation. *Strategic Management Journal*, 15, pp. 73–90.

Hughes, T., O'Regan, N. and Sims, M. A. (2009). The effectiveness of knowledge networks: An investigation of manufacturing SMEs. *Education + Training*, 51, pp. 665–681.

Huizingh, E. K. (2011). Open innovation: State-of-the-art and future perspectives. *Technovation*, 31, pp. 2–9.

Jakubik, M. (2008). Experiencing collaborative knowledge creation processes. *The Learning Organization*, 15, pp. 5–25.

Jashapara, A. (2011). *Knowledge Management: An Integrated Approach*. Prentice Hall, Harlow.

Kolb, D. A. (1984). *Experimental Learning: Experience as the Source of Learning and Development*. Engelwood Cliffs, NJ, Prentice Hall.

Lee, S., Park, G., Yoon, B. and Park, J. (2010). Open innovation in SMEs. An intermediated network model. *Research Policy*, 39, pp. 290–300.

Lichtenthaler, U. and Lichtenthaler, E. (2009). A capability-based framework for open innovation: Complementing absorptive capacity. *Journal of Management Studies*, 46, pp. 1315–1338.

Lowik, S., van Rossum, D., Kraaijenbrink, J. and Groen, A. (2012). Strong ties as sources of new knowledge: How small firms innovate through bridging capabilities. *Journal of Small Business Management*, 50, pp. 239–256.

Markus, L. M. (2001). Toward a theory of knowledge reuse: Types of knowledge reuse situations and factors in reuse success. *Journal of Management Information Systems*, 18, pp. 57–93.

McAdam, R. and Reid, R. (2001). SME and large organisation perceptions of knowledge management: Comparisons and contrasts. *Journal of Knowledge Management*, 5, pp. 231–241.

Mitchell, R. and Boyle, B. (2010). Knowledge creation measurement methods. *Journal of Knowledge Management*, 14, pp. 67–82.

Miller, W. L. and Morris, L. (1999). *Fourth Generation R&D: Managing Knowledge, Technology and Innovation*. John Wiley & Sons, New York.

Nejatian, M., Nejati, M., Zarei, M. H. and Soltani, S. (2013). Critical enablers for knowledge creation process: Synthesizing the literature. *Global Business and Management Research*, 5, p. 105.

Nonaka, I. (1991). The knowledge creating company. *Harvard Business Review*, 69, pp. 96–104.

Nonaka, I. and Konno, N. (1998). The concept of "ba": Building a foundation for knowledge creation. *California Management Review*, 40, pp. 40–54.

Nonaka, I. and Takeuchi, H. (1995). *The Knowledge-Creating Company*. Oxford University Press, Oxford.

Nonaka, I., Toyama, R. and Konno, N. (2000). SECI, Ba and leadership: A unified model of dynamic knowledge creation. *Long Range Planning*, 33, pp. 5–34.

Patton, M. Q. (2002). *Qualitative Research and Evaluation Methods*. 3rd ed. Sage. Thousand Oaks, CA.

Sankowska, A. (2013). Relationships between organizational trust, knowledge transfer, knowledge creation and firm's innovativeness. *Learning Organization*, 20, pp. 85–100.

Spicer, D. P. and Sadler-Smith, E. (2006). Organizational learning in smaller manufacturing firms. *International Small Business Journal*, 24, pp. 133–158.

Sparrow, J. (2005). Classification of different knowledge management development approaches of SMEs. *Knowledge Management Research & Practice*, 3, pp. 136–145.

Szarka, F. E., Grant, K. P. and Flannery, W. T. (2004). Achieving organizational learning through team competition. *Engineering Management Journal*, 16, pp. 21–31.

Thompson, M. and Heron, P. (2005). The difference a manager can make: Organizational justice and knowledge worker commitment. *The International Human Resource Management*, 16, pp. 383–404.

Ueki, H., Ueki, M., Linowes, R. and Mroczkowski, T. (2011). A comparative study of enablers of knowledge creation in Japan and US-based firms. *Asian Business & Management*, 10, pp. 113–132.

Von Krogh, G., Nonaka, I. and Rechsteiner, L. (2012). Leadership in organizational knowledge creation: A review and framework. *Journal of Management Studies*, 49, pp. 240–277.

Van de Vrande, V., De Jong, J. P., Vanhaverbeke, W. and De Rochemont, M. (2009). Open innovation in SMEs: Trends, motives and management challenges. *Technovation*, 29, pp. 423–437.

Wang, Z. and Wang, N. (2012). Knowledge sharing, innovation and firm performance. *Expert Systems with Applications*. 39, pp. 8899–8908.

Wee, C. N. J. and Chua, Y. K. A. (2013). The peculiarities of knowledge management processes in SMEs: The case of Singapore. *Journal of Knowledge Management*, 17, pp. 958–972.

Wynarczyk, P. (2013). Open innovation in SMEs: A dynamic approach to modern entrepreneurship in the twenty-first century. *Journal of Small Business and Enterprise Development*, 20, pp. 258–278.

Wong, K. Y. and Aspinwall, E. (2004). Characterizing knowledge management in the small business environment. *Journal of Knowledge Management*, 8, pp. 44–61.

Yin, R. K. (2009). *Case Study Research: Design and Methods*. 4th ed. Sage, UK.

Chapter 6

Knowledge Sharing and Open Innovation

Ardalan Haghighi Talab, Victor Scholten, and Cees van Beers

Faculty of Technology Policy and Management,
Delft University of Technology,
Jaffalaan 5, 2628 BX Delft, The Netherlands

Knowledge resources, mainly due to their causal ambiguity and inimitability, play a central role in shaping the competitive advantage of organizations. This chapter aims to illustrate a correspondence between knowledge types and organizational types in open innovation (OI) networks. It maps the knowledge types that shape diverse institutions of the economy as presented by the Triple Helix model: episteme at the academia, techne at the industry, and phronesis at the government. Each organization — beyond its institutional knowledge specialization — diversifies to incorporate the other two knowledge types in its knowledge integration portfolio. For example, a university may develop technologies and conduct responsible research and/or a firm may conduct scientific research and engage in corporate social responsibility activities. The implications of these institutional specialization and organizational diversification in OI networks are twofold: (a) organizations can gain a competitive edge by diversifying into a unique portfolio of

knowledge integration encompassing a novel proportion of episteme, techne, and phronesis and (b) to achieve the highest level
of knowledge integration, organizations belonging to diverse institutions can engage in inter-organizational knowledge sharing to
meta-integrate their institutionally specialized and organizationally
diversified knowledge types.

1. Introduction

Knowledge plays a crucial role for firms in developing new ideas,
novel innovations, and eventually sustained competitive advantage.
Universities, small and multinational firms in industry, and governmental authorities collaborate in networks to develop new knowledge,
acquire external knowledge, and/or put the available knowledge into
practice. Knowledge is the key to the competitiveness of organizations
and regions (Huggins and Izushi, 2007). The knowledge base of an
economy can be defined as the capacity and capability to create new
ideas, thoughts, and processes to innovate products and services.
Translating these into economic growth increases the value of economy and generates wealth (Huggins and Izushi, 2007). From a firm's
viewpoint, knowledge can increase the productive capacity of the
traditional factors of production (e.g. material, land, labor, capital)
via its facilitative role by increasing their efficiency and effectiveness
via technology as described by the production function. Additionally,
knowledge can enable the transformation of the production function
to produce new products, services, and processes, i.e. the enabling role
of knowledge. The resource-based view (RBV) of the economy gives
knowledge a privileged status compared to the other resources, e.g.
material, land, labor, or capital (Peteraf, 1993). This is mainly due to
higher causal ambiguity of knowledge resources, which enhances
inimitability. Also, the idiosyncrasies of each organization further
assure inimitability of knowledge-based resources and capabilities.
Path dependency of knowledge-based resources and capabilities contributes to the inimitability, further intensifying the role of knowledge
in gaining and maintaining a competitive advantage. Unlike the finite

resources (i.e. material, land, labor, capital), knowledge as an infinite resource can produce increasing returns (Dodgson, 1993). While the finite resources decrease in the course of the production process, knowledge increases, among other means, by cross-learning via knowledge sharing.

Thus, many organizations have become increasingly dependent on knowledge-based resources to gain sustained competitive advantage (Barney, 1991; Argote and Ingram, 2000; Tsoukas and Vladimirou, 2001; Grant, 2002; Argote *et al.*, 2003). Moreover, due to the increasing complexity of technologies, organizations, in particular small and medium-sized enterprises (SMEs), cannot develop all required knowledge internally and therefore aim to collaborate with external actors (Powell *et al.*, 1996). Due to the high cost and uncertainty involved in research and development, creating in-house knowledge or utilizing existing knowledge by a single organization is not always possible (Hardy *et al.*, 2003). In order to acquire resources that cannot be developed internally — due to economic and/or technological constraints — organizations collaborate with external parties (Powell *et al.*, 1996). These knowledge collaborations with external parties are studied in the field of OI (Chesbrough, 2003; Scholten and Temel, 2014). Inter-organizational knowledge collaboration (IKC), as a domain of Knowledge Management (KM), deals with the challenges organizations face in the co-creation and co-utilization of knowledge resources in OI (Laursen and Salter, 2006).

If today's organizations' value creation is mainly knowledge-based, and if the core rationale of inter-organizational collaboration in OI is to co-create/co-utilize knowledge, the taxonomy of knowledge should be related to organizational types. Also, such a taxonomy should shape the rationale of OI. Understanding the knowledge roles of organizations helps to better align and orchestrate their actions. To understand inter-organizational knowledge interactions in domains of OI, it is necessary to understand how the organizational types are associated with the knowledge taxonomy.

Instead of epistemology or terminology, this chapter concerns the taxonomy of knowledge. The building of a taxonomy is the first basic step to shape KM activities (Guarino, 1997). This means that a practical taxonomy, even in the absence of philosophical epistemology and/or distinctive terminology (of data, information, and knowledge), provides common ground for understanding, helping SMEs to strategically position themselves in the market, and efficiently allocate their internal and external knowledge resources. A consistent taxonomy of knowledge helps SMEs in capitalizing on their internal resources (i.e. existing knowledge), and it directs the knowledge search strategy to benefit from the matching partners in OI (i.e. external knowledge). Taxonomy comprises naming an all-inclusive set of categories to specify knowledge types. A comprehensive taxonomy possesses discriminant aptitude in distinguishing the knowledge types with ideally no overlap (internal consistency), and a one-to-one attachment of those all-inclusive and distinct labels to the real-world cases (external consistency). An internally and externally consistent taxonomy furnishes the practitioners and researchers with valuable perspective and has the potential to help find answers to the challenges of IKC in OI specifically and enhance our understanding of KM.

Several dichotomous taxonomies have been proposed in the literature: declarative vs. procedural (Minsky, 1975), descriptive vs. procedural (Holsapple *et al.*, 1996), tacit vs. explicit (Nonaka and Takeuchi, 1995), and local vs. global (Novins and Armstrong, 1998). Managing knowledge, subjected to dichotomous taxonomies, has been challenging in the past as particular knowledge, e.g. the process knowledge of converting light to electricity, cannot easily be assigned to one side of a dichotomy. In this example, such process knowledge is both declarative and procedural, has tacit and explicit dimensions at once, and is seen as both local and global. Furthermore, the unification or merger of taxonomies is also far from a consensus. This chapter, instead of a dichotomous mutually exclusive taxonomy, provides a link between the Aristotelian knowledge is taxonomy (i.e. episteme, techne, and phronesis) and organization types. This chapter argues that: first, the typology of organizations on an institutional level (e.g. university as an institution or the institution of business) is critically dependent on and shaped by the knowledge taxonomy. Universities, firms, and government institutions are primarily specialized forms to create and utilize knowledge in its distinctive forms. In brief, the Aristotelian knowledge taxonomy corresponds with the Triple Helix model (Leydesdorff and Etzkowitz, 1998). Second, organizations (e.g. a specific university or a firm) create and utilize secondary and tertiary types of knowledge. A university may diversify into the world of industries to make technologies. An industrial organization (e.g. an SME) may diversify into the world of universities to conduct scientific research. Third, extending the view in which "the *firm* is conceptualized as an institution for integrating knowledge" (emphasis added, Grant, 1996b, p. 109), all organizational types, including firms, universities, and governmental organizations, are considered as knowledge integrators, especially when collaborating through OI. It follows that the highest level of integration takes place by meta-integration of knowledge of multiple organizations and organizational types through IKC in an OI setting.

Section 2 of this chapter outlines the Aristotelian knowledge taxonomy. Also, a widely applied taxonomy of know-what, know-how, know-why, etc. in this section is shown to lack internal and external consistency. Section 3 sketches the link between the Aristotelian knowledge taxonomy and the organizational typology (Triple Helix model) through specialization. Section 4 illustrates the diversification strategy of organizations with regard to knowledge taxonomy and outlines the cross-tabulation of the knowledge taxonomy and organizational type. The diversified roles of organizations are outlined. Section 5 extends the taxonomy beyond the boundary of one organization and reflects on IKC in OI as a meta-integration process. Section 6 concludes.

2. Background

Practitioners and academics, supposed to act upon knowledge collaboration challenges, need to have an understanding of the forms the substances under their actions may take. A taxonomy is the main provider of such an understanding. Yet, "the field of KM pay scant attention to the ontological ground of knowledge" (Butler, 2006, p. 4). To enable the management of knowledge, the first step is to clarify: What is knowledge? This fundamental question "has intrigued some of the world's greatest thinkers from Plato to Popper without the emergence of a clear consensus" (Grant, 1996b, p. 110). This chapter does not aim to contribute to or settle these philosophical epistemological debates. Instead, it aims to provide a new perspective by integrating the established taxonomies to describe the real-world heterogeneities of organizations and inter-organizational collaborations. As an illustration of this approach, one does not need to know the essence of fire to warm up a pot. This chapter is exclusively about the taxonomy of knowledge, i.e. what are the distinct knowledge forms. Internal consistency promises this distinctness. External consistency puts it into test by detecting the real-world distinct manifestations of a distinct taxonomy.

Holsapple and Joshi (2002, p. 48) argue that "Commentators on the knowledge management scene often strive to draw distinctions between the notions of data, information, and knowledge. Some of these same commentators, as well as others, proceed to use the terms knowledge and information interchangeably". There is indeed inconsistency in the definitions and terminologies, and an ongoing debate is challenging the terminology of knowledge, information, and data. For instance, Keen and Tan (2007) believe that while it is important to understand KM terms, it is unproductive for researchers (and even less productive for practitioners) to get focused on trying to precisely define these terms at the expense of furthering KM research. In the same vein, Schwartz (2006, p. 11) asserts that "the distinction between data, information, and knowledge can be conveniently ignored: not treated as irrelevant for a philosophical debate, mind-body discussion, or a metalevel, object-level analysis, but not essential to the fundamental mission of knowledge management". Investigating a knowledge taxonomy indeed does not necessitate a strict terminology to differentiate between data, information, and knowledge. Knowledge types can be defined, independent from a distinction between information and data. Thus, apart from the epistemology and the terminology debates surrounding knowledge and knowledge management within OI fields, this chapter continues by describing a taxonomy and its organizational and inter-organizational implications.

2.1. *Aristotelian knowledge taxonomy: Episteme, techne, and phronesis*

In Book VI of The Nicomachean Ethics (N.E.) (Aristotle, 1976), Aristotle describes five intellectual virtues (p. 1139b) of: *epistêmê* (science), *tékhnê* (technical reason), *phrónêsis* (prudence or practice-oriented ethics), *sophía* (theoretical wisdom), and *noûs* (intuitive intelligence).

Scholars interpret these virtues differently (e.g. compare Flyvbjerg, 2001, 2006; Eikeland, 2008). This section describes the knowledge types aiming at a taxonomy that shapes the diverse organizational types and their knowledge interrelationships.

Episteme regards the general universal and eternal knowledge. Its aim is to understand the governing principles that the universe — for the most part (*hôs epì tò polú*) — works anywhere, anytime. The aim of epistemic knowledge is understanding, as the ultimate end, regardless of possible applications of that understanding. Of course, epistemic knowledge can be put in action or act as a basis for production.

> *With Aristotle it [i.e. episteme] meant something like studying for the purpose of understanding and truth, without intervening, and without the study being subordinated to or serving to promote any immediate plans for action of any kind* (Eikeland, 2008, p. 46).

Techne (art) is strictly differentiated from episteme by having the main focus on making and producing artifacts as an artisan. Techne is the intellectual virtue of production. Products and services are made existent by the artisan owing mainly to her techne. The distinction between episteme and techne does not imply that attaining epistemic knowledge does not rely on techne or vice versa. For instance, nuclear fission power plants as an artifact are rooted in epistemic knowledge of nuclear physicists. Also, the scientists developing epistemic knowledge of nuclear fission rely heavily on artifacts (measurement devices and alike in laboratories and elsewhere) to arrive at the general, universal, and eternal knowledge of nuclear fission. Techne had historically played a crucial role in the development of episteme, e.g. in studies ranging from the galaxies to an individual organic cell by producing a range of devices from telescopes to microscopes. Similarly, techne relies on episteme and is reinforced by it. Looking at building a house (a classic example from Aristotle's explanation of techne) or shipbuilding, there are general epistemic principles, for instance, on material science, statics, and/or hydraulics without which an artifact cannot function. Techne is making and materializing that includes and adheres to general principles. In short, episteme and techne, although distinct in nature, are constantly interacting to facilitate and enable the other. The interplay of episteme and techne is at the core of university-industry interaction in OI.

Phronesis is translated to prudence. It is a normative deliberation on action and its consequences with regard to a particular situation at hand. The term can be more precisely defined by its contrast to episteme and techne. First, phronesis is different from episteme in that it is not derived from a set of general, universal, and eternal principles. Phronesis is more concerned with the particular of here and now in relation to ethical bearings of a specific action in light of the general ethical rules. Phronesis, given the ethical principles, is a deliberation to crystallize the relation between the particular (contingent conduct) and the universal (ethical principle) (Gadamer, 1975).

Thus, well separated from the invariant principles of episteme, phronesis is not meant to apply anywhere, anytime. This does not imply that phronesis is without principles. Indeed, the principles are given by the ethical virtues.

> *[ethical] Virtue ensures the rightness of the end we aim at, prudence [phronesis] ensures the rightness of the means we adopt to gain that end (N.E., p. 1144a).*
>
> *Nor is Prudence a knowledge of general principles only: it must also take account of particular facts, since it is concerned with*

action, and action deals with particular things (emphasis added, N.E., p. 1141b).

While episteme is a deliberation of the universe by which one understands the principles of the universe as an external entity, phronesis regards one's actions and evaluates them based on one's ethical principles that one chooses to adhere to internally. The source of variation in episteme is not in one's control, while phronesis variation is chosen by one. "As two practical intellectual virtues, 'phrónêsis and tékhnê concern things that we ourselves can control, i.e. decide on, choose, initiate, change, develop, or stop, so that the change and variation depends on us" (Eikeland, 2008, p. 79). Variation and choice in praxis concern the circumstances which may defy the general ethical rules and axioms. For example, honest divulging of information as a general ethical virtue is "normally manifested in honest acts, but arguably practical wisdom (phronesis) in this area does not always mandate honest acts" (Swanton, 2001, p. 50) in all circumstances. Several ethical virtues, as universal codes of good conduct, may eventually come at a trade-off in a particular situation. Phronesis is the intellectual virtue to settle the case in those circumstances. Phronesis can thus be seen as a normative evaluation of actions on the spot. A directive statement — on the right course of action — is the output of phronesis as a practical intellectual virtue. "Prudence (i.e. phronesis) issues commands, since its end is a statement of what we ought to do or not to do" (N.E., p. 1143a).

Sophia as the highest level of theoretical intellectual virtues is achieved by combining nous and episteme. *Nous* regards intuitive intellect whose source is not clear to the knower. Integrating nous (intuition) in the KM context is thus challenging. The mysterious and often serendipitous source of intuition has made it unreachable to the scholarly examination in general (Osbeck, 1999) and KM and OI fields specifically. The scholarly body of literature considers intuition as an input from the subconscious mind (Agor, 1986; Crossan *et al.*, 1999; Miller and Ireland, 2005). The linkage between intuition and the subconscious opens a door to accommodate intuition in the confines of KM literature. That is, by nourishing knowledge types at the conscious level, subconscious intuition will be empowered. Exposure to episteme, techne, and phronesis at conscious level is likely to increase the chance of intuitive understanding at the subconscious level. Schwartz (2006, p. 13) stressing the interrelationship between techne and phronesis (and "to a certain extent epistémé") proposes that "support for the noûs within knowledge management may, in fact, be derived from our treatment of these two contributing types of knowledge." Thus, Sophia (wisdom), having nous and episteme as its components, is reliant on the integration of episteme, techne, and phronesis.

SMEs are commonly seen as the integrators of techne. However, the Aristotelian taxonomy opens room for SMEs to contribute in at least two other distinct knowledge types. SMEs may position themselves to delve into episteme and conduct research as a commercial R&D lab at a small/medium scale. The SME consultants are a manifestation of taking this path in epistemic knowledge integration. Also, SMEs may choose to integrate phronesis and deliberate the ethical bearings of a particular action (or policy). Normatively anticipating the consequences of other organizations' actions can be found as the knowledge specialization of policy analyst SMEs or corporate social responsibility (CSR) consultants.

2.2. *The know-X taxonomy*

The literature of KM frequently utilizes a taxonomy of knowledge including but not limited to: know-why, know-what, know-that, know-how, know-who, know-where, know-when, and so on. This taxonomy is noted as know-X hereafter. The historical foundation of this taxonomy is not clear, and scholars refer to fairly recent notations of this taxonomy. For example, Capurro (2004, p. 53) cites the work of Zahn *et al.* (2000) in linking this taxonomy with that of Aristotle: "know-how: 'techne', know-why: 'episteme', know-what: 'phronesis' [...] we may add: know-where, know-when, know-who". The linkage between the latter three knowledge forms and the all-inclusive taxonomy of Aristotle is not described in their work. Similarly, Flyvbjerg (2006) explains that "whereas episteme concerns theoretical know-why and techne denotes technical know-how, phronesis emphasizes practical knowledge and practical ethics" (p. 56). The position of phronesis in know-X taxonomy is not detailed in his work. Quite differently, Ryle (1945) discusses taxonomies of knowing-that *vis-à-vis* knowing-how.

The know-X categories are not as distinctive as Aristotle's taxonomy in that, epistemic know-how, explaining the general, universal, and eternal principles of a process, are not clearly distinguished from technical know-how, regarding the execution/making of that process, or phronesis know-how, deliberating on how should an action take place to be an ethically just process. How the universe works, how the universe can be put to work, and how the human actions should be performed are all amalgamated in the know-how category of the know-X taxonomy. In this sense, the know-X taxonomy does not exhibit external consistency. Essentially, different real-world manifestations are attached to one conceptual category. For example, how a material can be used to generate electricity from light has: (1) an epistemic side, in the principle of photovoltaic phenomenon, (2) a technical side, in making ingot/photovoltaic cells/photovoltaic panels, as well as (3) a phronesis side, in the socially, environmentally, and economically just manner in which the electricity should be generated from light to be ethical. Know-how can hence pertain to different types of knowledge.

The know-what category in this taxonomy also incorporates the three Aristotelian concepts at once and cannot be used in strict differentiation and may confuse KM analysis and understanding: knowing what epistemically (to understand), technically (to make), and phronetically (to be ethically just). Know-when and know-where similarly have three distinct Aristotelian aspects. Put in the context of the previous example, when/where (in principle) a photovoltaic effect yields more electricity, vs when/where a solar power plant yields more electricity, vs when/where a solar farm should be installed.

The know-why of phronesis is attributed to the ethical principles emerging from the ethical virtue. The answer of phronesis' knows-why is, without any exception, "good or bad for man" (N.E.,

p. 1140b). Know-why in face of techne concerns the purpose of an artisan or an artifact. The knowledge of "why a techne" defines its application and the purpose behind making is that techne is not an end in itself. Epistemic know-why, in the strict sense of not considering any application, regards the universal and eternal principles and/or causes. Yet, knowing "why a principle holds" or "why X causes Y" stays out of reach of episteme.

> *Scientific Knowledge is a mode of conception dealing with universals and things that are of necessity; and demonstrated truths and all scientific knowledge [since this involves reasoning] are derived from first principles. Consequently the first principles from which scientific truths are derived cannot themselves be reached by Science* (N.E., p.1140b).

For instance, the principle behind (i.e. why) the values of the physical constants, for instance, those of the gravitational constant [G], the speed of light [c], or Planck's constant [h], cannot be reached by episteme. Episteme may find what are those values, but "why those specific values?" is not epistemically reachable. Also, why matter and energy equate (at all or specifically) by $E = mc^2$ and not any other relationship is out of reach of episteme. In the photovoltaic example, "why photons and electrons interact at all" cannot be reached by science. Thus, know-why in this taxonomy has three distinct aspects: principles, purposes, and ethical virtue in which the epistemic know-why is confined to only provide a mechanism.

Such know-why, as a causal mechanism, itself is an epistemic know-how. The know-why of photovoltaic effect, as an instance, ultimately equates knowing the mechanism by which a photon excites an electron, i.e. an epistemic know-how. Further, one who explores to attain epistemic know-why without arriving at the ultimate principles discovers epistemic know-how. This type of mismatch hampers the know-X taxonomy's internal consistency when know-why equates know-how in epistemic knowledge.

Furthermore, the distinctions between the know-X categories are not described systematically. It is up to the reader to distinguish between, for instance, know-what and know-why in a cause–effect representation: consider A causes B. Is this understanding a know-what as in "knowing what causes B" or a know-why as in "knowing why B". This amalgamation further hampers the internal consistency of the know-X taxonomy. Moreover, the set is also not confined to a limited number of types: know-X taxonomy is still open-ended.

To conclude, know-X taxonomy in its current form lacks both internal and external consistency. To alleviate the inconsistencies, the know-X taxonomy needs a systematic definition to define and defend the current blur borders between its categories. Utilization of the know-X taxonomy in understanding, managing, or evaluating knowledge-related practices in industrial, academic, and governmental organizations is expected to be fruitless if not misleading.

3. Institutional Specialization

This section aims at sketching a manifestation of the Aristotelian knowledge taxonomy in the real-world to assert its external consistency.

Diverse institutions of the economy are argued to be a manifestation of the Aristotelian knowledge taxonomy. Eikeland (2008, p. 45) observes that: "Western institutions, and their divisions of labor, are undoubtedly partly a product of how Aristotle has been interpreted through the centuries".

It is however not necessary that the taxonomy shapes the institutions. It is equally possible that the taxonomy of Aristotle was derived from examining institutions relevant and present in the economy in his days. "When Aristotle illustrates what he means he uses examples from professional disciplines" (ibid, p. 39). In either case, the foundation of the Aristotelian knowledge taxonomy and its manifestation can provide an understanding of the knowledge and the institution of organization's types at once.

First, knowledge exploration and exploitation derive from *combining (integrating)* knowledge. In an individual's mind, new knowledge is created by combining it with existing knowledge. Also, intuitive knowledge is understood by linking and combining the out-of-the-blue knowledge with existing knowledge to ascribe it a meaning. The need for combination to render meaning sets the rational of conscious exposure to promote subconscious intuition as depicted earlier.

Similarly, a particular episteme, techne, or phronesis is meaningful in combination with a set of *a priori* established knowledge. For instance, knowing that "photons interact with electrons" in isolation, from the knowledge about the electron's orbits of an atom, energy content of a photon, and many more facts prevents that specific isolated knowledge fact from leading to scientific understanding. No knowledge piece can be utilized in isolation. The process of combination is necessary when knowledge is utilized in techne. Techne needs to be combined with a set of related knowledge pieces to become applicable. In the same example as above, in isolation from the knowledge of the semiconductor material, the chemistry of the needed impurity for a p–n junction, and many more knowledge pieces, one cannot technically produce any artifact to harness photoelectric energy, e.g. a photovoltaic cell. Thus, exploration and exploitation of knowledge involve "knowledge combination".

Second, from a resourced-based viewpoint (RBV), knowledge is regarded as the paramount source of sustained competitive advantage. "As the literature makes increasingly clear, a knowledge-based view is the essence of the resource-based perspective. The central theme emerging in the strategic management resource-based literature is that privately held knowledge is a basic source of advantage in competition" (Conner and Prahalad, 1996, p. 477). Reflected from the RBV assertions, it can be stated that: "(R)resource and capability-based advantages are likely to derive from superior access to and integration of specialized knowledge" (Grant, 1996a, p. 376). Thus, on the organizational level as well, knowledge is pooled to achieve an advantage. The combination of knowledge in an organization also extends the scope of bounded rationality since Simon's bounded rationality assures the insufficiency of one mind to possess and process all knowledge. Combining knowledge of multiple minds in an organization decreases the restrictions on a single mind's rationality.

[T]he "data" from which the economic calculus starts are never for the whole society "given" to a single mind which could work out the implications, and can never be so given (Hayek, 1945, p. 519).

It follows that "If the strategically most important resource of the firm is knowledge, and if knowledge resides in specialized form among individual organizational members, then the essence of organizational capability is the integration of individual's specialized knowledge" (Grant, 1996a, p. 375). The conclusion is that knowledge needs a combination at the individual as well as organizational levels. Hence, an organization can be regarded as a machine to integrate specialized individual knowledge. Knowledge in an organization is constituted of a coalesce of specialized knowledge of organizational members. In the same vein, an organization's capacity to "generate new combinations of existing knowledge" is described by Kogut and Zander (1992, p. 391) as "combinative capabilities". The resolution is that organizations in general, and SME's particularly, are knowledge integrating machines which first combine individual members' knowledge, and, second, integrate external knowledge in light of the initially combined knowledge. Organizations further specialize in integrating specific types of internal and/or external knowledge.

It follows that organizations, as specialized knowledge integrating machines, should resemble the knowledge taxonomy (as their integration material) in their institutional typology. Epistemic knowledge can be seen as the main knowledge type integrated by universities (as an institution rather than a particular university). A university's institutional core purpose is to find (for the sake of understanding) the general, universal, and eternal principles with which the universe works. Technical knowledge is leveraged mainly by an integration process in industrial organizations i.e. institution of business. The institution of business mostly concerns the making/production of products and/or services. Phronesis, to deliberate on what is good and bad for a man, is achieved by integrating that type of knowledge as the main purpose of governments and governance institutions. These include the non-governmental organizations (NGOs), societal/environmental activist groups, and similar institutions of governance.

4. Organizational Diversification

Although by institutional specialization the primary role of each major institution regards one category of the Aristotelian knowledge taxonomy, organizations are not, *per se*, confined to combine only one knowledge type. Secondary and tertiary knowledge types are also integrated to a certain degree, by each particular organization. Neither all universities are purely theoretical nor all industries purely practical. Organizations integrate episteme, techne, and phronesis in different proportions. Indeed a university, primarily dealing with integrating epistemic knowledge for the sake of understanding, may find it strategically advantageous to valorize its epistemic knowledge through technology development, i.e. integrating technical knowledge and epistemic knowledge. Within the field of OI, technical universities and academic spin-offs are the real-world examples of an organization diversifying in the integration of epistemic and technical knowledge types. Commercial R&D centers, as well as consultancy firms, are examples of organizations which diversify in integrating epistemic knowledge into the core technological knowledge integration. Both universities and firms may incorporate phronesis in their knowledge integration operations. Responsible research and innovation (RRI) and corporate social responsibility (CSR) are two manifestations that emphasize the inclusion of stakeholders and the role of considering one's accountability toward others when conducting innovations (Pavie *et al.*, 2014). Both universities and firms include these notions to support their diversification and integration of phronesis in their operations. Table 1 outlines examples of these primary, secondary, and tertiary roles played by the diverse organizational types.

For example, a commercial R&D facility can be seen as a techne-based organization which secondarily coalesces episteme. To demonstrate the accuracy of the taxonomy by manifestation, an example is provided. Consider an individual active in two organizations with different types, for instance, an academic working also in a commercial R&D. In the two roles, that individual will combine

Table 1. Knowledge Taxonomy and Organizational Roles

| Organization type | Knowledge taxonomy | | |
	Episteme	*Techne*	*Phronesis*
University	1st Role	2nd Role	3rd Role
	Science	Technical Uni.	RRI, Ethics
Industry	2nd Role	1st Role	3rd Role
	R&D, Consultancy	Technology	CSR
Government	Outsourced	Outsourced	1st Role
			Legislation

the knowledge types in differing proportions. The knowledge type approaches and the proportion of emphasis change as (s)he switches between the two organizations. Being in academia, the urge for understanding and being an arms length away from application is dominating since science deals with the general, universal, and eternal. The very same person within the R&D activities of an SME deals more extensively with the applicability and making where pure understanding without production potential loses its relevance.

Further, there is a contrast between phronesis and the other two knowledge types: episteme and techne. The contrast regards the possibility of delegation of specialized knowledge to an expert. While episteme and techne can be delegated to the scientist and technologist, phronesis does not escalate by following advice or orders.

> *We do not all study medicine in order to become healthy. Instead we follow orders and recommendations, and get treatment from the experts who have, since medicine is mainly a technical art of making [poíêsis]. But in ethics we cannot simply take the orders or advice of others who possess phrónêsis in the same way as we follow the advice from a doctor knowing medicine. Following the advice or orders from other individuals presumed competent is not sufficient in relation to the requirements for ethical virtue* (Eikeland, 2006, p. 35).

Thus, phronesis is the intellectual virtue necessary in every knowledge portfolio and is not delegated as a specialized knowledge to a specialized organization. Conversely, episteme and techne can be sourced out. In other words, although governments can outsource episteme and techne, for instance, to get evidence-based decision-making and/or infrastructure development, universities and firms cannot (and should not) outsource phronesis and need to deliberate on their actions as part of their organizational internal knowledge integration. This does not mean that there is no need for a specialized institution to safeguard and promote phronesis, in that not all actors are ethically concerned and the presumption of goodwill of all actors does not match the reality. This final note solely posits that phronesis, although being watched over and promoted by governments and governance structures, has to be attended by all organizational types.

For SMEs particularly, the integration of phronesis can particularly be seen as a source of competitive advantage. SMEs who proactively deliberate on their operations and perform based on ethical considerations and anticipation of each particular action and its implications (i.e. responsible innovation) are strategically ahead of the competitors who merely comply with the generally set bottom-line regulations. Products and services of SMEs, which are ethically deliberated, possess an advantage in delivering higher value to the client.

5. Knowledge Meta-integration in Open Innovation

As explicated earlier, knowledge combination is the essence of individual and organizational knowledge creation. Organizations, in this perspective, are seen as knowledge integrators of teams of individuals. OI can be similarly seen as a meta-integration of knowledge by teams of organizations. This section aims at sketching a link between the Aristotelian knowledge taxonomy and IKC in OI.

Wisdom (i.e. Sophia in Aristotle's taxonomy) is a meta-integration of nous (empowered by techne and phronesis) and episteme, hence a coalesce of all Aristotelian knowledge types. Wisdom can be considered the state in which principles, their consequences in practice, and their ethical bearings are known at once in a holistic approach encompassing all types in all fields of knowledge.

> *But we also think that some people are wise in general and not in one department [...] Hence it is clear that Wisdom must be the most perfect of the modes of knowledge. The wise man therefore must not only know the conclusions that follow from his first principles, but also have a true conception of those principles themselves* (N.E., p.1141a).

Achieving such an overarching repertoire of reinforcing episteme, techne, and phronesis in all fields is indeed challenging, demanding, and time consuming. However, a meta-organization can deliver such knowledge integration by incorporating diverse organizational types specialized in diverse knowledge types. Several fields of knowledge can be integrated within and between the three categories of knowledge. Such overarching integration can be studied in the case of IKC in OI. In IKC, diverse organizational types pool knowledge resources of diverse types and join forces in integrating them to arrive at meta-knowledge, i.e. a coalesce of episteme, techne, and phronesis.

To achieve that level of integration, special attention needs to be directed at idiosyncrasies of cross-boundary knowledge sharing: IKC requires awareness of organizations and organizational members about the processes of absorption and dissemination. In the cross-boundary absorption and dissemination, there is a special need to adjust and demonstrate a fit for the frames of understanding and aims of organizational main knowledge type to stay relevant. The double process of dissemination and absorption should be congruent in a sense that the sender takes into account what the receiver can or is willing to understand (i.e. customized articulation of knowledge). The receiver should also take into account what the sender could actually mean by the conveyed message and with what aim (i.e. correctly inferring knowledge). The receiver should bear in mind that the frames of understanding and aim of the sender are in accordance with the specialized knowledge type. Also, to effectively disseminate knowledge, to utilize it elsewhere, one should carefully take into account the prior knowledge escalated in the cognitive system of the recipient and consider the aims of such person in digesting the new input. For example, the Deficit model of knowledge transfer — i.e. shortcomings of decision-makers as the recipients to interpret and use research evidence (Ward *et al.*, 2009) — needs to be extended by adding the shortcomings of the knowledge provider in framing the knowledge in an understandable and relevant format (i.e. deficit of dissemination capacity). KM research must take into account the very fundamental congruence of the knowledge collaborating partners. Successful collaboration requires both articulation and digestion in light of the core knowledge taxonomy of the collaborating partners: (1) that knowledge is conveyed to recipients in a format that is relevant to them and enables them to comprehend it, and (2) that knowledge is interpreted by the recipients in accordance with the intellectual virtues of the source. Thus, SMEs in meta-integration of knowledge in OI need to first frame their input in congruence with their partner organization's aims and capacities: the message framing in knowledge dissemination is the key to a successful knowledge collaboration. Second, in absorbing external knowledge, SMEs need to tune in with the partner organization's frame of reference and intellectual virtue set: adaptive attentiveness in knowledge absorption is essential in a successful knowledge collaboration.

6. Conclusion

Considering the prominent role of knowledge in shaping the competitive advantage of organizations, this chapter illustrated a distinct correspondence of knowledge types and organizational types within the field of OI. The Aristotelian knowledge taxonomy of episteme, techne, and phronesis is shown to possess internal and external consistency in mapping the knowledge types which shape diverse institutions of the economy and their multifaceted networks contained by the Triple Helix model: episteme at the university, techne at the industry, and phronesis at the government. Specialized institutions combine and integrate specific Aristotelian knowledge types.

SMEs that collaborate through OI strategies are advised to sketch their strategy in light of the core competence arising from their institution's primarily specialized knowledge type.

In OI networks, each organization further diversifies by incorporating secondary and tertiary knowledge types in its integration portfolio. A university may develop technologies, and/or a firm may conduct research. SMEs can further gain a competitive edge by diversifying into a unique portfolio of knowledge integration encompassing a novel proportion of episteme, techne, and phronesis.

To achieve the highest level of knowledge integration in OI, organizations collaborate to integrate all three specialized knowledge types in diverse fields. SMEs on this path can team up with other organizations from different institutions which integrate different knowledge types and/or different proportion of knowledge types to attain the aims of OI. In doing so, special attention needs to be paid to knowledge absorption and dissemination processes to be in congruence with the partner organization's institution and knowledge portfolio.

References

Agor, W. H. (1986). The logic of intuition: How top executives make important decisions. *Organizational Dynamics*, **14**(3), pp. 5–18.

Argote, L. and Ingram, P. (2000). Knowledge transfer: A basis for competitive advantage in firms. *Organizational Behavior and Human Decision Processes*, **82**(1), pp. 150–169.

Argote, L., McEvily, B. and Reagans, R. (2003). Managing knowledge in organizations: An integrative framework and review of emerging themes. *Management Science*, **49**(4), pp. 571–582.

Aristotle (1976). *The Nicomachean Ethics* (abbreviated as N.E.), translated by J. A. K. Thomson, revised with notes and appendices by Hugh Tredennick, Introduction and Bibliography by Jonathan Barnes. Harmondsworth: Penguin.

Barney, J. (1991). Firm resources and sustained competitive advantage. *Journal of Management*, **17**(1), pp. 99–120.

Butler, T. (2006). An antifoundational perspective on knowledge management. In: D. G. Schwartz (Ed.), *Encyclopedia of Knowledge Management*, pp. 1–9. Hershey, PA: Idea Group Reference.

Capurro, R. (2004). Sceptical knowledge management. In *Knowledge Management: Libraries and Librarians Taking Up the Challenge* (Vol. 108). Walter de Gruyter. IFLA publications, pp. 47–58.

Chesbrough, H. (2003). The era of open innovation. *Sloan Management Review*, 44(3), pp. 35–41, Spring.

Conner, K. R. and Prahalad, C. K. (1996). A resource-based theory of the firm: Knowledge versus opportunism. *Organization Science*, 7(5), pp. 477–501.

Crossan, M. M., Lane, H. W. and White, R. E. (1999). An organizational learning framework: From intuition to institution. *Academy of Management Review*, 24(3), pp. 522–537.

Dodgson, M. (1993). Organizational learning: A review of some literatures. *Organization Studies*, 14(3), pp. 375–394.

Eikeland, O. (2006). Phrónêsis, Aristotle, and action research. *International Journal of Action Research*, 2(1), pp. 5–53.

Eikeland, O. (2008). *The Ways of Aristotle: Aristotelian Phronesis, Aristotelian Philosophy of Dialogue, and Action Research* (Vol. 5). Peter Lang.

Flyvbjerg, B. (2001). *Making Social Science Matter: Why Social Inquiry Fails and how it can Succeed Again*. Cambridge University Press.

Flyvbjerg, B. (2006). Making organization research matter: Power, values, and phronesis. *The Sage Handbook of Organization Studies*, 2nd ed. Thousand Oaks, CA, Sage, pp. 370–387.

Gadamer, H. G. (1975). *Truth and Method*. Trans. W. Glen-Dopel, London: Sheed and Ward.

Grant, R. M. (1996a). Prospering in dynamically-competitive environments: Organizational capability as knowledge integration. *Organization Science*, 7(4), pp. 375–387.

Grant, R. M. (1996b). Toward a knowledge-based theory of the firm. *Strategic Management Journal*, 17(S2), pp. 109–122.

Grant, R. M. (2002). The knowledge-based view of the firm. *The Strategic Management of Intellectual Capital and Organizational Knowledge*, pp. 133–148.

Guarino, N. (1997). Understanding, building and using taxonomies. *International Journal of Human-Computer Studies*, 46(2), pp. 293–310.

Hardy, C., Phillips, N. and Lawrence, T. B. (2003). Resources, knowledge and influence: The organizational effects of interorganizational collaboration. *Journal of Management Studies*, 40(2), pp. 321–347.

Hayek, F. A. (1945). The use of knowledge in society. *The American Economic Review*, 35(4), pp. 519–530.

Holsapple, C. W. and Joshi, K. D. (2002). Knowledge management: A threefold framework. *The Information Society*, 18(1), pp. 47–64.

Holsapple, C. W., Whinston, A. B. Benamati, J. H. and Kearns, G. S. (1996). *Instructor's Manual with Test Bank to Accompany Decision Support Systems: A Knowledge-based Approach*. West Publishing.

Huggins, R. A. and Izushi, H. (2007). *Competing for Knowledge: Creating, Connecting and Growing*. Routledge.

Keen, P. and Tan, M. (2007). Knowledge fusion: A framework for extending the rigor and relevance of knowledge management. *International Journal of Knowledge Management* (IJKM), 3(4), pp. 1–17.

Kogut, B. and Zander, U. (1992). Knowledge of the firm, combinative capabilities, and the replication of technology. *Organization Science*, 3(3), pp. 383–397.

Laursen, K. and Salter, A. (2006). Open for innovation: The role of openness in explaining innovation performance among UK manufacturing firms. *Strategic Management Journal*, 27(2), pp. 131–150.

Leydesdorff, L. and Etzkowitz, H. (1998). The triple helix as a model for innovation studies. *Science and Public Policy*, 25(3), pp. 195–203.

Miller, C. C. and Ireland, R. D. (2005). Intuition in strategic decision making: Friend or foe in the fast-paced 21st century? *The Academy of Management Executive*, 19(1), pp. 19–30.

Minsky, M. (1975). A framework for representing knowledge. *Computation & Intelligence*. American Association for Artificial Intelligence, Menlo Park, CA, pp. 163–189.

Nonaka, I. and Takeuchi, H. (1995). *The Knowledge-creating Company: How Japanese Companies Create the Dynamics of Innovation*. Oxford University Press.

Novins, P. and Armstrong, R. (1998). Choosing your spots for knowledge management. *Perspectives on Business Innovation*, 1, pp. 45–54.

Osbeck, L. M. (1999). Conceptual problems in the development of a psychological notion of "intuition". *Journal for the Theory of Social Behaviour*, 29(3), pp. 229–249.

Pavie, X., Scholten, V. and Carthy, D. (2014). *Responsible Innovation: From Concept to Practice*. World Scientific.

Peteraf M. A. (1993). The Cornerstones of competitive advantage: A resource-based view. *Strategic Management Journal*, 14(3), pp. 179–191.

Powell, W. W., Koput, K. W. and Smith-Doerr, L. (1996). Interorganizational collaboration and the locus of innovation: Networks of learning in biotechnology. *Administrative science quarterly*, pp. 116–145.

Ryle, G. (1945). Knowing how and Knowing that: The Presidential Address. In *Proceedings of the Aristotelian society* (Vol. 46), pp. 1–16. Aristotelian Society, Wiley.

Scholten, V. and Temel, S. (2014). Open Innovation, Chapter 27. In *Global Innovation Science Handbook*, McGraw-Hill Professional, New York.

Schwartz, D. G. (2006). Aristotelian view of knowledge management. *Encyclopedia of Knowledge Management*, pp. 10–16.

Swanton, C. (2001). A virtue ethical account of right action. *Ethics*, 112(1), pp. 32–52.

Tsoukas, H. and Vladimirou, E. (2001). What is organizational knowledge? *Journal of Management Studies*, 38(7), pp. 973–993.

Ward, V., House, A. and Hamer, S. (2009). Knowledge brokering: The missing link in the evidence to action chain? *Evidence & Policy: A Journal of Research, Debate and Practice*, 5(3), pp. 267–279.

Zahn, E., Foschiani, S. and Tilebein, M. (2000). Wissen und Strategiekompetenz als Basis für die Wettbewerbsfähigkeit von Unternehmen. In Die *Ressourcen-und Kompetenzperspektive des Strategischen Managements*, pp. 47–68. Deutscher Universitätsverlag.

Chapter 7

Comparing Open Innovation of Innovative Food SMEs with SMEs in the Seed and High-Tech Industries — An Analysis of 15 SMEs in the Netherlands

Onno Omta*, Frances Fortuin*, and Niels Dijkman[†]

*Department of Business Administration,
Wageningen University, The Netherlands
[†]Soil and More International Ltd, The Netherlands

Various studies have shown that open innovation (OI) has become a basic requirement for the long-term survival of high-tech companies. However, also in an artisanal sector like the food industry OI has become increasingly important. To discover the extent to which innovative food and seed improvement SMEs can learn from high-tech small and medium-sized enterprises (SMEs), in 2011 the authors conducted a comparative study of OI. The overall conclusion was that the degree to which food SMEs are able to collaborate with other SMEs, knowledge institutions and government agencies have become key for success in innovation, also in the food sector. Valuable learning points for food SMEs included, increasing the number of go/ no-go moments; using clear performance indicators during the whole OI process; providing remuneration for innovation performance; and capturing the lessons learned after the OI process. Considering the risk of opportunistic behavior, innovative food SMEs should take the protection of intellectual property (IP) more seriously in the future, as is already the case in the seed improvement sector.

1. Introduction

No business can afford not to adapt to such changing circumstances. Research shows that innovation has become a basic requirement for long-term survival in the market. Traditionally, this was thought to apply chiefly to high-tech industries, such as consumer electronics, mobile telephony, and the computer industry, where one product generation follows the other with dizzying speed. In these industries, we see that businesses dominant during one period often have trouble keeping up with the competition in the next. Nokia is a good example. And then there are businesses that seemed to have been wiped out, yet came back even stronger: Apple, for example, with the iPhone.

Innovative products and unexpected propositions are important for surviving the competition. Creativity is especially important at the start of the innovation process (also known as the "fuzzy front end"). The problem, especially for large businesses, is that the structural principles that make them effective in managing business processes (leading to operational excellence) provide innovators little or no room to maneuvre. Small and medium-sized companies (SMEs) are generally regarded as highly flexible and innovative and thought to be more innovative than large companies (e.g. Ziegler, 1994). Therefore, in this chapter, we focus on SMEs.

Innovation is becoming increasingly complex, and often also more expensive. These factors make it impossible, or nearly so, for individual businesses to develop and introduce new products and processes independently. Innovation has become an unavoidable interplay of various parties who combine their knowledge and turn problems into design requirements. This is how they create opportunities. In the past several years, the term open innovation (OI) introduced by Chesborough (2003) has thus become a key concept. This term characterizes the shift to a system in which chain partners, knowledge institutions, governmental bodies, and even competitors work together to develop new products and processes quickly and effectively.

Also in the food industry, OI has become increasingly important. The food industry operates in a market that is more turbulent than ever, characterized by global competition, fast changing consumer tastes, and high demands for sustainability in terms of consumer health, animal welfare, and the environment. According to Sarkar and Costa (2008), there is rapid growth in the number of OI projects. One explanation is that more than 90% of the sector consists of SMEs. However, because they have limited resources for in-house R&D, they must maintain a broad network of partners to provide them with scientific and technological input (Knudsen, 2007). Reinmöller *et al.* (2010, in Dutch) found that collaboration with high-tech companies can produce high returns for food companies. This appears to support Ebersberger and Herstad's (2011) position on the impact of external innovation expenditure:

A positive impact is found in those countries which are the farthest away from the technological frontier.

Countries, and probably also companies, thus make use of the knowledge of pioneers to strengthen their own innovative capacity.

Within the larger agrifood industry, the plant breeding industry is the most important one in the Netherlands (see also Appendix 1). Over the past three decades, the vegetable breeding industry has become more and more consolidated due to many mergers and acquisitions. As a result, the top 10 vegetable breeding companies now account for over 85% of the vegetable seed market in the world (Agricultural Economics Research Institute, The Hague 2014), and

Table 1.   Overview of Important Vegetable Breeding Companies in the Netherlands, Liu *et al.* (2015)

	Private family-owned companies	Part of multinational companies
Large[a]	• Rijk Zwaan • Enza Zaden • Bejo Zaden	• Monsanto Vegetable Seeds • Syngenta Seeds • Nunhems (Bayer Crop Science)
Small[b]	• Pop Vriend Seeds • Agrisemen	• Nickerson-Zwaan (Vilmorin and Cie) • Takii Europe (Takii Japan)

Notes: [a] Large: with more than 1000 employees; [b]Small: with 10–100 employees.

most of these top 10 companies originated in the Netherlands or have important R&D facilities in the Netherlands (see Table 1).

They spend on average 25% of their sales on Research and Development (R&D). In this respect, they are clearly among the global leaders. Due to climate differences and culturally determined consumer preferences, the R&D laboratories of innovative seed companies are located throughout the world. The development time in the seed sector is also reminiscent of high-tech sectors. It takes 6–12 years to bring a new variety to the market. The failure rate is also similar: only 1 in 20 cultured varieties ever makes it to the market.

To discover the extent to which innovative food and seed companies can learn of OI in high-tech companies, in 2011 the authors conducted a comparative study of OI in food and high-tech SMEs. The study participants were eight innovative companies in the plant breeding industry; three innovative food SMEs; and four high-tech SMEs in the Netherlands. Most of the interviewees were general managers of an SME and managers who were directly involved in collaborative projects. Every respondent was asked to complete a questionnaire for a number of OI projects the company had been involved in.

The chapter is structured as follows. In Section 2, we start with the definition of innovation and the management literature regarding the factors related to the success of innovation. Thereafter, we zoom in on OI, in particular, related to customer involvement. Section 3 presents the main findings of the study comparing food with seed and high-tech SMEs, while in Section 4 the main conclusions are drawn.

2. Theory

2.1. *Innovation, definition, and importance*

The economist Schumpeter (1934) defines innovation as a process of creative destruction, where the quest for profit pushes companies to innovate constantly, breaking old rules and establishing new ones. For Schumpeter, innovation implies not only the introduction of new products but also the successful commercialization of new combinations, based on the application of new materials and components, the introduction of new processes, the opening of new markets, or the introduction of new organizational forms. In this chapter, we use the definition of innovation of Johnson *et al.* (2008): Innovation is the conversion of new knowledge into a new product, process, or service and the putting of this new product, process, or service into use, either via the marketplace or by other processes of delivery.

Tidd *et al.* (2005) categorize innovation in product/services, process, position, and paradigm innovations. Product innovation includes changes in products or services; process innovations are changes in the way in which they are created and delivered; position innovations are changes in the context in which the products/services are introduced; and paradigm innovations include changes in the underlying business model. The degree of novelty can differ from incremental (minor changes, e.g. line extensions) to radical (major changes, new to the market/world products).

Currently, innovation is widely recognized as one of the major drivers of business success. The American Management Association (AMA) concluded, based on a survey of 1,396 top executives in large multinational companies, that more than 90% of them consider innovation to be (extremely) important for their company's long-term survival, with over 95% considering that this will still be the case in 10 years' time (Jamrog, 2006). A study among nine leading food processing companies in the Netherlands revealed that in the food and beverages industry also innovation is important for sustainable business success (Fortuin and Omta, 2009). In this study, the authors found that the importance attached to innovation by the company's executives, and the quality of the innovation process, as assessed by its food engineering staff, show a significant positive correlation with the company's financial position relative to its closest competitors.

Most companies organize the innovation process in projects, defined as determined plans and routes of development and implementation with the aim to deliver a new product to the market, or new (manufacturing) processes to business. Nowadays, most companies use cross-functional teams to carry out the innovation projects, since many studies proved cross-functional teams to have more chance of being successful (e.g. Griffin, 1997; Tidd *et al.*, 2005). Team members who bring in specific expertise from R&D, financing, marketing, manufacturing, and procurement usually co-operate from the early stage of an innovation project till the product actually gets introduced to the market.

2.2. *Open innovation*

According to Chesbrough (2003), innovative companies increasingly realize that the "closed" model of innovation, in which the internal R&D department exclusively provides for new products and processes to foster the company's growth, does not work anymore in the current highly dynamic business environment. As proven empirically by Caloghirou *et al.* (2004), interacting with external partners enables a firm to access a variety of new knowledge — a phenomenon they have termed "enhanced absorptive capacity" — which increases innovative performance. The ability to identify potential network partners and maintain existing relations with current partners is thus of crucial importance. Huston and Sakkab (2006) refer to this new paradigm of OI as "Connect and Develop", instead of "Research and Develop".

Figure 1 shows that in OI the boundaries of a firm become blurred. Ideas and technologies are not only developed internally,

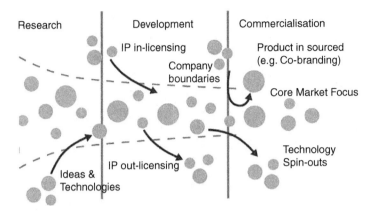

Figure 1. Open Innovation, Chesbrough (2003)

but also originate outside the company. The firm licenses in and, if necessary, also licenses its own knowledge out to companies that can use it to create more value. Spin-out companies put products on the market — at some distance — on the basis of technologies they do not consider core technologies. At the same time, they buy products from other firms in order to complement their product portfolio beyond their core competencies.

Actually, OI works like a lever. An individual business only has to do part of the work itself; other firms do the rest. This generates income and accelerates the innovation process. And yet OI project participants are left with plenty of managerial issues: above all, how an organization can profit the most from others' expertise while still retaining enough potential value itself. It is hence a balancing act. On one hand, businesses want to be open and make use of others' know-how. On the other hand, they need to protect themselves in order to prevent competitors from running off with their profit-making expertise. This is a constant source of tension. In order to maximize the leverage and minimize the risks, businesses must find partners with complementary knowledge and skills. Preferably, partners with a comparable organizational culture, for example, in terms of decision-making and planning.

Fortuin and Omta (2007, 2009) demonstrate that there are big cultural differences between firms that tend to have long gaps between various product generations and those in which this time is short. Examples of the former are firms in aircraft construction, pharmaceuticals, and the food sector (especially seed improvement). In consumer electronics, mobile telephony, and the computer industry, on the other hand, one product generation comes on the heels of another. With innovation, time perspective is essential.

An OI project is called an "innovative alliance" when a firm collaborates with just one partner. When there are several partners, it is a "network collaboration". The first of the two forms is the most common, most likely because of its advantages: innovative alliances are easier to manage and make it easier to reach agreement about property rights. However, there can be a downside: as there are fewer participants with diverse backgrounds, creativity may be diminished and some competencies may be lacking.

Traditional collaboration usually looks like a regular project, with a defined goal, start date, and endpoint. In contrast, the collaboration of chain partners in OI projects continues beyond the end of the project. When competitors work together, this is usually in the form of precompetitive collaboration projects, after which the original innovation partners resume their competitive roles. In practice, OI processes are difficult to manage effectively, especially if they involve a network of partners. It is an art — or a science — to ensure that collaboration does not get bogged down in endless consultation and compromise seeking.

At the same time, OI is not only about collaboration. When there is a high degree of specialization, a firm can limit the complexity of the innovation process by outsourcing part of the process to specialized organizations or knowledge institutions. This does, however, place high demands on the firm in terms of absorptive capacity: the firm's ability to acquire new knowledge or expertise and to put it to use to set up innovative activities in order to respond actively to a constantly changing environment. This is also demanding for personnel, who must be able to understand complex technological innovations and integrate them into business processes. In addition, there is a need for specialized alliances or network managers capable of managing an extensive internal and external network, as in OI projects.

A large-scale empirical study in Europe by Ebersberger and Herstad (2011) shows that — in general — OI has a positive impact on the innovative potential of a business. OI incorporates several dimensions: taking a broad view of developments, collaborating concretely in a process, and seeking external knowledge (external innovation expenditure[a]). This might include making use of contract R&D, sourcing expertise tied into machines or components, or establishing licenses or patents. If a firm is focused solely on this search for external know-how, the collaboration will actually have a negative impact. A business must know what it is and what it is capable of, and it must experience the "why" of knowledge development. Enough attention must be devoted to creating and maintaining its own absorptive capacity. Ebersberger and Herstad (2011) say:

First, make sure your own competencies are satisfactory. Only then will the lever begin to work, and can you profit from open innovation.

2.3. *Partners in OI*

Figure 2 clearly shows that building and maintaining an external network is now crucial for the survival of innovative food firms. Until 2000, only 15–20% of innovative food companies collaborated with suppliers, clients, and knowledge institutions. Since then, these collaborations have become more common: up to 45% with suppliers and 30–35% with clients and knowledge institutions. The rate of collaboration with competitors is the lowest and

---

[a] *External innovation expenditure* involves arm's length contracting related to the procurement of technology "embodied" in machinery and components, the purchase of problem-solving capabilities through contract R&D, or the acquisition of technology and capabilities in the form of patents or licenses. External innovation expenditure is, for example, less contingent on a firm's internal capabilities or absorptive capacity than search and screening activities or collaboration for innovation.

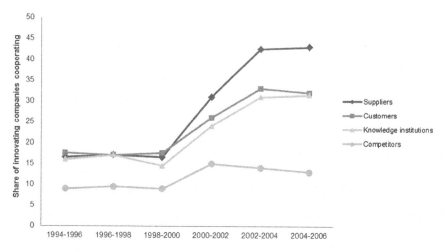

Figure 2. Percentage of Innovative Dutch Food Firms that Collaborate with Various Partners in OI Projects, Dutch Community Innovation Survey (CIS)

also shows the least increase, from 10% until the year 2000, and then up to only 15%. Interestingly enough, the Dutch Community Innovation Survey (CIS) database reveals that the pattern of collaboration between innovative food firms is very comparable to that in high-tech sectors. This is true for both the increase and the distribution among the various types of partners.

2.4. Open innovation in the food and seed industry

OI is becoming increasingly important, also in the food and seed sector. According to Sarkar and Costa (2008), there is rapid growth in the number of OI projects. One explanation is that more than 90% of the sector consists of SMEs, which are generally regarded as highly flexible and innovative. However, because they have limited resources for in-house R&D, they must maintain a broad network of partners to provide them with scientific and technological input (Knudsen, 2007).

Figure 3 shows that the food sector is just in the middle of the continuum from closed innovation to OI: on par with consumer electronics, just behind pharmaceuticals and biotechnology, but ahead of semiconductors. Furthermore, the sector is increasingly

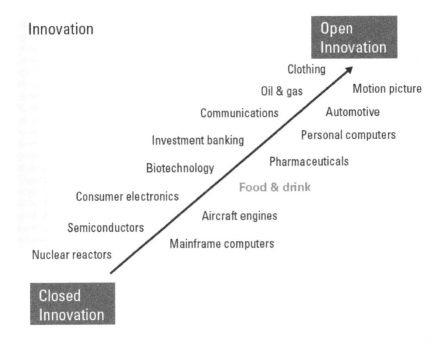

Figure 3.   Various Industries Arranged on a Continuum from Closed to OI, Paul Isherwood, Director Innovation and External Networks at GSK

active. The food industry is moving progressively in the direction of OI. Food firms are making a strategic choice to focus more intensively on their core competencies. They are looking beyond the walls of their own organizations, actively seeking knowledge, technology, and partners to implement a portion of the innovation process.

The boundaries between various industries, such as food, pharmaceuticals, and cosmetics, are also rapidly blurring. As shown in Figure 4, food firms involved in probiotics are patenting more frequently, both independently and in partnership with pharmaceutical companies.

The development of probiotics really started after the market launch of "Activia", the innovation breakthrough from Danone in 1987. Activia was the first yoghurt based on probiotics. This product aids digestion due to the addition of the Bifidus Regularis bacteria. We can see that the increase in number of patents since

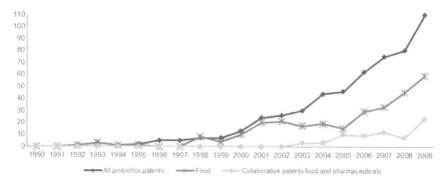

Figure 4.   Development of the Number of Probiotics Patents from 1990 to 2010
Source: Adapted from Bornkessel *et al.* (2015).

1999 has been nearly linear, with an obvious acceleration in the food sector in 2005. Furthermore, in 2009, we see an indisputable climb in the number of patents based on collaboration between food and pharmaceuticals firms. Recently, though, the European Food Safety Authority (EFSA) dismissed many health claims — to the disappointment of many food firms.

Until recently, there was no empirical evidence for the true relevance of OI in the food sector. Wubben *et al.* (2015) have shown convincingly that OI became increasingly important for innovative food firms during the period 1994–2006, especially since 2000 (see also Figure 2). This convincing evidence emerged from the responses to six serial Community Innovation Surveys (CIS) by more than 1300 innovative food firms.

Cees 't Hart, the former CEO at Friesland Campina, presented a beautiful example of collaboration based on specialized roles. Regarding activities of their cheese, butter, and powdered milk division, he said:

> For the marketing of these products, collaboration with the marketplace plays an important role. We can do it all ourselves, but sometimes specialised companies can do it much better. Besides, market forces are so strong that you can't always beat them.

3. Results

Altogether, 32 OI projects were reviewed, of which 27 were successful (i.e. they resulted in the expected outcome) and five were not
successful (the desired outcome was not achieved or the projects
were terminated prematurely). In the seed sector, 15 successful and
2 unsuccessful OI projects were reviewed. The three innovative food
SMEs were involved in three of these successful projects and the two
that failed. This result was compared to the one failed and nine successful OI projects that involved a high-tech SME (see Figure 5).

In this research study, it became clear that seed companies should be
seen as high-tech. The companies employed on average 487 people, 144
of whom (almost 30%) were directly involved in innovation, and 16 in
OI projects (11% of the innovation personnel). Although the number of
FTE in the high-tech SMEs was lower (163), a larger percentage of the
staff members — 108 (66%) — was involved in (open) innovation projects. In the innovative food companies, about 30 of the (on average)
100 personnel were involved in some way in open or in-house innovation projects. The percentage of sales generated by new products put on
the market in the previous three years was somewhat lower for the seed
companies than for the high-tech SMEs: 37% vs about 50%.

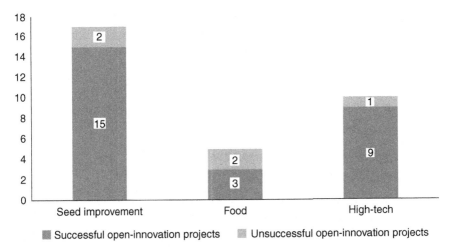

Figure 5. (Un-) successful Open Innovation Projects in the Sectors Seed
Improvement, Food and High Tech

The fact that these companies also reported about 50% turnover from new products demonstrates just how innovative the selected SMEs in the food sector were. Interestingly, the average lifecycle of product generations in all sectors was comparable, namely nine years. The participating companies in the seed industry applied for an average of 8–9 patents (breeder's rights) in the previous three years, compared to 5–6 applications among high-tech SMEs. In contrast, SMEs in the food sector applied for not even one patent.

Innovation leads to distinctive character, and this ensures better margins for innovative companies. Indeed, all of the companies reported that they were more profitable than their competitors (on average 4–5 on a 7-point scale). All of the respondents also believed that their companies generally introduced products onto the market sooner than the competition (from 4.6 for high-tech SMEs to 6.3 for innovative food companies on a 7-point scale).

For a correct interpretation of the results, it is important to remember that although the food and high-tech SMEs were carefully selected, they were relatively few in number. The results presented can therefore only give an indication. Moreover, the deviations in size of the food, seed, and high-tech companies may to some extent explain the differences found. Indeed, just the fact that the larger companies are more professionally organized could alone be responsible for some of the differences, particularly in the reward policy for innovation, performance indicators, and lessons learned. We note, however, that even taking this into account, the differences found are striking. Nevertheless, to validate the results, a larger number of high-tech and food companies would need to be reviewed.

3.1. The innovation process in the participating firms

When asked about the organization of the innovation process, all of the firms indicated that they focused considerable attention on communication between R&D and marketing. The two departments met on average weekly to monthly to discuss the innovation projects.

The authors of this study investigated the innovation process and the OI projects by means of semi-structured interviews in which open questions were combined with closed questions based on a 7-point scale. When asked about the organization of the innovation process, all of the firms indicated that they focused considerable attention on communication between R&D and marketing. The two departments met on average weekly to monthly to discuss the innovation projects.

More significant differences among the firms emerged when we asked about structured "go" or "no-go" moments. These were least frequent (once every 9 months to a year) in the innovative food firms, compared to biweekly to monthly in the high-tech SMEs. Table 2 provides an overview of the answers to the closed questions.

Table 2. Answers to the Closed Questions Posed During the Comparative OI survey Among Three Innovative Food SMEs, Eight Plant Breeding SMEs and Four High-Tech SMEs (Successful Collaborations)

	Innovative food	Plant breeding	High-tech SMEs
Reward system that promotes innovation	1.3	4.5	3.9
Use of performance indicators	2.7	4.1	5.4
Capturing of lessons learned	2.7	4.0	5.3
Degree of complementarity in the collaboration	6.3	4.9	5.1
Degree of trust in the partner(s)	5.3	5.6	5.6
Would you want to work together again with the same partner(s)?	6.7	6.1	6.1
Willingness to make additional investments	5.0	5.4	4.8
Development of new products in the OI project	6.3	6.2	5.1
Development of new processes in the OI project	5.7	4.1	3.0
Risk that confidential information will be leaked	3.0	2.7	4.1
Prior confidentiality agreements	3.0	6.3	5.0
Prior agreements on property rights and returns	3.0	5.9	6.8

Notes: 7-point Likert scale questions: from 1 = not at all to 7 = very much/to a great extent.

The differences in reward policies to promote innovation were striking: From "nearly non-existent" (1.3 on a 7-point scale) in the innovative food firms to "very common" in high-tech SMEs and in the seed sector (3.9 and 4.6).

There was also a clear difference in the use of key performance indicators and capturing of lessons learned at the end of an innovation process: From "seldom" in the innovative food firms to "often" in the seed improvement sector and even "very often" in the high-tech SMEs.

4. Conclusions

4.1. *Successful OI projects*

As could be expected, the respondents were generally satisfied with the collaboration in the successful innovation projects. How well partners complement each other in OI projects is comparable in the high-tech and food sectors: between 4.9 and 6.3 on a 7-point scale. The partners generally trust each other and would like to work together again. There is also a clear willingness to make extra investments should that be necessary.

Innovative food firms often develop new processes together with ingredient and machinery suppliers. This type of collaboration is clearly less common among seed companies and much less common among the high-tech SMEs.

Not only *process* but also *product* innovation is vitally important for the seed and food firms studied. Product development within the collaboration is even more important for innovative food SMEs and seed companies than for the high-tech SMEs.

The frequency of contact was about the same in all of the collaborations. On average, partners met face-to-face once a month, for example, during progress reviews, and communicated by telephone, Skype, or e-mail on a weekly or biweekly basis.

Personnel exchange is clearly more common among high-tech firms than in the food sector. This was the case in all OI projects in the high-tech sector. On average, personnel were exchanged 142 hours per month for 7.5 months among the high-tech SMEs compared to 97 hours per month for 5 months in the research institute. In the seed sector, 13 exchanges took place, but these were comparatively shorter, namely 15 hours for two months. Personnel exchange was almost non-existent in the food sector. This may be related to the relatively lower level of education among workers in the food sector.

Despite the importance of confidentiality (with respect to recipes for example), firms in the food and seed sectors clearly estimate less risk that confidential information will be leaked than do firms in the high-tech sector. This may explain why the innovative SMEs in the food sector pay much less attention to confidentiality agreements than the high-tech SMEs. The seed companies did not appear to be concerned about this because they made solid contractual agreements to start with. When it comes to property rights, revenues, and results, the SMEs in the food sector clearly make fewer prior agreements than the high-tech SMEs and the seed companies.

4.2. *Unsuccessful OI projects*

Considering the limited attention innovative SMEs in the food sector pay to confidentiality and the establishment of property rights, it is not surprising that these firms in particular encountered opportunism in working with partners in the unsuccessful OI projects (6.0 vs 1.5 in the seed sector; the high-tech sector did not indicate any problems). Interestingly, agreements were apparently made at this conjuncture — after the fact. By then it was clearly too late.

It thus appears to be important, especially for the innovative SMEs in the food sector, to make clear agreements in advance. One of the directors of an innovative food company had this to say:

For me, innovation is a passion. In the past when I began working on innovation projects with others I always assumed they were as passionately committed as I was. But I learned my lesson over the years and am now definitely less trusting. It felt at times like the partner was stabbing me in the back.

4.3. Learning experiences for innovative SMEs in the food sector

Innovative food SMEs, in particular, can learn something about professionalism in and around the organization of the R&D process from high-tech SMEs. Valuable points are the number of go and no-go moments, performance rewards for innovation, the use of performance indicators during the innovation project, and the capturing afterward of lessons learned. Precisely because it is so important to reach agreements in advance on property rights and confidentiality, it is remarkable that the innovative SMEs report omitting this step. Considering the risk of opportunistic behavior by one or more partners, innovative SMEs could clearly learn a lesson here. We expect that the protection of IP may, and should, be taken more seriously in the future, as is already the case in the seed improvement and high-tech sectors.

Slowly but surely, the world is developing into a network economy. Countries are becoming more interconnected and competition more international. In this global network economy, businesses can no longer focus only on short-term returns. Knowledge and flexibility have become survival skills; investment in innovation and knowledge development is therefore indispensable. In order to arrive at successful innovations, a public–private collaboration between businesses, knowledge institutions, and government is also gaining in importance. This makes the success of businesses increasingly dependent on the degree to which they can collaborate in both domestic and international networks. The food industry is no exception: intense competition, complex new technologies, and highly demanding consumers (motivated in part by NGOs) call for multidisciplinary, rapidly available solutions. Innovation is a prerequisite for future successes. An often-heard criticism of the food sector is that it is characterized by certain conservatism and, by extension, a lack of collaboration. This chapter demonstrates the benefits of collaboration. Although not always easy to realize — dependent as it is on human interactions — it is essential.

5. Concluding Remarks

This chapter provides a general introduction on the factors important for success in innovation and demonstrates the need for collaboration in OI for SMEs facing a world of ever more intensive competition, more complex new technologies, and highly demanding customers. The results of a comparative study of OI in food, seed, and high-tech SMEs give the reader some in-depth insights in how innovative SMEs across sectors differ in the extent to which they master OI processes. The results show that all 15 SMEs report to be more profitable than their competitors (on average 4–5 on a 7-point Likert scale). Respondents also believe that their companies generally introduce products onto the market faster than competitors. Interesting differences among the firms emerge when their innovation processes and OI projects are compared.

In the innovation process, the food firms' use of structured "go" or "no-go" moments, reward policies to promote innovation, and key performance indicators were strikingly lower than in the high-tech firms, with the seed industry taking an intermediate position. A closer look at the OI projects of the companies in the study reveals that innovative food firms often develop new processes together with ingredient and machinery suppliers. This type of collaboration is clearly less common among seed companies and much less common among the high-tech SMEs. Personnel exchange, on the other hand, is found to be clearly more common among high-tech firms than in the food sector.

It is concluded that innovative food SMEs are active in the field of OI, but in particular, can learn something about professionalism in and around the organization of the R&D process from high-tech SMEs. The overall conclusion is that the degree to which SMEs across industries are able to collaborate with other SMEs, knowledge institutions, and government agencies has become a key factor for success in innovation.

Acknowledgments

Our gratitude goes to the businesses that participated in the interviews, thereby offering us valuable insight into their thoughts and actions.

References

Agricultural Economics Research Institute (2014). Plant Reproduction Materials. A Dutch Motor for Export and Innovation, LEI, Netherlands.

Bornkessel, S., Bröring, S. and Omta, S. W. F. (2015). Crossing industrial boundaries at the pharma-nutrition interface in probiotics: A lifecycle perspective. *PharmaNutrition*, 3(4), pp. 29–37.

Caloghirou, Y., Kastelli, I. and Tsakanikas, A. (2004). Internal capabilities and external knowledge sources: Complements or substitutes for innovative performance? *Technovation*, **24**, pp. 29–39.

Chesbrough, H. W. (2003). *Open Innovation: The New Imperative for Creating and Profiting from Technology*, Harvard Business School Press, USA.

Ebersberger, B. and Herstad, S. J. (2011). Product innovation and the complementarities of external interfaces. *European Management Review*, 8(3), pp. 117–135.

Fortuin, F. T. J. M. and Omta, S. W. F. (2007). Aligning R&D to business. A longitudinal study of BU customer value in R&D. *International Journal of Innovation and Technology Management*, 4(4), pp. 393–414.

Fortuin, F. T. J. M. and Omta, S. W. F. (2009). Innovation drivers and barriers in food processing. *British Food Journal*, 111(8), pp. 839–851.

Griffin, A. (1997). PDMA research on new product development practices: Updating trends and benchmarking best practices. *Journal of Product Innovation Management*, **14**, pp. 429–458.

Huston, L. and Sakab, N. (2006). Connect and develop: Inside Procter & Gamble's new model for innovation. *Harvard Business Review* (March), pp. 60–72.

International Seed Federation (2014), Seed Imports and Exports, http://www.worldseed.org/isf/seed_statistics.html.

Jamrog, J. J. (2006). *The Quest for Innovation: A Global Study of Innovation Management 2006–2016*, Human Resource Institute, University of Tampa, USA.

Johnson, G., Scholes, K. and Whittington, R. (2008). *Exploring Corporate Strategy*, 8th ed. Pearson ed. Limited, UK.

Knudsen, M. P. (2007). The relative importance of interfirm relationships and knowledge transfer for new product development success. *Journal of Product Innovation Management*, 24(2), pp. 117–138.

Liu, Z., Jongsma, M. A., Huang, C., Dons, J. J. M. and Omta, S. W. F. (2015). The sectoral innovation system of the dutch vegetable breeding industry. *Wageningen Journal of Life Sciences (NJAS)*, **74–75**, pp. 27–39.

Plantum (2014). Leading Position, https://www.plantum.nl/321519619/Basis-for-the-Green-Economy.

Reinmöller, P., Verwaal, E. en Dijkman, N. C. (2010). Corporate development en de rol van bedrijfsnetwerken, *ABN AMRO*, p. 48.

Sarkar, S. and Costa, A. I. A. (2008). Dynamics of open innovation in the food industry. *Trends in Food Science & Technology*, 19, pp. 574–580.

Schumpeter, J. A. (1934). *Theory of Economic Development*, Harvard University Press, USA.

Tidd, J., Bessant, J. and Pavitt, K. (2005). *Managing Innovation: Integrating Technological, Market, and Organizational Change*, 3rd ed. John Wiley & Sons, USA.

Wubben, E. F. M., Batterink, M., Kolympiris, C., Kemp, R. and Omta, S. W. F. (2015). Profiting from external knowledge: The impact of different external knowledge acquisition strategies on innovation performance. *International Journal of Technology Management*, 69(2), pp. 139–165.

Ziegler, T. R. (1994). Explaining organizational diseconomies of scale in R&D: Agency problems and the allocation of engineering talent, ideas, and effort by firm size. *Management Science*, 40(6), pp. 708–729.

Appendix 1: How Innovative is the Dutch Plant Breeding Industry?

After one century of development of the plant breeding business, the Netherlands has become the major exporter in the world of starting materials of plants, representing an increasing export value of 2.5 billion euro (Plantum, 2014). Dutch companies enjoy positions as global market leaders in plant reproduction material (seeds, cuttings, plantlets for ornamentals, potatoes, flower bulbs, grasses, and vegetable seeds). This position is based on craftsmanship, entrepreneurship, and innovation, and as a result, the Dutch breeding industry is cited as one of the most innovative in the world (Agricultural Economics Research Institute, The Hague, 2014). Particularly in the vegetable breeding sector, companies with their basis and main premises in the Netherlands account for about one third of the worlds' vegetable seed exports and one eighth of the world vegetable seed imports (International Seed Federation, 2014). This makes the Netherlands both the largest vegetable seed exporting as well as importing country. Over the past three decades, the vegetable breeding industry has become more and more consolidated due to many mergers and acquisitions. As a result, the top ten vegetable breeding companies now account for over 85% of the vegetable seed market in the world (Agricultural Economics Research Institute, The Hague 2014) and most of these top ten companies originated in the Netherlands or have important R&D facilities in the Netherlands (see Table 1). Since over 100 years, most plant breeding companies are clustered in the Seed Valley, referring to the area between Enkhuizen and Warmenhuizen in the Netherlands. In this area, 21 innovative seed companies, specializing in breeding, production, and sales of high-quality seeds and basic plant material. This cluster also includes suppliers of services and machines specific to the seed sector. These companies work closely together on OI projects supported by government and knowledge institutions. This can, for instance, be illustrated by the four plant breeding companies that together own Keygene, a molecular genetics research institute in Wageningen, which has laboratory facilities in the US and China. Keygene has drastically accelerated the R&D process in seed improvement, thanks to techniques such as seed selection based on genetic mapping. In addition, Keygene offers a platform for OI for SMEs via the Keygene Innovators Club.

Chapter 8

ALITE: Open Innovation and Experimentation in a Small Learning Organization

Joaquín Alegre, Francisco Romera,
Ana García-Granero, and Anabel Fernández-Mesa

University of Valencia, Av. de Blasio Ibáñez, 13, 46010 València, Spain

Open innovation (OI) is being regarded as a new paradigm in understanding innovation processes. Being rooted in previous research in collaboration for innovation, it is currently widely used both in academic and practitioner analyzes. While OI is a common procedure in the context of large manufacturing firms, how do small firms cope with collaborations with large technology suppliers is an issue that deserves further attention. This study looks at how OI and knowledge management (KM) are undertaken in a successful, innovative, and small Spanish firm: ALITE. This 35-employees' firm is managed as a learning organization that favors experimentation as a basic procedure to be creative, solve problems, and create new internal knowledge. Using a qualitative methods approach, we scrutinize how internal knowledge obtained through experimentation in a small shop-floor is integrated with external knowledge flows coming from large suppliers to achieve successful innovation outcomes. Interestingly, ALITE emphasizes the internalization of core activities and the creation of internal knowledge through experimentation to the detriment of external knowledge transfers. Finally, we connect our findings to the OI and KM literature and we highlight a number of important implications for small creative companies.

1. Introduction

Nowadays, innovation and knowledge management (KM) are key issues for any organization. Innovating is a complex and risky process though. Organizations need to be able to identify, assimilate, and apply external knowledge (Lane *et al.*, 2006). No company possesses all the knowledge it needs to innovate. Useful external knowledge might come from universities and research institutes, consultants, suppliers, competitors, or customers (OECD, 2005; Chen *et al.*, 2011; Ferreras-Méndez *et al.*, 2016). As a result, external knowledge search strategies, absorptive capacity, and open innovation (OI) are critical for firms to generate new products and processes (Ferreras-Méndez *et al.*, 2015; García-Granero *et al.*, 2014).

Innovation also requires combining external knowledge with internal knowledge in order to come up with new solutions, new technologies, or new products. R&D activities and experimentation generate new internal knowledge which represents an important asset of the firm (Thomke, 2001; Alegre and Chiva, 2008; Alegre *et al.*, 2013). Managers should consider their firms as learning organizations if they are to make the most of external and internal knowledge.

In order to integrate external and internal knowledge activities within the innovation process, the academic community is extensively using the concept of OI. Chesbrough (2003) called the attention of the research community by understanding innovation not as a process constrained to the organization's boundaries but instead as a new model in which firms created and commercialized innovation by looking for opportunities beyond the firms' boundaries. Recently, Chesbrough and

Bogers (2014) defined OI as "a distributed innovation process based on purposively managed knowledge flows across organisational boundaries, using pecuniary and non-pecuniary mechanisms in line with each organisation's business model". Knowledge inflows leverage external knowledge through internal processes; knowledge outflows leverage internal knowledge through external commercialization processes.

Previous research provides empirical findings on the interplay between OI and knowledge flows, but they are rather limited to large firms and high-tech contexts. Further research is still required for SMEs (Van de Vrande *et al.*, 2009). Moreover, within the context of SMEs, we argue that the challenges encountered when managing knowledge and undertaking OI might be different in a 240 employees' medium enterprise than in a 35-employees' small enterprise. Size is a relevant issue even within the category of SMEs. Important factors such as resource endowment, bargaining power, and leadership for innovation projects might be clearly more favorable in the case of a medium enterprise while communication and flexibility can be extraordinarily boosted in the case of a small one.

The objective of this study is to analyze how OI and KM are undertaken in a successful, innovative, and small Spanish firm: ALITE. This firm is managed as a learning organization that favors experimentation as a basic procedure to be creative, solve problems, and create new knowledge. ALITE has successfully faced a number of important technological challenges in the last decade.

Our methods for this case study are in line with Yin's (2015) guidelines. First, we used archival data on ALITE. Then, we design a semi-structured interview with ALITE CEO: Mr. Miguel Angel Alite. In November 2016, the four authors of this study visited ALITE facilities at Villarrobledo and carried out the interview. The interview was registered. Additional information was provided subsequently by several phone calls.

With this case study, we scrutinize how internal experimentation and knowledge flows are used in order to achieve innovation outcomes in the particular case of a small firm of 35-employees. Finally, we highlight a number of important implications for OI, KM, and innovation strategy in a small creative company.

2. The Company

ALITE is a small family firm located in Villarrobledo (Albacete, Spain) and devoted to the design, development, and production of trailers, semi-trailers, and accessories for the automotive truck sector. In 2016, it had 35-employees and a turnover of approximately 4 million euros: clearly a small enterprise according to the European Commission (2003) standards. It has over 40 years of experience in this activity and currently, the third generation of the family is managing the firm. Mr. Miguel Angel Alite, CEO since 2008, is an aeronautical engineer who graduated from the Polytechnic University of Madrid. Being a former employee in Madrid at the Spanish National Aerospace Technical Institute (INTA), he decided to come back to Villarrobledo to get involved in the management of the firm.

Today ALITE's main line of business is trailers production. They are the largest Spanish producer of mobile floor trailers. In 2016, ALITE has manufactured 60 vehicles with watertight floor.

ALITE has recently developed with the financial participation of the Center for Industrial Technological Development (CDTI) a research and development (R&D) project called "Prototype watertight transport RSU". The outcome of the project has been a new type of vehicle to transport municipal solid waste (MSW). The novelty of this project is a mobile floor that is completely watertight. This project has been granted a patent.

With the help of this successful project, ALITE has been granted the INNOVATIVE SME SEAL from the Spanish Ministry of Economics and Competitiveness. Recently, the Spanish newspaper with the greatest circulation, EL País, published a special report on ALITE on October 14th, 2016 highlighting the firm's innovation achievements.

3. The Business Model

ALITE provides products and solutions that other companies do not provide. Reliability, flexibility, and innovativeness are the basic cornerstones of their business model. Regarding the production process, the shop floor can be organized in different ways; some areas can be devoted to project-based production when required. Some other parts of the shop floor are robotized, especially for design issues and welding operations. Robotization boosts the number of production possibilities at a reasonable cost. Products can be customized following the customers' specific requirements. ALITE aims to be a problem-solver for its customers. For example, this is the reason why they always design new solutions using standard components that are easy to find worldwide at a reasonable price. This empathy with the customer situation is clearly a relevant strength for ALITE in the trailer industry.

> *Anyone can buy our product and if it breaks you can buy standard tools and materials to fix the product yourself* — The CEO said.

Employees are a key resource in ALITE. The basic selection requirement is that employees have to be passionate about what they do. They should be motivated with the challenges encountered in the shop floor. Solving problems should make them happy. According to Mr. Alite, "this makes them terribly dynamic and proactive". There is a lot of variety in employees' profile: three engineers, experienced workers in welding and assembling operations, and even a medical doctor in the mechanics testing section on the shop floor. Experimentation constitutes part of the company's DNA. Because of the firm's size, there is a lot of control as well as feedback on the activities developed. Management is always involved in experimentation activities. ALITE's CEO is rather enthusiastic about experimentation. At ALITE, communication is very important: engineers, mould-makers, and assemblers work together, side-by-side, while manufacturing the products. By doing so, they learn together, thus favoring knowledge creation and knowledge sharing. Experiment failures and successes generate a substantial amount of learning that is reported, stocked, and shared throughout the organization. As new solutions and new designs are developed, new knowledge is created and is stored in security copies the firm generates on a daily basis. In line with this, Yan and Yan (2016) underscore that the entrepreneur's knowledge about products and technologies has a direct and positive impact on the innovation in small businesses.

My main assets are electronic files. One design is useful to improve the next one. We start from the very beginning and build new knowledge — The CEO said.

Design and simulation are important tasks at ALITE. By using design and simulation, software engineers can explore new technical options and solutions efficiently. Moreover, they can share their solutions and interact with customers.

The work plan is organized by autonomous groups of six workers under the responsibility of a manager who organizes the team tasks on a daily basis. The problems that arise in day-to-day operations are normally solved by their own workers.

The company has a passion for knowledge and technology. As the CEO states, they always want to be at the frontier of knowledge and technology. Adopting a rigorous and scientific approach, they usually make a study of the state-of-the-art on any particular new issue they face. All projects start from scratch and represent an opportunity for knowledge creation.

Miguel Angel Alite says that ideas arise because engineers work on the machine with the assembler and other operations workers. The culture of the company facilitates that all employees are initiated in diverse tasks.

ALITE normally does not formalize the amount of resources they invest in R&D. Because of its size, ALITE does not have a formalized R&D department. They do informal R&D and lots of experimentation. All in all, the R&D investments could fluctuate to around 35–40% of the turnover of the company per year. This exceptionally high R&D investment attests the extraordinary innovative capacity of ALITE.

4. The "Moving Floor" Project in ALITE

In the current context of transport of goods by road, the vehicles with the greatest capacity of load by volume and weight are those of the articulated type; that is those that incorporate a towing vehicle or tractor which is mechanically coupled with a semi-trailer which constitutes the receptacle for receiving and transporting the loads. The mobile floors installed on semi-trailers are an effective and efficient solution for loading and unloading any type of fragmented or packaged good. A mobile floor consists of a hydraulic drive system consisting basically of three hydraulic cylinders, a distributor that controls the movement of the cylinders, and a set of blades positioned longitudinally to the axis of the vehicle. The proper movement of the blades by means of their hydraulic drive will allow the "floor or mobile floor" to carry out the loading or unloading process of the goods as required.

Since the emergence of the first mobile floor system (American patent of the 1950s) until today, the design has not undergone any conceptual variation. Only the design of the various components has been optimized to increase its performance and lighten weight.

In this scenario, it can be easily deduced that this loading and unloading system may be suitable for the transport of municipal solid waste (MSW). However, there is a constraint that is a major obstacle to their total implementation in this sector: MSW is made up of solid materials but also has a liquid component, the proportion of which varies according to the type of waste, and this is known as leachate. In order to avoid the filtration of extremely fractionated or powdery materials, a watertight joint is usually installed between the slats of the movable floor. Moreover, underneath the sealing gasket of each sheet, a collection channel or tray is installed to prevent dripping between the seals. The collection channel is directed toward the tank located at the back of the vehicle.

This system offers a reasonable solution for the transport of wet or low-fluid components. However, experience has shown that the MSW leachate components are generally much higher than expected. Thus, it is completely impossible to control the level of leachate, and so the vehicles pour leachate during transport.

Other solutions were implemented such as installing a continuous complete tray underneath the sheets throughout the vehicle's loading surface and placing the hydraulic drive system in the upper front. This mobile floor system, called "leak proof" (watertight) is manufactured today by the two largest manufacturers of mobile

Table 1.   Comparison Between State-of-the-Art Vehicles and Watertight Floor Improvement Proposed by ALITE

	State-of-the-art	ALITE watertight floor
Maximum run mass (Kilogram) (MRM)	10300	9090
Load volume (cubic meter)	85.3	91.1
Maximum load per year (365 runs) Tonne for 1 of 34.000 Kilograms	8650.5	9092.15
Annual transported volume (365 runs) cubic	31134	33288
Increase % weight load	increase of 12%	
Increase % load in volume	increase of 7%	

Notes: The mobile floor lorry maximum measures are: load zone length (13.520 mm breadth), loading zone (2.480 mm), and height from ground (4.000 mm).

floor worldwide: the American Walking Floor and the Dutch Cargo-Floor.

In September 2011, ALITE delivered the first 11 semi-trailers with watertight mobile floor for the urban solid waste treatment plant that CESPA (an environmental division of FERROVIAL) operates for the Environmental Consortium of the Provincial Council of Albacete (Spain).

Table 1 shows a comparison between the vehicles corresponding to the "state-of-the-art" vehicle manufactured by ALITE at the end of 2011 and the new vehicles that ALITE proposed to develop through their R&D project "Prototype watertight transport RSU".

The optimization efforts offered are based on three main lines of action:

1. Reduction of the vehicle vacuum mass: To increase the maximum weight capacity of the vehicle.
2. Increase in the volume of internal load of the load drawer: Through increasing volume load capacity of the vehicle.
3. Guarantee the hermetic closure of the mobile floor assembly. To achieve the sealing of the vehicle loading zone, the moving floor equipment will be integrated into the structure of the vehicle

chassis and the enclosure itself. This changes the manufacturing process, from having independent suppliers for the chassis, mobile floor, and enclosure: now, it must be passed to a single assembly, and designed and manufactured together.

In 2015, ALITE started on this new idea based on the improvement of the most advanced commercial vehicles on the market, which were also manufactured by them at the end of 2011. ALITE started by improving the commercial components. However, they realized that this improvement of the components also implied manufacturing almost the entire vehicle.

5. Challenges ALITE Encounters in Managing OI

5.1. *First attempt to collaborate*

The first approach for developing this innovation project was to ask for collaboration the main suppliers of the walking floor system, WALKING FLOOR and CARGO FLOOR in order to develop the commercial components. None of these companies were interested in the new system proposed by ALITE because the potential market estimation was small. The improvement of the commercial components included an improved WATERTIGHT walking floor system. However, the niche market integrates only those companies interested in waste collection, where a lorry with an improved WATERTIGHT walking floor system is really necessary. In Spain, these companies sum up to approximately 85. This was the first challenge ALITE faced in developing their innovation, their main suppliers were not interested in co-developing the innovation. In fact, the CEO of CARGOFLOOR visited the company and said it was an attractive project though it was not in the interest of CARGOFLOOR to develop it.

> We (ALITE) did not have the necessary structure to manufacture the production equipment. But they (Cargofloor) were not interested in collaborating in the project and they would be asking for

their component to be paid at an after-sales price (paying 3 times more) — The CEO said.

Thus, the second approach for developing the innovation was to develop internally an improved watertight walking floor system. As explained above, the development of this improved system required the company to internalize part of the production of the vehicle. For this purpose, ALITE started looking out for other partners that could participate in the project. They first tried to approach a German multinational company for robotic expertise in welding, but this attempt failed:

We tried to collaborate with a German multinational company but there was no way. This German multinational company was not interested in collaborating with a small company — The CEO said.

After the failure with a German multinational company, they looked out for firms with a similar culture to theirs, and they succeeded. Concretely, they approached ABB and ESAP, Swedish suppliers that could offer them a similar solution to that of the previous company.

ABB helped and collaborated closely. Despite being a multinational, ABB has a very familiar and easy-going climate... ABB seemed to me a dynamic entrepreneurship-oriented company — The CEO said.

Mr. Alite found that collaboration with ABB was easy and fruitful. This is an important issue because the transfer of knowledge also depends on the development of an atmosphere of trust and collaboration (Omerzel, 2010).

Subsequently, they approached several public organizations: the metal-mechanic industry association of Castilla La Mancha (ITECAM), the University of Castilla La Mancha, and the local Centre for the

Development of Industrial Technology (CDTI). ITECAM association facilitates dialogue and cooperation between firms of the same industry. In addition, ITECAM facilitated ALITE's contact with the other two public organizations, the University of Castilla La Mancha and CDTI. Through the collaboration with the University, ALITE obtained specialized human resources, and through the collaboration with CDTI, the firm obtained public financial resources with advantageous return conditions (about the 80% of the financial resources obtained was returned with a low interest rate, 20% not repayable).

> *It was through ITECAM that we started collaborating with The University of Castilla la Mancha. We accessed to their employment pool. And during the last year, we have hired two industrial engineers." "We partnered with ITECAM and they told us about CDTI. They helped us present the already established proposal and in one week it was approved* — The CEO said.

Users were also involved in the project since the very beginning. Actually, it was since the projects' starting point that ALITE regularly interacted with the user FERROVIAL, a leading infrastructure and services operator in Spain.

5.2. *Internalization*

Once the scope of external collaborations was defined for this project, it was clear to the CEO that ALITE was going to have to internalize the core issues: the design of the final product and the design of the production equipment. External collaborations were to play an important role in the project, but the internalizing process and product design and execution represented a huge challenge for a 35-employees firm.

> *We are manufacturers of first equipment, and we do not really subcontract anything in the production process. We are the final product manufacturers.*

> *Now we manufacture the whole vehicle. The only thing we buy are the wheels from Michelin and some other components such as axles and suspensions systems, brake systems and light systems; we manufacture the rest. We design, manufacture, integrate and market, entirely in Villarobledo* — The CEO said.

Internalization is well aligned with the company's business model. By internalizing, they face design and production problems on their own and they create lots of new knowledge. Therefore, they make sure to have all the know-how that is required. This way of proceeding allows ALITE to be reliable, flexible, and effective in new technology developments. Internalization goes well with the passion for technical challenges at ALITE.

> *It is not a question of price, but also a question of doing it better* — The CEO said.

Moreover, the CEO highlights that by internalizing he (a) optimizes resources by keeping people employed in crisis time and (b) keeps people motivated.

5.3. *The role of human resources*

But, how does ALITE keep people motivated by internalizing most of its production process? The CEO stresses that by creating their own products and not depending so much on suppliers, workers are motivated into thinking that they have been involved in the entire process. It's a challenge with immediate feedback.

> *My engineers are in love with what they do. They design what they want and then they have the equipment to test the new designs. This provides immediate feedback* — The CEO said.

The CEO considers that human capital is the most important resource and that this resource needs to be optimized.

SMEs are experts at optimizing. We try to always seek to do as much as you can with the resources you have.

The starting point is very important. Small companies do not have important organisational inertias. We can start from scratch — The CEO said.

ALITE manages to do so by generating self-managed, polyvalent, and dynamic teams. This is why the hiring process is not based on academic qualifications but on competences, such as responsibility, dynamism, and coherence.

Interestingly, the firm is capable of favoring a climate where individuals are creative and innovative. The CEO and his team are always looking for experimentation and they always face problems by looking at them from scratch. ALITE can be regarded as a small learning organization (Senge, 1990; Dixon, 1997; Dess *et al.*, 2014). Experimentation and creativity, polyvalence and flexibility, autonomy, fluid communication, team work, and an emphasis on creating and storing new knowledge are important features in this small firm. Interestingly, control is an important issue at this firm. ALITE's size favors spontaneous and adaptive control both between peers in operations activities as well as between top management and the whole organization.

6. Open Innovation and Knowledge Creation in SMEs

For the development of this innovation project, ALITE faced certain challenges due to the fact that innovation processes are complex organizational processes (Love *et al.*, 2011; Hogan and Coote, 2014). Specifically, SMEs face particular challenges which are associated with the limited capacity these types of firms have to develop internally all the innovation processes, and the need for external partners in this process (Van de Vrande *et al.*, 2009). In this context, the use of external partners is necessary to develop innovations. This is known as OI (Dahlander and Gann, 2010; Vanhaverbeke *et al.*, 2014; West *et al.*, 2014; Bogers *et al.*, 2016). In the following section, we will explain the main points of this perspective.

It is important to highlight that the idea of OI (Chesbrough, 2003) emerges from the analysis of certain large firms that deviated from traditional practice based on vertically integrated models in the 20th century (West *et al.*, 2014). However, OI is not understood as the abandonment of vertically integrated models based on traditional R&D practices but instead, the increase of sourcing of external technologies, as well as controlled outflows of internal technologies seeking new markets through outbound licensing (Chesbrough *et al.*, 2016; West *et al.*, 2014).

This novel approach to innovation has caused an avalanche of interest in the academic community and beyond, but as recently highlighted, it should polish some aspects in order to overcome relevant pitfalls (West *et al.*, 2014; Vanhaverbeke *et al.*, 2014). One of the important limitations, originates because the first contributions of OI (Chesbrough, 2003) were based on the study of large firms, and later research has mostly focused on these types of firms, paying less attention to smaller firms (Van de Vrande *et al.*, 2009).

Many papers have called attention for further analysis of SMEs in the context of OI and knowledge creation. Huizingh (2011) points out that more research is needed in order to identify how SMEs benefit from their collaborations with external agents. More recently, Vanhaverbeke and colleagues (2014), in their review of OI literature, specifically highlighted the need to study SMEs specificities, their motivations, and the challenges they face in the context of OI. From a more general KM perspective, Durst and Edvardsson (2012) point out that prior research in KM has tended to emphasize large firms, and assuming that SMEs are abundant in most of the economies around the world they find this situation unsatisfactory.

Some previous research gives us some hints on the motivations and challenges that SMEs might be encountering in managing OI. Van de Vrande *et al.* (2009) highlight that smaller firms increased collaboration with external partners which is especially relevant because smaller firms often suffer from limited resources, and so collaborating with external agents helps them access to these resources. Following this line of research, Colombo *et al.*, (2014) examine the intra-industry diversification choices of European SMEs software companies that collaborate with open software community. They show that SMEs diversify less, but that those that manage to be active collaborators are more diversified and that this is the case when SMEs possess adequate internal technological resources. Thus, previous research seems to suggest that even though SMEs do their best to access and exploit external resources, some absorptive capacity is needed. It seems that we know more about why SMEs need to access external resources but we do not know so much about how they do so and to which degree.

7. Conclusions

Literature has focused on analyzing how large firms perform OI and has applied these recipes to SMEs. The case of ALITE shows that SMEs, and specifically those that are smaller, diverge from OI performed in large firms.

This case study on ALITE and its "moving floor project" provides new evidence on this research stream on different issues. First, this case study focuses on a small firm. We argue that small enterprises might be facing quite different situations from medium enterprises.

Second, ALITE case is a good example of a learning organization with some specific and original features: it is a small learning organization, it pays a lot of attention to KM, and it emphasizes control in all its creative activities. Although important, control is normally not emphasized in findings of the learning organization literature (Mallén *et al.*, 2016; Chiva, 2017).

Third, quite interestingly, ALITE explores OI possibilities, and finally makes the decision to internalize almost everything. This is due to the impossibility to participate in the project of CARGO FLOOR, the European market leader in moving floor trailers, as well as to ALITE's idiosyncrasy and business model. Internalization is an important characteristic of ALITE that is a part of its culture. By maintaining activities internally, control is enhanced. Moreover, the CEO underscores that the employees are more motivated, reinforcing the idea that a better product is offered. Also, employees are kept busy, thus optimizing the firm's most valuable resource.

However, for some specific issues, ALITE is able to partner with some external agents and benefits from their collaboration. Collaborators have quite different profiles: public organizations such as CDTI, ITECAM, or University of Castilla La Mancha, as well as international multinational companies such as ABB.

In sum, a small firm like ALITE does not seem to engage in high degree of OI (multiple partners, extensive joint R&D projects, or outbound practices) as in the case of large firms, but when they do, they do it selectively and with those partners that share a similar culture. Most of their innovation process is developed internally, and interestingly the case shows that smaller firms can benefit from internalization in terms of optimizing human resources and keeping them motivated when this is combined with a culture oriented toward innovation. In this sense, the CEO encourages their employees to feel autonomous and engage in new ideas and solutions in their daily job. Lastly, the CEO highlights that by being more closed and not so open, more workers are needed and this contributes to employment in the region. Different from other firms studied previously, most of them large, ALITE seems to attribute additional internalization benefits to those of asset specificity and cost, but rather factors related to control of the process and discretion to adapt the product, motivation of their human resources, and contribution to the territory.

At present, ALITE fits quite well the technological leader profile on Freeman's (1974) innovation strategies classification: lots of experimentation and offensive R&D investments, exploration, passion for learning, and creating new things. On the other hand, CARGO FLOOR fits well with the market leader profile. Currently, ALITE is involved in international markets. Their technical solutions might be useful in other countries. Because of their successful innovation projects and their internationalization, ALITE is quite likely to grow. This will represent a new important strategic challenge for an organization that is used to facing technical challenges on the shop floor.

References

Alegre, J. and Chiva, R. (2008). Assessing the impact of organizational learning capability on product innovation performance: An empirical test. *Technovation*, 28, pp. 315–326.

Alegre, J., Sengupta, K. and Lapiedra, R. (2013). Knowledge management and innovation performance in a high-tech SMEs industry. *International Small Business Journal*, 31, pp. 454–470.

Bogers, M., Zobel, A. K., Afuah, A., Almirall, E., Brunswicker, S., Dahlander, L. and Hagedoorn, J. (2016). The open innovation research landscape: Established perspectives and emerging themes across different levels of analysis. *Industry and Innovation*, pp. 1–33.

Chen, J., Chen, Y. and Vanhaverbeke, W. (2011). The influence of scope, depth, and orientation of external technology sources on the innovative performance of Chinese firms. *Technovation*, 31, pp. 362–373.

Chesbrough, H. and Bogers, M. (2014). Explicating Open Innovation: Clarifying an Emerging Paradigm for Understanding Innovation. In: H. Chesbrough, W. Vanhaverbeke and J. West (Eds.), *New Frontiers in Open Innovation*. Oxford: Oxford University Press, pp. 3–28.

Chesbrough, H. W. (2003). *Open Innovation: The New Imperative for Creating and Profiting from Technology*, 1st Ed. Harvard Business Press.

Chesbrough, H., Vanhaverbeke, W. and West, J. (2006). Open Innovation: Researching a New Paradigm Open Innovation: A New Paradigm for Understanding Industrial Innovation. In: H. Chesbrough, W. Vanhaverbeke and J. West (Eds.), *Open Innovation: Researching a New Paradigm*. Oxford: Oxford University Press, pp. 1–12.

Chiva, R. (2017). The learning organization and the level of consciousness. *The Learning Organization*, 24, pp. 119–126.

Colombo, M. G., Piva, E. and Rossi-Lamastra, C. (2014). Open innovation and within-industry diversification in small and medium enterprises: The case of open source software firms. *Research Policy*, 43, pp. 891–902.

Dahlander, L. and Gann, D. M. (2010). How open is innovation? *Research Policy*, 39, pp. 699–709.

Dess, G. G., Lumpkin, G. T. and Eisner, A. B. (2014). *Strategic Management: Text and Cases*. McGraw-Hill. New York.

Dixon, N. M. (1997). The hallways of learning. *Organizational Dynamics*, 25, pp. 23–34.

Durst, S. and Edvardsson, I. R. (2012). Knowledge management in SMEs: A literature review. *Journal of Knowledge Management*, 16, pp. 879–903.

Freeman, C. (1974). *The Economics of Industrial Innovation*. 1st Ed. Harmondsworth: Penguin Books.

Ferreras-Méndez, J. L., Fernández-Mesa, A. and Alegre, J. (2016). The relationship between knowledge search strategies and absorptive capacity: A deeper look. *Technovation*, 54, pp. 48–61.

Ferreras-Méndez, J. L., Newell, S., Fernández-Mesa, A. and Alegre, J. (2015). Depth and breadth of external knowledge search and performance: The mediating role of absorptive capacity. *Industrial Marketing Management*, 47, pp. 86–97.

García-Granero, A., Vega-Jurado, J. and Alegre, J. (2014). Shaping the firm's external search strategy. *Innovation, Management, Policy and Practice*, 16, pp. 417–429.

Hogan, S. J. and Coote, L. V. (2014). Organizational culture, innovation, and performance: A test of Schein's model. *Journal of Business Research*, 67, pp. 1609–1621.

Huizingh, E. K. (2011). Open innovation: State of the art and future perspectives. *Technovation*, 31, pp. 2–9.

Lane, P. J., Koka, B. R. and Pathak, S. (2006). The reification of absorptive capacity: A critical review and rejuvenation of the construct. *Academy of Management Review*, 31, pp. 833–863.

Love, J. H., Roper, S. and Bryson, J. R. (2011). Openness, knowledge, innovation and growth in UK business services. *Research Policy*, 40, pp. 1438–1452.

Mallén, F., Chiva, R., Alegre, J. and Guinot, J. (2016). Organicity and performance in excellent HRM organizations: The importance of organizational learning capability. *Review of Managerial Science*, 10, pp. 463–485.

OECD (2005). The Measurement of Scientific and Technological Activities. Proposed Guidelines for Collecting and Interpreting Technological Data. Oslo Manual. Paris: OECD.

Omerzel, D. G. (2010). The impact of knowledge management on SME growth and profitability: A structural equation modelling study. *African Journal of Business Management*, 4, pp. 3417–3432.

Senge, P. (1990). *La Quinta Disciplina. Como impulsar el aprendizaje en la organización inteligente*, 1st Ed. Editorial Garnica Barcelona.

Thomke, S. (2001). Enlightened experimentation. The new imperative for innovation. *Harvard Business Review*, 79, pp. 66–75.

Van de Vrande, V., De Jong, J. P., Vanhaverbeke, W. and De Rochemont, M. (2009). Open innovation in SMEs: Trends, motives and management challenges. *Technovation*, 29, pp. 423–437.

Vanhaverbeke, W., Chesbrough, H. and West, J. (2014). Surfing the New Wave of Open Innovation Research. In: H. Chesbrough, W. Vanhaverbeke and J. West

(Eds.), *New Frontiers in Open Innovation*. Oxford: Oxford University Press, pp. 281–295.

West, J., Salter, A., Vanhaverbeke, W. and Chesbrough, H. (2014). Open innovation: The next decade. *Research Policy*, **43**, pp. 805–811.

Yan, J. and Yan, L. (2016). Individual entrepreneurship, collective entrepreneurship and innovation in small business: An empirical study. *International Entrepreneurship and Management Journal*, **12**, pp. 1053–1077.

Yin, R. K. (2015). *Qualitative Research from Start to Finish*, 2nd ed. Guilford Publications.

Chapter 9

Mitigation of Knowledge Risks in Open Innovation

Haley Wing Chi Tsang and Rongbin W. B. Lee

Knowledge Management and Innovation Research Centre (KMIRC),
Department of Industrial and Systems Engineering,
The Hong Kong Polytechnic University, Hong Kong

In recent times, open innovation (OI), which involves collaboration with business partners and utilization of open resources in outside environment, is gaining popularity and importance in small and medium-sized enterprises (SMEs). While OI offers many advantages, SMEs need to be aware that they may expose their hard-earned knowledge, expertise, or other valuable knowledge assets to others when participating in sharing and co-developing knowledge. They must first understand the status and characteristics of their knowledge assets and then assess their readiness to enter OI. The chapter therefore introduces the Culture Space (C-Space model) for SMEs to use to organize and classify their total knowledge with the aim to identify what can be shared and what must be protected during OI. The chapter moves on to explain that when knowledge is not managed well, problems, threats, or dangers, referred to as knowledge risk, may arise and offset the advantage that can be gained from OI. The chapter describes four common types of knowledge risk and shows how to assess them individually. It also suggests how to mitigate these risks. Finally, a case study done in China is presented to illustrate the knowledge risk assessment and mitigation.

1. Introduction

Traditionally, enterprises keep their innovation secrets to themselves and everything is done by their own staff. However, such closed innovation is almost impossible nowadays as no enterprise can have all the know-how necessary to develop new products and services on its own. Even if this could be done, the development cost would be high and the cycle would be much longer. Further, enterprises should work closely with all their stakeholders in the value supply chain from suppliers to customers in the product initialization stage. This newer, more effective, and potentially more rewarding development model, being innovative itself, is known as open innovation, as opposed to the closed innovation traditionally practiced.

At first, OI appears to be monopolized by large corporations or global enterprises as managing an innovation project involving more than one party calls for expertise, strong R&D collaborative skills, and a team of specialists. This, however, is an illusion only; in fact, there is a wide spectrum of OI opportunities and projects of smaller scale that can be handled comfortably and beneficially by many small and medium-sized enterprises (SMEs). As OI by its very nature involves the exchange of knowledge and know-how among many parties, enterprises should consolidate and classify their knowledge assets to identify their strengths and weaknesses and to decide what types of knowledge should be acquired and could be shared in the project. This can be done through a systematic classification of knowledge assets and assessment of their knowledge risks first. In this way, an enterprise can holistically review the positive side and downside of knowledge exchange to make better decisions on whether or not to proceed with OI. In addition, the enterprise should also examine the risk mitigation strategy for managing knowledge risks in an OI environment.

This chapter first describes the types of knowledge assets possessed by an enterprise and then illustrates what knowledge risks an

SME would face and the methods used to assess the risks. A case study is provided. Based on the foregoing, how knowledge risks can be mitigated in OI in the context of SMEs is discussed.

2. Open Innovation and SMEs

Open innovation is a term coined by Professor Henry Chesbrough which dates back to the 1960s. In the past, most innovation processes, involving idea generation, design, sourcing, manufacture, and product promotion, were all carried out inside an enterprise (Chesbrough, 2004) and all the research-related activities took place in the internal research and development (R&D) department (Van de Vrande *et al.*, 2009). This is the familiar set-up for large corporations having the required financial capital to invest in future growth. The R&D department was usually charged with the mission of preventing competitors from entering the same market segment (Van de Vrande *et al.*, 2009). In OI, an enterprise selects some parts of the innovation process for co-development with external parties or to be based on public domain knowledge/technology rather than developing all aspects internally.

2.1. *From large enterprises to SMEs*

In the early days, the OI arena was crowded with larger companies (Gassmann *et al.*, 2010). IBM, Apple, and P&G have undertaken OI projects with good success for quite some time, an outcome in line with the finding by Sisodiya *et al.* (2013) who show there is a positive correlation between company performance and the degree of adoption of OI. For the majority of SMEs, OI was still relevant, though it less viable for those enterprises having smaller business sizes and limited human and financial resources to use the OI model for creating new products or services. Their small size and being less well-known than large corporations make their scope of business contact limited, preventing them from accessing or attracting a larger pool of potential partners and talented people with new ideas in the market. However, because of the substantial increase in workers' mobility, entrepreneurial funds, and public domain information and knowledge in the global economy (Van de Vrande *et al.*, 2009), the OI model has become more viable to SMEs. In addition, the smaller size and the simpler and less bureaucratic organizational structure are well suited for forming partnerships with outsiders (Edwards *et al.*, 2005). Some scholars even forecast that SMEs may become major players in the OI market (Zeng *et al.*, 2010) due to their flexibility and agility. Some examples are worth mentioning. Devan Chemicals, a Belgium SME manufacturing chemicals for the textile industry, partnered with top textile companies to develop chemicals to be sold at a high price, thus making good profits (Vanhaverbeke *et al.*, 2008). Two SMEs in Denmark, Quilts, and Jaga, are other examples. Using OI, Quilts makes products to provide a healthy sleeping experience for customers and Jaga has developed an eco-friendly heater (Vanhaverbeke *et al.*, 2012).

2.2. *Modes of open innovation*

According to Professor Chesbrough (2004), firms should make use of ideas internally generated or available externally in addition to paths on either side of the firm's boundary to reach the market in an attempt to raise their technological competence level. Basically, there are two directions in OI, inward and outward, put forward by Kim and Park (2010) who summarized the concepts of OI. In the inward approach, new ideas are sourced from outside, partnerships are formed with external parties, and capital is invested in promising high-technology start-up companies. In the outward approach, patents are sold to outside parties and internal units are spun off. Besides these two directions, more and more types of OI directions are now available as enabled by the widespread use of powerful cloud platforms.

The two prominent types are crowdsourcing and crowdfunding. In the former, a well-defined task or project which may even include the generation of innovative ideas is outsourced by issuing open calls to a large group of unidentified people in the public, often known as the "crowd". This new mode of accomplishing new products, especially innovative ones, has received much attention recently from the public (Frey *et al.*, 2011) and business enterprises alike to create benefits, including economic value (Buecheler *et al.*, 2010). In the latter, capital is usually raised over the Internet from a large number of people sharing a common interest and scattered in many locations to provide the needed capital to support the realization of a new project or idea. Crowdfunding has also become a popular way for consumers to get involved in and influence the production of a prototype of a new product or the manufacturing of a limited number of units (Rayna and Striukova, 2015). Recently, crowdfunding was used by entrepreneurs to raise funds for start-up businesses without securing finance from venture funds or borrowing money from a bank (Mollick, 2014).

As a result of the options and flexibility available for adopting OI, an SME now has a new way to create new products or services (Sisodiya *et al.*, 2013), and more resources such as outside expertise and specialized equipment are available for development. Further, SMEs can also learn closely the needs of customers and co-create inventions together.

3. Classification of Knowledge Assets

OI involves the exchange of know-how and skills among various parties. Enterprises have expressed valid concerns in launching OI in regard to the extent of disclosure needed for their hard-earned knowledge. Such a concern may be more evident in SMEs which rely on only a small pool of specialization and top confidential know-how to differentiate themselves in the market. To reduce these, it is critical for the enterprise to conduct a classification of its knowledge asset portfolio before the launch of such projects. This classification can also assist an enterprise to know to what extent knowledge and skills should be shared with the external partners or released to the public in the execution of the OI project. An initial assessment of the readiness of an enterprise for an OI business model can then be undertaken.

In the framework developed by Boisot (1987), the Culture Space (C-Space) model, as shown in Figure 1, knowledge is classified by considering two factors, namely, codification and diffusion. The codification factor refers to the degree to which knowledge is converted to text, images, sound, or films and stored in a suitable medium for re-use,

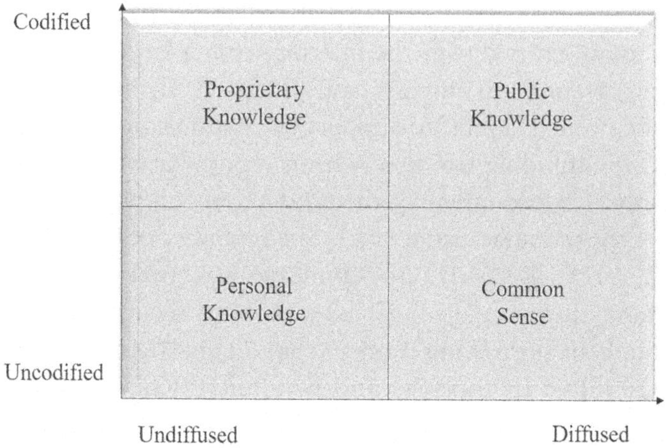

Figure 1.   Types of Knowledge Based on Boisot (1987)

extension, or enhancement. The diffusion factor refers to the degree to which knowledge is being tightly confined within a boundary and possessed by its originator. Based on "undiffused" to "diffused" on the horizontal axis and "uncodified" to "codified" on the vertical axis, four distinct quadrants can be classified for ease of analysis as shown in Figure 1: (i) personal knowledge which is "uncodified" and "undiffused"; (ii) proprietary knowledge which is "codified" and "undiffused"; (iii) public knowledge which is "codified" and "diffused"; and (iv) "common sense" which is "uncodified" and "diffused".

Public knowledge (in the form of books, videos, and press releases etc.) should be promoted widely for easy access by consumers and users. Proprietary knowledge (such as documents on how to produce the products and the mechanisms involved) is usually restricted for internal use and is classified according to the purpose for which it is intended. For instance, an enterprise may need to open up some of their knowledge for the purpose of tendering or outsourcing, etc. Different levels of access rights may be granted according to the sensitivity of the types of knowledge and the partners' roles. Personal knowledge, which is often tacit in nature and owned by a small pool of staff, or expertise needs to be protected. Those which contain the critical know-how should become the propriety knowledge of the enterprise. On the other hand, the personal knowledge and experience that could be used by the front-line staff to increase operational efficiency, service quality, and productivity should be shared with as many staff as possible to become "common sense". A lot of companies worry about knowledge leakage and loss to their competitors. As such, they must have a holistic view of their knowledge position and know which aspect of knowledge should be strengthened within the enterprise and which aspect should be made more open.

4. Knowledge Risks in an OI Environment

In any organization, the huge amount of knowledge handled, the intangible nature, and the variety and complexity often make effective knowledge management (KM) an issue at both the strategic and operational levels. In SMEs, such an undesirable situation gets worse compared to larger corporations because SMEs usually do not have the required know-how, human, financial, or system resources to undertake KM (Schiuma *et al.*, 2012). If the SME is in the knowledge-intensive or technology-driven industry, the lack of resources will make the KM issue more acute because of the more important role played by knowledge in their business. One direct result of improper KM is the creation of risk which impacts on an enterprise's short-term or long-term well-being.

4.1. *Four types of knowledge risk*

Classifying knowledge assets in an SME is the first step in adopting OI in business. Understanding the risks associated with knowledge is the next step. In general, risk refers to the likelihood of danger, threat, loss, or something undesirable happening in the future. Billington (1997) also includes in risk definition uncertainties about the difference between what actually occurs and what is expected, and opportunities for enhancement and growth. It follows that knowledge risk refers to the likelihood of impact on an organization and uncertainty about future events taking place when knowledge is managed improperly. There is more than one way to classify risk in business. The Committee of Sponsoring Organizations of the Treadway Commission divides risk into strategic risk, operation risk, reporting risk, and compliance risk (Curtis and Carey, 2012); while the Casualty Actuarial Society (2013) identifies four types of risk: hazard risks, financial risks, operational risks, and strategic risks. These two common enterprise risk management (ERM) frameworks are more suitable for larger enterprises and are more focused on conventional risks. Both suffer from the fact that knowledge risk is not specifically or is hardly dealt with.

In the context of OI in SME where the role of knowledge is more important than ever, a specific, pertinent classification of knowledge risk is put forward. Knowledge risk can be divided into four types of risk as shown in Figure 2: knowledge loss risk, knowledge leakage risk, knowledge obsolescence risk, and knowledge shortage risk. The former two are related to the outward flow of knowledge and the latter is related to the insufficient inflow of knowledge from outside.

Effective management of these risks is important, especially in OI, which calls for knowledge exchange among many external parties. When an SME becomes engaged in OI, it is more likely impacted by these risks than larger counterparts in the same market, as explained below.

(A) **Knowledge loss risk:** The first type of knowledge risk is the knowledge loss risk, which refers to the decrease in an enterprise's knowledge repositories in systems, processes, and employees, resulting in loss of value. For many SMEs, knowledge loss risk is the most

Figure 2.   Four Types of Knowledge Risk

common knowledge risk faced, and this is therefore discussed in greater detail than the other three.

Knowledge residing in employees is very commonly not codified in SMEs, and one of the reasons is that it is difficult to do so (Edvinsson and Sullivan, 1996). This situation can be a threat to SMEs when employees, particularly those in key positions who have good knowledge of the company business, resign or retire (Schiuma *et al.*, 2012). Such situations cause more problems to SMEs when compared to the large companies (Durst and Edvardsson, 2012) because SMEs have smaller business size and less favorable working conditions, making staff replacement a somewhat slow process. In general, employee turnover and lack of control procedures to capture and retain knowledge in the operation and management of an SME can cause many problems. Massingham (2008) identified four areas affected by employees leaving: output, productivity, organization memory, and learning.

In general, the damage caused by knowledge loss is inversely proportional to the size of an enterprise. Therefore, SMEs may suffer more, because they usually have a relatively much smaller knowledge repository on which they depend, compared to multinational corporations (MNCs). Further, SMEs usually compete in the market more on their special knowledge or skills (though limited in scope but used to the fullest extent) and other intangible resources rather than on land and equipment and financial resources, which normally are scarce (Desouza and Awazu, 2006). Any loss of knowledge may result in a great survival threat to the business of SMEs. Larger enterprises, however, are more resilient to knowledge loss because of their having more major business lines.

In a survey of 107 large and small companies done by Enkel *et al.* (2009), it was found that knowledge loss was identified as one of the most important risks in OI.

(B) **Knowledge leakage risk:** Knowledge leakage risk refers to risk caused by knowledge leaked to the outside, unauthorized parties, or the public because of errors in the system procedures or staff carelessness. Though the enterprise still retains and owns the leaked knowledge, such leaked knowledge decreases in its value to the enterprise because competitors may take advantage of the leaked information to increase their know-how or improve their production, marketing, or R&D strengths.

(C) **Knowledge obsolescence risk:** Knowledge obsolescence risk refers to problems caused by a certain part of the existing knowledge becoming no longer useful to the enterprise, owing to advances in technology, change in the business environment, or changes in business operations, corporate objectives, or strategies.

(D) **Knowledge shortage risk:** Knowledge shortage risk refers to potential problems or impacts caused by a shortage of knowledge to meet technological or business needs. Such shortage can arise from rapid expansion, inadequate training of new staff, and long learning curves.

5. Knowledge Risk Assessment

A checklist is designed to assess the risk level of each of the above four categories of knowledge risk (loss, leakage, obsolescence, and shortage) which are then averaged to come up with an overall enterprise knowledge risk index. There are three risk factors under each of the knowledge risk categories. The respondent gives a score of 1–6 for each risk factor addressed. A higher value means a higher risk. The risk factors are summarized in Tables 1–4 for each type of knowledge risk.

Table 1. Assessment Factors for Knowledge Loss Risk

Risk factor
High employee turnover
Insufficient retention process
Low managerial commitment

Table 2. Assessment Factors for Knowledge Leakage Risk

Risk factor
Low information technology security
Improper intellectual properties (IP) handling
Insufficient protection measures

Table 3. Assessment Factors for Knowledge Obsolescence Risk

Risk factor
Low R&D intensity
Insufficient external collaboration
Rapid technological/market change

Table 4. Assessment Factors for Knowledge Shortage Risk

Risk factor
Inadequate training
Poor learning culture
Poor talent management

An enterprise-wide knowledge risk assessment enables an enterprise to assess both its weakness and opportunities. When the scores of knowledge loss or leakage risk are high, the enterprise should consider protection measures and delay the decision of adopting OI until the knowledge loss or leakage does not pose a serious threat to the enterprise. When the levels of knowledge obsolescence and shortage risk are high, the enterprise should consider seriously the need to seek external stimulation and input through an OI approach. This would raise the capabilities of the enterprise and its staff with better technologies, skills, or knowledge from new partners.

When an enterprise has taken an inventory of its existing knowledge assets, understood the different types of knowledge risk and their potential impacts, and learnt how initial knowledge risk assessment can be done, the enterprise can move on to the next critical stage of the risk management process — risk mitigation. Risk mitigation refers to the actions taken to reduce the adverse effects of risk events when they occur.

To reduce knowledge loss, one effective way is to codify all essential business knowledge into the enterprise's repositories (archives and documents) as much as possible. Also, SMEs usually depend on a small group of core staff to compete with large companies in the market. Therefore, what really matters is to have an effective human resources policy in place to retain and motivate key staff to reduce knowledge loss due to employee turnover. With the right people who are dedicated and loyal in the enterprise, SMEs should not be so fearful of knowledge loss or leakage due to operational errors. In knowledge leakage, the knowledge is usually already codified and only a copy flows out from the enterprise into the hands of unintended parties. The proprietary knowledge that is at risk (please refer to Section 1.3 for details) should be classified and access rights to it should be restricted.

On the other hand, knowledge becomes obsolete when there is a slow inflow of new knowledge. Knowledge shortage becomes acute when the knowledge flow among staff is slow and the essential knowledge is not shared and transferred adequately. To address the adverse effects caused by knowledge shortage and obsolescence, a good way is to accelerate the inflow of new, pertinent knowledge through OI. The lifecycle of useful knowledge or technology can be surprisingly short nowadays. Increasing the influx of new or innovative knowledge will certainly make up for the loss of old knowledge because of obsolescence and add much needed knowledge to solve any shortage problem. Therefore, it can be seen that a comprehensive knowledge risk assessment helps an enterprise to identify both threats and opportunities in OI.

6. Case Study of Knowledge Risk Assessment in an SME

6.1. *Findings*

A case study on the knowledge risk assessment of an SME in China has been conducted. The SME is an electronic component manufacturer actively considering OI opportunities. During the study, four departments participated in the assessment: human resources, production, engineering, and marketing. The senior management of each department assessed the knowledge risks of the enterprise using the proposed risk assessment checklist. The average of the ratings given by the four department representatives are presented as shown in Figures 3–7 and in Tables 5–9.

6.2. *Analysis and recommendations*

In the case studied, knowledge loss has a higher risk than the other three types of knowledge risk, and this warrants further

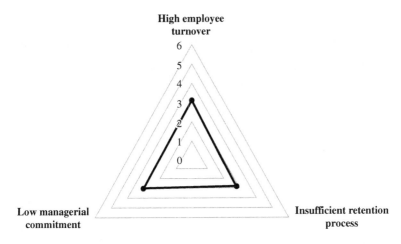

Figure 3.   Radar Diagram of Knowledge Loss Risk Factor Levels

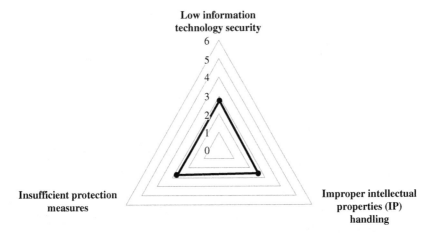

Figure 4.   Radar Diagram of Knowledge Leakage Risk Factor Levels

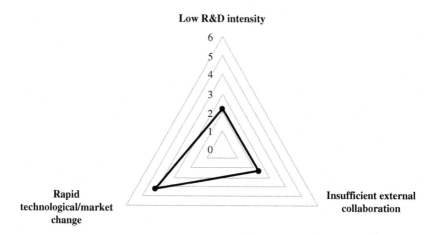

Figure 5.   Radar Diagram of Knowledge Obsolescence Risk Factor Levels

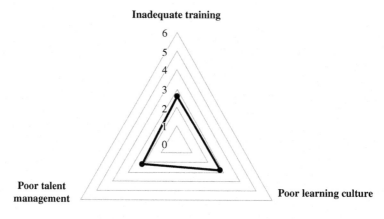

Figure 6.   Radar Diagram of Knowledge Shortage Risk Factor Levels

investigations. The relatively high risk factor for employee turnover (a score of 3.12) indicates the possibility that the turnover may be higher than the industry average. Second, the knowledge leakage risk is not high (2.65) and "Improper IP handling" has the lowest level, possibly indicating that management pays sufficient awareness and effort to IP. Third, in knowledge obsolescence risk, the R&D risk factor has the lowest value. This implies that the enterprise puts sufficient

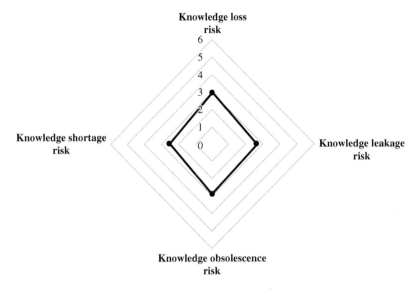

Figure 7.   Overall Risk Level of Each Risk Type

Table 5.   Results of Knowledge Loss Risk Factor Level

Risk factor	Score*
High employee turnover	3.12
Insufficient retention process	2.75
Low managerial commitment	3
Average	*2.95*

Note: * The score ranges from 1 to 6.

Table 6.   Results of Knowledge Leakage Factor Level

Risk factor	Score*
Low information technology security	2.69
Improper IP handling	2.56
Insufficient protection measures	2.71
Average	*2.65*

Note: * The score ranges from 1 to 6.

Table 7. Results of Knowledge Obsolescence Risk Factor Level

Risk factor	Score*
Low R&D intensity	2.12
Insufficient external collaboration	2.31
Rapid technological/market change	4.2
Average	*2.88*

Note: * The score ranges from 1 to 6.

Table 8. Results of Knowledge Shortage Risk Factor Level

Risk factor	Score*
Inadequate training	2.56
Poor learning culture	2.8
Poor talent management	2.14
Average	*2.5*

Note: * The score ranges from 1 to 6.

Table 9. Overall Knowledge Levels

Dimension	Risk score*
Knowledge loss risk	2.95
Knowledge leakage risk	2.65
Knowledge obsolescence risk	2.88
Knowledge shortage risk	2.5
Total knowledge risk	*2.75*

Note: * The score ranges from 1 to 6.

emphasis on R&D. Fourth, in the knowledge shortage risk, the average risk factor level is the lowest among the four types of risk. In particular, "poor talent management" has the lowest score, which may mean that ample training resources and opportunities for career development are available in the company. Generally speaking, as shown in Tables 9 and 10, the individual risk levels are not high,

Table 10.   Risk Score Description

Risk score	Description
4.75–6	Very high risk
3.5–4.75	High risk
2.25–3.5	Low risk
1–2.25	Very low risk

though that of knowledge loss risk, being the highest, requires closer attention.

To mitigate knowledge risks in the SME under study, several recommendations are made. For knowledge loss risk, the human resources director should review the effectiveness of the current staff retention program, especially for high-performance or talented staff. At the same time, a thorough review of current knowledge retention procedures in each department should be reviewed for enhancement. For knowledge leakage risk, one practical way to reduce leakage risk is to install safety measures in the document management system (such as control function on a photocopier to prevent confidential information from being copied or distributed). For knowledge obsolescence risk, as technology and market change rapidly in the industry, the SME should seriously consider more collaboration with external partners. To reduce the knowledge shortage risk, the enterprise should review their training and recruitment programs, foster a better learning culture, and promote more knowledge and experience sharing among staff.

6.3. *Deviations in the assessment of risk factors among departments*

As mentioned earlier, four department representatives participated in the assessment. Each of them assessed the knowledge risks of the enterprise from their own perspective, and the results from each department vary as shown in Figure 8. This is expected, but a detailed examination of the difference may help reveal gaps for

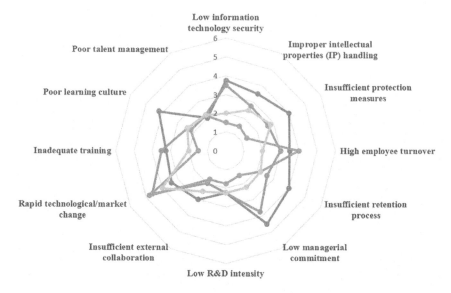

Figure 8.   Deviations in Assessment of Risk Factors

Table 11.   Top Three Risk Factors Having Highest Deviations in Ratings

Risk factors	Standard deviation, σ	Range	Highest level	Lowest level
Low managerial commitment	2.25	3	4.5	1.5
Insufficient information system security	1.11	2.25	3.75	1.5
Insufficient protection measures	1.09	2.67	4	1.33

Note: The average standard deviation is 0.76 and the average of range is 1.68.

improvement. Table 11 shows the three risk factors having the highest standard deviations. "Low managerial commitment" has the highest deviation among the corresponding departments. This may mean each department understands and views managerial commitment quite differently, and so quite different scores are given. The high deviation in "insufficient information security" may be accounted for by the possibility that all departments except engineering may not adequately understand what information security means in daily work or technologically, making their scores appear to be given randomly (so a large range occurred). Finally, the reason for the third highest deviation in "insufficient protection measures" may be that different protection measures are adopted in different departments or the same enterprise-wide set of measures is interpreted in different ways by each department. Overall, to address the said likely inconsistencies among departments in understanding the same term or question, there should be more interdepartmental communication and enterprise-wide dissemination of regulations and policies.

The relatively low knowledge risk rating may be due to the fact that normally the respondents from the senior management may consciously or unconsciously give a higher rating as they do not want to reveal the true situation (when it is poor) of their enterprise to outsiders. At the same time, the ratings given by the respondent are unavoidably subjective. This is an inherent weakness of all methods based on a checklist-type survey. To overcome this drawback, a validation in the form of interviews with on-site staff or a site visit could also be performed to ensure the reliability of the results.

7. Conclusion

Four types of knowledge risk have been identified and discussed, namely, knowledge loss, knowledge leakage, knowledge obsolescence, and knowledge shortage. A checklist, in which there are four important criteria (the four types of knowledge risk), each with three accompanying risk factors, is proposed. It can be adopted by an enterprise to perform a systematic and comprehensive assessment of important knowledge risk factors. The risk factor levels obtained in an assessment can then be used for prioritization of resources to manage knowledge risks. Alternatively, the same checklist adopted by two or more enterprises provides a common basis for comparison of risk factor levels between them. In other words, if an enterprise is benchmarked against the best practice one, areas of improvement can be identified for the former enterprise.

On the other hand, the same kind of assessment provides an enterprise actively considering or already engaging in OI important information for risk/reward analysis at the beginning of or during an OI project. If the risk factor levels of knowledge loss and/or leakage are high, an OI project should not be started or it should be slowed down if already in progress unless the loss or leakage is brought to an acceptable low level. If the risk factor levels of knowledge obsolescence and/or shortage are high, an enterprise new to OI should actively pursue it. An enterprise in the middle of OI should accelerate its pace, taking advantage of OI which, by its nature, can increase the inflow of new knowledge from partners or the market to mitigate these two risks. Further, as the OI project in an enterprise moves on, the same assessment done at different time points will yield results that can be compared and serve as a tool to monitor the effectiveness of risk mitigation in a time period to initiate timely, appropriate corrective mitigation actions. Finally, in the case study for an SME, apart from the overall picture of risk ratings of the enterprise obtained by the assessment, communication problems and differences in practice between different units in an organization can also be revealed.

References

Billington, J. (1997). A few things every manager ought to know about risk. *Harvard Management*, 2(3), 1–12.

Boisot, M. H. (1987) *Information and Organizations: The Manager as Anthropologist.* Fontana, London.

Buecheler, T., Sieg, J. H., Füchslin, R. M. and Pfeifer, R. (2010). Crowdsourcing, open innovation and collective intelligence in the scientific method-a research agenda and operational framework. *Proceedings of the 7th ALIFE Conference*, pp. 679–686.

Casualty Actuarial Society (2003). *Overview of Enterprise Risk Management.* Retrieved December 01, 2016 from https://www.casact.org/area/erm/overview.pdf.

Chesbrough, H. (2004). Managing open innovation. *Research-Technology Management*, 47(1), pp. 23–26.

Curtis, P. and Carey, M. (2012). *Risk Assessment in Practice.* Retrieved October 20, 2016 from http://www.coso.org/documents/COSOAnncsOnlineSurvey2GainInpt 4Updt2IntrnlCntrlIntgratdFrmwrk%20-%20for%20merge_files/COSO-ERM%20Risk%20Assessment%20inPractice%20Thought%20Paper%20 OCtober%202012.pdf.

Desouza, K. C. and Awazu, Y. (2006). Knowledge management at SMEs: Five peculiarities. *Journal of Knowledge Management*, 10(1), pp. 32–43.

Durst, S. and Edvardsson, I. R. (2012). Knowledge management in SMEs: A literature review. *Journal of Knowledge Management*, 16(6), pp. 879–903.

Edvinsson, L. and Sullivan, P. (1996). Developing a model for managing intellectual capital. *European Management Journal*, 14(4), pp. 356–364.

Edwards, T., Delbridge, R. and Munday, M. (2005). Understanding innovation in small and medium-sized enterprises: A process manifest. *Technovation*, 25(10), pp. 1119–1127.

Enkel, E., Gassmann, O. and Chesbrough, H. (2009). Open R&D and open innovation: Exploring the phenomenon. *R&D Management*, 39(4), pp. 311–316.

Frey, K., Lüthje, C. and Haag, S. (2011). Whom should firms attract to open innovation platforms? The role of knowledge diversity and motivation. *Long Range Planning*, 44(5), pp. 397–420.

Gassmann, O., Enkel, E. and Chesbrough, H. (2010). The future of open innovation. *R&D Management*, 40(3), pp. 213–221.

Howe, J. (2014). Crowdsourcing. Retrieved December 28, 2016 from http://crowdsourcing.typepad.com/

Kim, H. and Park, Y. (2010). The effects of open innovation activity on performance of SMEs: The case of Korea. *International Journal of Technology Management*, 52(3/4), pp. 236–256.

Massingham, P. (2008). Measuring the impact of knowledge loss: More than ripples on a pond? *Management Learning*, 39(5), pp. 541–560.

Mollick, E. (2014). The dynamics of crowdfunding: An exploratory study. *Journal of Business Venturing*, 29(1), pp. 1–16.

Poetz, M. K. and Schreier, M. (2012). The value of crowdsourcing: Can users really compete with professionals in generating new product ideas? *Journal of Product Innovation Management*, 29(2), pp. 245–256.

Rayna, T. and Striukova, L. (2015). Open innovation 2.0: Is co-creation the ultimate challenge? *International Journal of Technology Management*, 69(1), pp. 38–53.

Schiuma, G., Durst, S. and Wilhelm, S. (2012). Knowledge management and succession planning in SMEs. *Journal of Knowledge Management*, 16(4), pp. 637–649.

Sisodiya, S. R., Johnson, J. L. and Grégoire, Y. (2013). Inbound open innovation for enhanced performance: Enablers and opportunities. *Industrial Marketing Management*, 42(5), pp. 836–849.

Van de Vrande, V., De Jong, J. P., Vanhaverbeke, W. and De Rochemont, M. (2009). Open innovation in SMEs: Trends, motives and management challenges. *Technovation*, 29(6), pp. 423–437.

Vanhaverbeke, W., Van de Vrande, V. and Chesbrough, H. (2008). Understanding the advantages of open innovation practices in corporate venturing in terms of real options. *Creativity and Innovation Management*, 17(4), pp. 251–258.

Zeng, S. X., Xie, X. and Tam, C. M. (2010). Relationship between cooperation networks and innovation performance of SMEs. *Technovation*, 30(3), pp. 181–194.

Part 3
The Future

Chapter 10

Open Innovation and Knowledge Management in SMEs: What Comes Next?

Susanne Durst* and Serdal Temel[†]

*University of Skövde, Högskolevägen 1, 541 28, Skövde, Sweden
and Universidad del Pacífico, Lima, Peru
[†]Ege University, Erzene Mahallesi, Gençlik Caddesi,
35040 Boronova, İzmir, Turkey

The aim behind this final chapter is to propose and discuss a number of topics that could build the basis for future research regarding the interplay between knowledge management (KM) and open innovation (OI) in SMEs.

1. Outline

This book has provided several examples of what the interplay between open innovation (OI) and knowledge management (KM) in SMEs looks like or could look like, respectively, which was the aim of this book. In this concluding chapter, the editors of the book will address some possible future research directions that hopefully will stimulate interest in starting research activities of existing as well as new researchers in the area.

2. The Need of Discussing OI from a Risk Perspective

In comparison with the study of collaborative innovation (von Hippel, 2007), the study of OI is still at an early stage. This not only refers to the study of OI in SMEs but also to the study of OI in general. Therefore, it is hardly surprising that the discussion about OI still has a positive connotation. If some reports are to believed, OI is one of the key solutions to every business challenge, including both current and future ones. OI is considered as positive and beneficial for all types of organizations in order to remain competitive. It is believed that OI helps companies access external knowledge either with lower cost or even no cost (D'Este *et al.*, 2015). It is also assumed that all companies or external partner such as consumers, competitors, and research organizations are ready for collaboration (Chesbrough, 2006). But often they are not, or collaboration is not as easy as it was thought. Another issue with OI is experience and management skills. It is argued that all companies are good candidates for OI, but without in-house innovation experience and management skills it may not be true (Damanpour, 1991; Kock, 2016). Consequently, all companies should sooner rather than later begin with their OI activities.

A very similar situation is apparent with the study of KM, although more established than the study of OI; the former continues to show an emphasis on seeing knowledge as something positive as something of value. Only recently, some researchers have turned to the study of the risky aspects, the downside of knowledge. To make use of the full potential of knowledge, one needs to understand both sides of the coin, therefore this recent development can be assessed as both timely and relevant and will help us to expand our understanding of knowledge and therefore its management. Given the attention OI has achieved in recent years and thus the expectations raised, it is therefore high time to have a stronger focus on possible negative consequences of OI as well. Indeed, there is a need for studies that address the downside of opening up a smaller firm. Research findings would contribute to an increased account-ability of OI as a field of study and support practitioners in their decision-making processes regarding OI and its realization. Research is also needed that addresses the management of risks related to OI. What are these risks and how can they be addressed from an SME risk management approach? When would it be better not to involve the smaller firm in OI?

From a practical point of view, practitioners should ask them-selves about their risk tolerance as well as the level of risk they are willing to accept. The latter also refers to the acceptance of possible negative outcomes due to OI activities.

3. Consequences of Opening Up the Company

Another aspect we believe that deserves more attention and thus research is the consequences of opening a smaller firm. Because of the novelty of the topic of OI, activities and research have largely been centered on highlighting the possible benefits of OI, or success factors for initiating and implementing different OI strategies. What is lacking, however, are empirical insights into the consequences of having opened the company. Indeed, it would be interesting and relevant to start focusing on this part of the OI process in order to understand the actual effects of OI on companies and their develop-ment. For instance, SMEs can gain benefits from OI activities by taking advantage of features such as less bureaucracy, flexibility, and agility that are usually assigned to this category of firms (Parida *et al.*, 2012; Hafkesbrink and Kirkels, 2016).

Has the OI strategy materialized itself? And if yes, what were the driving forces behind it? If not, what went wrong and why? What are the actual outcomes of OI with regard to knowledge and organiza-tional development in companies? Does OI lead to better or even new products/services? And if so, why and how? Does OI contribute to other areas of the company and its development as well? If yes, to what areas and what is the contribution? On the other hand, what are the reactions to possible negative consequences of being involved in OI? Do they mean the end of engagement into OI? What are the consequences of opening the company between different categories of SMEs? What differences and/or similarities can be found? What forms of protection are preferred by smaller firms? What does a stronger opening of the company mean for the firm's knowledge management?

Finding answers to the questions raised above is of vital importance not only for smaller companies but also for specific sectors as well as countries. This is because the OI paradigm is being considered as the best way to increase the innovation skills of companies regardless of size. Over the years, different collaborative programs have been introduced with the aim of urging companies to collaborate. For instance, under Horizon 2020, in order to get funds, it is compulsory to collaborate with other companies to have access to external knowledge and thus increase the impact of activities at EU level. This situation not only increases the willingness and motivation for collaboration but also strengthens the KM in the companies concerned. The same kind of activities have also been started in some individual countries. For instance, in Turkey, under the Industrial Theses Program (SanTez), the only way for a smaller company to get government grants for either R&D or innovation projects is by collaborating with a university. Under some programs in Turkey, collaboration, is not compulsory but considered as an additional benefit. For example, if smaller companies collaborate with a university and apply for R&D funds from the Scientific and Technological Research Council of Turkey (TUBITAK), they can get an additional 10%. TUBITAK is the national public organization to support innovation and R&D projects of companies as well as academic institutions.

4. The Effectiveness of OI for Different Types of Companies

Another important issue that needs more research is the performance evaluation of OI activities. Environments that are characterized by finite resources need thorough analyzes of the cost-income ratio for justification. This applies to SMEs in particular. The readiness and speed of adoption of OI activities, among other issues, will certainly be facilitated by having access to tools and assessment methods. Ideally, these methods will be integrated into existing systems to make possible a harmonized system. The same applies to the need of having tools and methods for KM to see the outcomes of certain KM practices on the organization and its performance. Given the interplay between KM and OI, as shown in the previous chapters, smaller firms should try and find a solution for an integrative approach to these aspects and thereby, as mentioned above, make sure that this solution is also linked with the overall company infrastructure.

However, before the smaller firms start their KM-based OI activities, they should critically analyzes the company's readiness. It cannot be ruled out that the company is not ready due to cultural differences regarding the prospective partners, differences regarding the level of development of the country the SME is located in, lack of awareness of the activities' benefits, lack of skills and knowledge on how to initiate and implement the activities, etc. This underlines the need for a systematic and well-thought-out approach from the planning phase to the operational deployment of the KM-based OI, one that considers the possible ups and downs.

Prior research (e.g. Prencipe, 2000; Lichtenthaler, 2008) has given an impression of industrial differences regarding the implementation of OI, and thus its effectiveness. Due to the specific nature of sectors, implementation of OI may be different in manufacturing and service sectors. The products of manufacturing sectors are more tangible than the those of service sector, and therefore it is easier to collaborate with external partners during product development in the manufacturing sector. Gassmann (2006) assumed that sectors that are characterized by globalization, technology intensity, technology fusion, new business models, and knowledge leveraging are more inclined to OI. This clearly shows that researchers who are interested in contributing to the further development of the field need to take this into consideration and, based on this, design proper research projects. It also suggests the need for more cross-sector research projects, not only to show the differences between sectors/ industries but also to develop our understanding of the consequences of these differences regarding the perception of OI, the execution of OI, and the evaluation of OI outcomes.

In the context of this section, we should also address the outcomes of OI. In fact, it could be more than just improved or new products/services or higher returns; OI has the power to contribute to soft facts as well such as learning, knowledge creation, efficiency, and higher job satisfaction. This represents an area that also deserves more attention.

5. The Need for a Targeted KM-based OI Strategy

Given the complexity and uncertainty of innovation in general and OI in particular, and this in conjunction with the resource limitations, it would seem advisable for smaller firms to develop a targeted approach to both KM and OI. From prior research, we, unfortunately, know that often smaller firms have no (formal) strategies or strategies that are not well defined or not aligned with the overall firm strategy (Durst and Edvardsson, 2012). Smaller firms tend to follow an *ad hoc* approach which is more responsive to the attributes of flexibility and fast adaptability (Ibrahim and Ellis, 1990). On one hand, this approach seems clear, on the other hand, such an approach bears the risk that the finite resources are not utilized in the best possible way but are used with no clear focus, leading to expensive duplicative efforts which in the worst case results in closure of the company. Consequently, there is a clear need for the formulation of targeted KM-based OI strategies. It is important, in this context, that the formulation of OI is not all — the critical aspect will be to put the strategy into action. This also means that the companies will need to specify a number of tactics in order to meet this objective and be prepared to make adjustments to the strategy in the event of changes triggered by the company's internal or external environment. In addition, it is also possible that there is not just one strategy but several. Moreover, the issue of time will matter, i.e. when to have an OI approach and when to have a closed one. Finding this out will probably be based on learning-by-doing. Yet, with SMEs, this learning process should follow a systematic path, one that is based on a systematic KM approach rather than an *ad hoc* one.

Last but not least, we should also study firms that decide against OI in order to develop our understanding, as there might be good reasons out there that call for alternatives.

6. The Development of Suitable Skills and Competencies in SMEs

The chapters presented in this book have shown that different types of KM-based OI also require different types of skills and competencies. Therefore, there is high likelihood that the SMEs will realize that there is a mismatch between the skills and competencies needed and those at their disposal. Consequently, the firms in question will have to update their competencies and skills in order to increase the success of their planned activities. So, the question will be how best to develop these skills and competencies? How should it be done from a practical point of view in order to make sure that the company's overall business operations will be affected to the least extent possible? What kind of teaching/learning strategies would be the best to address the three different OI archetypes? Should the focus be on internal, external, or combined teaching/learning strategies? Who is offering those courses and seminars? How to transfer and retain the new (updated) knowledge in the best way? Would it require an amendment of the existing KM approach/system as well? If yes, in what way?

7. Selecting Suitable Partners

It is not new that networking with other actors is not only important for SMEs to complement and expand existing resources and skills for innovation but also to overcome the burden of smallness and its consequences. Additionally, the competitive and knowledge-driven business environment has resulted in, among other issues, shortened product lifecycle and has brought both collaboration and networks and KM to the forefront.

The studies that focused on the relationship between OI and collaboration with external partners have shown its important role on the companies' performance. For instance, Shan *et al.* (1994) emphasized that company performance is reduced when companies limit their partner search to their organizational boundaries. Similarly, Powell *et al.* (1996) investigated the impact of collaboration in the biotechnology sector and showed greater innovation performance when companies were actively involved in networking. Against this background, it would be interesting to study the quality of the relationship between OI and collaboration in smaller firms as well.

In this context, the question about with whom to collaborate is essential (Kirkels and Duysters, 2010); as we know the selection of partners has always been a critical issue for companies (Hafkesbrink and Kirkels, 2016). Given the specific nature of OI, one would assume an even more rigorous selection process. Therefore, it would be interesting to study how SMEs approach the selection process, whom they select, when, and why? Considering the OI archetypes and the different knowledge strategies/goals, it can also be assumed that the selection of a partner will be different depending on both the internal and external situation.

As OI is not limited to innovation, even though sometimes one gets the feeling that it is, it would be beneficial to study for what reasons SMEs adopt OI, and what the end results would be? OI may help smaller firms to strengthen their marketing skills by collaborating with partners who are good at marketing.

Additionally, it would be interesting to understand what types of contracts are specified between the partners. How do they vary depending on the form of OI? Are there preferences regarding the selection of partners in general and in specific situations, respectively? If yes, what are the reasons behind this? Moreover, one central precondition to ensure the availability of a broad range of partners is proximity (Maskell and Malmberg, 1999). To an extent, physical proximity can be complemented and strengthened by other forms of proximity such as cognitive, social, organizational, institutional, or social proximity

(Boschma, 2005). Therefore applying this concept, it would be interesting to find out how SMEs proceed when selecting partners.

8. The Consequences of Digitalization for OI and KM in SMEs

Finally, we may raise the question of the consequences of the digitalization for OI and KM in SMEs. According to the Gartner IT Glossary, digitalization is the use of digital technologies to change a business model and provide new revenue and value-producing opportunities; it is the process of moving to a digital business. Digitalization not only means a strategic reorientation but also a need for a cultural change (Jahn and Pfeiffer, 2014). The resulting changes will put an additional burden on the management of SMEs and call for even more targeted measures to make the best use of the existing resources. These changes will influence the smaller companies' approach to KM. Also, an analysis of the company's readiness for the age of digitalization is likely to point out knowledge gaps that need to be filled. These knowledge gaps might be filled through a particular OI strategy. For example, the company may miss the necessary IT and technological understanding and skills needed to make informed decisions; by starting to collaborate with a local or regional university, the company can establish links with students in higher semesters and thus get access to this type of knowledge. This could also lead to other forms of collaboration, such as attending courses related to digitalization, such as a digital business management or business modeling course.

9. Conclusion

In sum, we hope that the content provided in this book has not only contributed to a more fine-grained understanding of the interface between KM and OI in SMEs but also prompted an interest to continue pursuing this subject or even carry out requisite activities.

As it is well defined in previous chapters, including this one, KM and OI are two of the main strategies for enhancing smaller companies' competitiveness. Given its linkage, these two strategies need to be applied hand in hand. The editors hope this has become clear in the book.

Useful Sources

About Knowledge Management in SMEs

- https://realkm.com/km-in-small-and-medium-enterprises-smes/
- https://www.udemy.com/knowledge-management-tools-for-smes/
- http://ceur-ws.org/Vol-1226/paper46.pdf
- https://doi.org/10.1016/j.sbspro.2013.06.441
- http://www.mdpi.com/2078-2489/5/3/440/htm

About Open Innovation in SMEs

- http://www.openisme.eu/
- http://www.inspire-smes.eu/

About the interface between Knowledge Management and Open Innovation in SMEs

Congratulations, you have a very useful source in your hands!

References

Boschma, R. A. (2005). Proximity and innovation. A critical assessment. *Regional Studies*, **39**, pp. 61–74.

Chesbrough, H. W. (2006). *Open Innovation: The New Imperative for Creating and Profiting from Technology*. Harvard Business Press, Boston, MA.

Damanpour, F. (1991). Organizational innovation: A meta-analysis of effects of determinants and moderators. *Academy of Management Journal*, **34**(3), pp. 555–590.

D'Este, P., Amara, N. and Olmos-Peñuela, J. (2015). Fostering novelty while reducing failure: Balancing the twin challenges of product innovation. *Technological Forecasting and Social Change*, **113**(Part B), pp. 280–292

Durst, S. and Edvardsson, I. R. (2012). Knowledge management in SMEs: A literature Review, *Journal of Knowledge Management*, **16**(6), pp. 879–903.

Gassmann, O. (2006). Opening up the innovation process: Towards an agenda. *R&D Management*, **36**(3), pp. 223–228.

Hafkesbrınk, J. and Kirkels, Y. (2016). Open innovation in SMEs. In: A.-L. Mention, A. P. Nagel, J. Hafkesbrink and J. Dabrowska (Eds.), *Innovation and Education Reloaded; Nurtıring Skills for the Future*, Finland: Open innovation network-OI, pp. 282–301.

Ibrahim, A. B. and Ellis, W. H. (1990). *Entrepreneurship and Small Business Management*. Dubuque, Kendall / Hunt Publishing.

Jahn, B. and Pfeiffer, M. (2014). Die Digitale Revolution: Neue Geschäftsmodelle statt (nur) Neue Kommunikation. *Marketing Review St. Gallen: die neue Thexis-Marketingfachzeitschrift für Theorie und Praxis*, **31**(1), pp. 80–92.

Kirkels, Y. E. M. and Duysters, G. M. (2010). Brokerage in SME networks. *Research Policy*, **39**(3), pp. 375–385.

Kock C. J. (2016), Network externalities and open innovation. In: A.-L. Mention, A. P. Nagel, J. Hafkesbrink and J. Dabrowska (Eds.), *Innovation and Education Reloaded; Nurtıring Skills for the Future*, Finland: Open innovation network-OI, pp. 218–234.

Lichtenthaler, U. (2008). Open innovation in practice: An analysis of strategic approaches to technology transactions. *IEEE Transactions on Engineering Management*, **55**(1), pp. 148–157.

Maskell, P. and Malmberg, A. (1999). Localised learning and industrial competitiveness. *Cambridge Journal of Economics*, **23**(2), pp. 167–186.

Parida, V., Westerberg, M. and Frishammar, J. (2012). Inbound open innovation activities in high-tech SMEs: The impact on innovation performance. *Small Business Management*, **50**(2), pp. 283–309.

Powell, W. W., Koput, K. W. and Smith-Doerr, L. (1996). Interorganizational collaboration and the locus of innovation: Networks of learning in biotechnology. *Administrative Science Quarterly*, **41**(1), pp. 116–145.

Prencipe, A. (2000). Breadth and depth of technological capabilities in CoPS: The case of the aircraft engine control system. *Research Policy*, **29**(7), pp. 895–911.

Shan, W., Walker, G. and Kogut, B. (1994). Interfirm cooperation and startup innovation in the biotechnology industry. *Strategic Management Journal*, **15**(5), pp. 387–394.

Von Hippel, E. (2007). The sources of innovation. In: *Das Summa Summarum des Management*, C. Boersch and R. Eschen (Eds.), Springer, Wiesbaden, pp. 111–120.

Index